STORYTELLING IN EARLY CHILDHOOD

Storytelling in Early Childhood is a captivating book which explores the multiple dimensions of storytelling and story acting and shows how they enrich language and literacy learning in the early years. Foregrounding the power of children's own stories in the early and primary years, it provides evidence that storytelling and story acting, a pedagogic approach first developed by Vivian Gussin Paley, affords rich opportunities to foster learning within a play-based and language-rich curriculum. The book explores a number of themes and topics, including:

- the role of imaginary play and its dynamic relationship to narrative;
- how socially situated symbolic actions enrich the emotional, cognitive and social development of children;
- how the interrelated practices of storytelling and dramatisation enhance language and literacy learning, and contribute to an inclusive classroom culture;
- the challenges practitioners face in aligning their understanding of child literacy and learning with a narrow, mandated curriculum which focuses on measurable outcomes.

Driven by an international approach and based on new empirical studies, this volume further advances the field, offering new theoretical and practical analyses of storytelling and story acting from complementary disciplinary perspectives. This book is a potent and engaging read for anyone intrigued by Paley's storytelling and story-acting curriculum, as well as those practitioners and students with a vested interest in early years literacy and language learning.

Teresa Cremin is Professor of Education (Literacy), The Open University, UK.

Rosie Flewitt is Reader in Early Communication and Literacy, UCL Institute of Education, UK.

Ben Mardell is Project Director at Project Zero at the Harvard Graduate School of Education, USA.

Joan Swann is Emeritus Professor of English Language, The Open University, UK.

A much-needed resource for early childhood teachers and literacy educators! *Storytelling in Early Childhood: Enriching language, literacy and classroom culture* documents the value of play in an era when playtime for superhero stories and sand castles is crumbling under the harsh glare of teacher accountability. Inspired by Vivian Gussin Paley's groundbreaking work on storytelling and story acting, this contemporary collection is a refreshing respite and reminder that children still play to learn. Nine leading early childhood scholars provide thoughtful theorisation and convincing evidence of the power of children's play and storytelling and the richness of literacy learning, when their teachers take children seriously, listen deeply, and respond imaginatively.

Karen Wolhend, Indiana University, USA

This book brings together a section of research from different disciplinary perspectives, focusing on the important themes of the role of narrative, storytelling and imaginative play in children's learning. Centred on a timely revisiting of Vivian Gussin Paley's work, the authors bring new and contemporary insights into these themes. The book has many features that will engage different audiences.

The chapters report empirical work across international contexts, using a range of theoretical and methodological frameworks. Each chapter contributes to the vibrancy of research that brings together literacy, play, storytelling and drama. What also stands out is the quality of relationships between children and adults – a theme that recurred throughout Paley's distinguished work. The engagement with inclusion and diversity is embedded throughout the book, reflecting the commitment to democratic classrooms, pedagogies and relationships.

The interdisciplinary nature of the research projects reported here shows the strength of using different lenses, and what emerges when we think within and beyond disciplinary borders. The authors engage with some well-established theoretical ideas, but from new angles, and with a critical edge that provoke new questions and debates.

This book is multi-vocal and multi-modal in that there are many voices in the chapters – those of the children and the adults who work with them, of professional story actors and storytellers, all with a deep interest in children, and ways of working creatively with them. Inevitably, there is some well-justified critique of current policy frameworks that emphasise an acquisition model of literacy and language, and that ignore the complex social practices that are portrayed so vividly in this book. The authors all respect children's agency as fundamental to their engagement with literacy as part of everyday social practice.

The book offers theoretical, empirical and practical insights, and outlines new provocations for future research in this field. I recommend this as essential reading for students, researchers and practitioners in early childhood education, childhood studies, language and literacy studies, and playwork.

Elizabeth Wood, University of Sheffield, UK

Motivated by the work of Vivian Gussin Paley, this volume has a triple focus – children's own stories, acting them out, and all in the context of playful learning. While we rush children forward, we take the joy out of literacy; this book argues for a vibrant approach that is child-initiated, shared and highly collaborative. Collateral benefits such as perspective-taking and executive function skills associated with storytelling and acting abound.

Roberta Michnick Golinkoff, University of Delaware, USA

STORYTELLING IN EARLY CHILDHOOD

Enriching language, literacy and classroom culture

*Edited by Teresa Cremin, Rosie Flewitt,
Ben Mardell and Joan Swann*

Routledge
Taylor & Francis Group

LONDON AND NEW YORK

First published 2017
by Routledge
2 Park Square, Milton Park, Abingdon, Oxon OX14 4RN

and by Routledge
711 Third Avenue, New York, NY 10017

Routledge is an imprint of the Taylor & Francis Group, an informa business

British Library Cataloguing in Publication Data
A catalogue record for this book is available from the British Library

Library of Congress Cataloging in Publication Data
A catalog record for this book has been requested

ISBN: 978-1-138-93213-5 (hbk)
ISBN: 978-1-138-93214-2 (pbk)
ISBN: 978-1-315-67942-6 (ebk)

Typeset in Bembo
by Saxon Graphics Ltd, Derby
Printed and bound by CPI Group (UK) Ltd, Croydon, CR0 4YY

CONTENTS

FOREWORD

Vivian Gussin Paley

'Where did my story come from?' Walter asks, watching me write the final sentence of his dinosaur story. This week his hero is a mischievous dinosaur who is locked in jail but always finds a way to escape. Next week Walter will be a lion who eats dinosaurs. Whatever the cast of characters, Walter's classmates are as eager to help him act out the stories he dictates as they are to play with him in the blocks or on the playground.

'That's an interesting question, Walter,' I say. 'I wonder about the same thing.' I could tell him that lots of grownups are curious about the origins and purposes of this constant make-believing going on. We even create research projects and write papers to explain our theories and pose new questions.

However, the matter of where Walter's dinosaur story comes from is his query and he pursues his own answers. 'It's from my dreams,' he decides.

'I think you mean from your pretend dreams, Walter,' Andrea says. She is next on the list of those who signed up to dictate a story. Hers and Walter's will be acted out with all the other stories told that day. 'I mean like when you're in bed and you pretend to be someone else.' Andrea's 'someone else' is usually Baby Princess Rainbow, a role she takes in the doll corner as well.

I write Andrea's name at the top of her paper and await her story. The subject and words will be hers, and it is in the power of each storyteller to influence the culture and imagination of the group. We humans have much in common with other primates when we are young. But we alone tell stories. We all crawl, run, climb and jump. We play with siblings, pretend to fight, and find ways to communicate our joys and anxieties. We keep an eye on Mom while moving away from her in small steps, but only the human child invents plots and characters to accompany the full range of our feelings and experiences.

The narrative begins in the baby's crib and may well be the earliest design for storytelling. 'Peek-a-boo' sounds like the original lost and found plot, acted out of the fear of being left alone. What joy to act out these dramas again and again as the child grows older and, happily, a vehicle has been provided, free of charge. It is play and its natural counterpart storytelling, just a step away from play and recognizable by every child. Walter's dinosaur, first jailed and then escaped, is not so far from Peek-a-boo.

In *Storytelling in Early Childhood* our scholarly writers demonstrate their respect and admiration for the unique differences in each young storyteller and in the environment in which stories are told and dramatized. We are invited to study children from new perspectives and to re-examine our classrooms with awakened curiosity and creativity.

There is so much to wonder about: How do young children use their narrative talents to climb the ladder of social awareness and help others do the same? Why does the simple act of playing inside a story heighten its imagery and so easily serve the goals of literacy?

It is the theatre of the young we are being asked to reconsider. The world's oldest and most reliable tool of education is taking its proper place in the early childhood classroom and we will want to add our voices to the instructive and inspiring essays in this book. We want to know what has been lost in our children's early years and how we might find new ways to reset the clock. The children will have much to tell us if we listen to them carefully.

CONTRIBUTORS

Editors

Teresa Cremin is Professor of Education (Literacy) in the Faculty of Education and Language Studies at the Open University in the UK. Her sociocultural research focuses mainly on the consequences of teachers' literate identities and practices, and creative pedagogic practice in literacy, the arts and the sciences from the early years through to Higher Education. She has a particular interest in volitional reading and writing. Her research is frequently co-participative, involving teachers as researchers both in school and children's homes. A Fellow of the English Association, the Academy of Social Sciences, and the Royal Society of the Arts, Teresa is also a director of the Cambridge Primary Review Trust and a trustee of the UK Literacy Association. Teresa co-convenes the British Educational Research Association's Creativity Special Interest Group and is a member of the Economic and Social Research Council's Peer Review College. Previously she has served as President of the UK Reading Association and the UKLA and as a trustee of the Society for Educational Studies (SES), and as a board member of BookTrust and the Poetry Archive. Recent publications include: *Researching Literacy Lives: Building home school communities* (Routledge, 2015); *Building Communities of Engaged Readers: Reading for pleasure* (Routledge, 2014); and the co-edited (with Kathy Hall, Barbara Comber and Luis Moll) text, *The International Handbook of Research into Children's Literacy, Learning and Culture* (Wiley Blackwell, 2013). Her next book is *Writing Identity and the Teaching and Learning of Writing* (Routledge), edited with Terry Locke. Teresa is editor of the series *Teaching Creatively in the Primary School* (Routledge).

Rosie Flewitt is Reader of Early Communication and Literacy at University College London Institute of Education (UCL IOE) in the UK, and member of

MODE 'Multimodal Methodologies for Researching Digital Data and Environments' (http://mode.ioe.ac.uk/). Her research and teaching focus on the complementary areas of young children's communication, language and literacy development and inclusive education, with expertise primarily in multimodality and visual ethnography. Throughout her career she has refined multimodal methodological, analytic and theoretical frameworks for the study of how children make meaning through combinations of modes (such as spoken and written language, gesture, images and sounds) as they engage with written, oral, visual and digital texts at home and in early education. Recent work includes the development of cutting-edge participatory methods using digital technologies to investigate the lives of children living with disadvantage. Rosie has served on the TACTYC executive committee (http://tactyc.org.uk/), Froebel Trust Research Committee (http://www.froebel.org.uk/) and the Economic and Social Research Council Peer Review College. She is currently Editorial Board Member for *Journal of Early Childhood Literacy, Literacy and Visual Communication*. Recent publications include *Understanding Research with Children and Young People* (edited with Alison Clark, Martyn Hammersley and Martin Robb, 2013).

Ben Mardell is Professor in Early Childhood Education at Lesley University, USA. He is also the project director of The Pedagogy of Play, a research project at Project Zero at the Harvard Graduate School of Education. For the past 30 years, Ben has taught and conducted research with infants, toddlers, preschoolers and kindergartners. He recently helped write the new Boston Public School kindergarten curriculum that includes storytelling and story acting as a daily practice. Ben is a co-author of *Visible Learners: Promoting Reggio-inspired approaches in all schools* (Jossey-Bass), *Making Learning Visible: Children as individual and group learners* (Reggio Children) and *Making Teaching Visible: Documentation of individual and group learning as professional development* (Project Zero). He is the author of *From Basketball to the Beatles: In search of compelling early childhood curriculum* and *Growing Up in Child Care: A case for quality early education* (Heinemann).

Joan Swann is Emeritus Professor of English Language at the Open University, UK. At the Open University she was Director of the Centre for Language and Communication. She is a sociolinguist, with a particular interest in the analysis of spoken interaction. Her teaching and research cover English as a global language, language and identity, language and education, and language and creativity. Recent and current projects under this last heading include creativity in everyday language; the discourse of reading groups (how adults and children talk about literary texts); and storytelling, both professional storytelling performances and children's stories. Much of this work has been applied research carried out in educational contexts, including the evaluation of extracurricular reading projects, an immersive theatre project and storytelling and story acting with young children. Books include: *The Discourse of Reading Groups: Integrating cognitive and sociocultural perspectives* (with David Peplow, Paola Trimarco and Sara

Whiteley; Routledge, 2016); *English in the World: History, diversity, change* (edited with Philip Seargeant; Routledge, 2012); *Creativity in Language and Literature: The state of the art* (edited with Ronald Carter and Rob Pope; Palgrave Macmillan, 2011).

Contributors

Patricia ('Patsy') M. Cooper is Associate Professor and Director of Early Childhood Education at Queens College, CUNY, USA. A former classroom teacher and school director, she has been involved with Paley's 'storytelling curriculum' from all salient perspectives: classroom teacher, school director, teacher educator and researcher. Cooper is also the founding director of School Literacy and Culture at Rice University in Houston, Texas, a teacher education organisation engaged in dissemination and research around storytelling and story acting. Her first book, *When Stories Come to School: Telling, writing, and performing stories in the early childhood classroom*, describes various aspects of the impact of storytelling and story acting on classroom teachers and children, as do her multiple articles and chapters. Another book, *The Classrooms All Young Children Need: Lessons in teaching from Vivian Paley*, investigates the broad breadth of Paley's vision, encapsulated by Cooper as Paley's 'pedagogy of meaning' and 'pedagogy of fairness'. Cooper is past editor of the *Journal for Early Childhood Teacher Education*, where her editorial commentaries were devoted to the real lives of early childhood educators, and include 'Early childhood teacher educators as necessary mediators of research, practice, and change' and ' "Building better teachers" in early childhood teacher education'.

Dorothy Faulkner is a Senior Lecturer in Child Development and Honorary Associate in the Centre for Research in Education and Educational Technology at the Open University. Current research interests include creativity and early years education, narrative development and the impact of peer relationships on collaborative play and children's learning and problem solving. She has also contributed to several independent evaluations of the impact on schools of working with creative professionals. At the Open University, Dorothy has chaired the development of courses on child development and the psychology of education at undergraduate and master's level, as well as professional development materials for in-service teacher training. She has a special interest in developing practitioners' understanding of the use of play and narrative for enhancing young children's creative thinking skills. Together with Elizabeth Coates (Centre for Education Studies, Warwick University) and Iram Siraj-Blatchford (Institute of Education, University College London) she co-founded the *International Journal of Early Years Education* and is a member of its editorial board. Recent publications include the edited collections *Exploring Children's Creative Narratives* (Routledge, 2011) and *Progress, Change and Development in Early Childhood Education and Care: International perspectives* (Routledge, 2016).

Natalia Kucirkova is a senior lecturer in Early Years and Childhood Studies at Manchester Metropolitan University, UK. Her research concerns innovative ways of supporting shared book reading, digital literacy and the role of personalisation in early years. Natalia's doctoral research inspired the development of the Our Story tablet/smartphone app. She is the founding convenor of the Children's Digital Books and Literacy Apps Special Interest Group of the United Kingdom Literacy Association. Most recently, Natalia was involved in the production of the Massive Open Online Course 'Childhood in the digital age' by Open University and FutureLearn and a national survey of parents' perceptions of children's media use at home with BookTrust. Her publications have appeared in *First Language, Computers & Education, Cambridge Journal of Education, Communication Disorders Quarterly* and *Learning, Media & Technology*.

Gillian Dowley McNamee is Professor of Child Development and Director of Teacher Education at Erikson Institute in Chicago, Illinois, USA. She works closely with early childhood teacher candidates during their preparation for teaching as well as long term with teachers in schools, particularly those working with children growing up in challenging social and economic situations. Her expertise is in language and literacy development, and in the work of Russian psychologist Lev Vygotsky. She has worked extensively with the storytelling and story-acting activities as developed by Vivian Gussin Paley. She has been a Spencer Fellow with the National Academy of Education, and received a Sunny Days Award from Children's Television Workshop/Sesame Street Parents in 1998. Gillian's new book, *The High Performing Preschool: Story acting in Head Start classrooms* describes the achievements of African American and Latino children engaging in storytelling and story acting during a school year, and the teaching practices that make their learning possible. She is also co-author of *Early Literacy* (Harvard University Press, 1990), *The Fifth Dimension: An after school program built on diversity* (Russell Sage Foundation, 2006), and *Bridging: Assessment for teaching and learning in early childhood classrooms* (Corwin Press, 2007).

Ageliki Nicolopoulou is Professor of Psychology and Global Studies at Lehigh University, USA. She is a sociocultural developmental psychologist whose interests include young children's narrative activities and their role in the construction of reality and identity; the peer group and peer culture as social contexts for children's development, socialisation, and education; and the foundations of emergent literacy. One long-term line of research has explored the ways that participation in Paley's storytelling and story-acting practices can help promote narrative development among low-income preschoolers. She has numerous publications in an interdisciplinary range of journals including *Child Development, Developmental Psychology, Human Development, Early Education and Development, Early Childhood Research Quarterly, Narrative Inquiry, Discourse Studies, The American Journal of Play, Mind, Culture, & Activity*, and *Storyworlds*, as well as chapters in edited volumes. She co-edited (with Scales, Almy and Ervin-

Tripp) a volume on *Play and the Social Context of Development in Early Care and Education*, published by Teachers College Press (1991). More recently she edited a special issue of *Cognitive Development* (2005) on *Play and Narrative: Commonalities, differences, and interrelations.*

INTRODUCTION

Teresa Cremin, Rosie Flewitt, Ben Mardell and Joan Swann

Over the past twenty years, a considerable body of research by applied linguists, educationalists, and child psychologists has established the developmental significance of storytelling and imaginary play during early childhood. This book foregrounds the power of children's own stories and their dictation and dramatisation in the early years classroom. It provides empirical evidence that storytelling and story acting, a pedagogic approach pioneered by Vivian Gussin Paley (1990), affords rich opportunities to foster learning within a play-based and language-rich curriculum. Narrative and imaginary play are widely recognised as valuable strategies for the development of spoken language and literacy within early years and elementary classrooms. Nonetheless in accountability cultures, where early years educators are pressured by the 'drive to literacy' and policy expectations regarding contested concepts such as 'reading readiness' (Whitebread and Bingham, 2012), practitioners often find it hard to make space for children's own stories. Drawing on studies in the USA and the UK, this edited collection illustrates and explores the multiple dimensions of Paley's storytelling and story-acting approach and shows how these interrelated practices enhance language and literacy learning, and contribute to an inclusive classroom culture that embraces young children's diverse interests and learning needs.

Paley's child-centred and play-based philosophy is well-known and well-respected internationally (Paley, 1981, 1984, 1986, 1988, 1990, 1992, 1997, 2001, 2004). Many researchers have recognised Paley's perceptive accounts of children's narrative engagement (e.g. Booth, 2005; Fox, 1993; Gupta, 2009; Nicolopoulou, 2005) and educators interested in early learning have also acknowledged her sensitive understanding of the value and significance of child play (e.g. Craft, 2002; Whitehead, 2004; Wood and Attfield, 2005; Wright, 2010). Her work has made a rich contribution to both theoretical discussions and to professional practice, particularly in the USA and in England (e.g. Cooper, 2009; Lee, 2015; Pound and

Lee, 2011). In relation to her advocated practice of storytelling and story acting, researchers in the USA and the UK have sought to theorise this and understand more fully the nature of its contribution. In the US Nicolopoulou and her colleagues have undertaken a body of empirical work focused upon this practice (e.g. Nicolopoulou, 1997, 2002; Nicolopoulou and Richner, 2004; Nicolopoulou et al., 2014). Alongside this is the work of Cooper (1993, 2005, 2009), Gupta (2009) and McNamee (McNamee et al., 1985; McNamee, 2015). In England, speech therapists Typadi and Hayon (2010) investigated the potential of Paley's storytelling and story-acting practice for promoting communication and language development, and more recently a team of interdisciplinary scholars have researched the wider social and cognitive impacts of this practice in early years education (e.g. Cremin et al., 2013; forthcoming).

Based on new empirical studies, this volume further advances the field, offering new theoretical and practical analyses of storytelling and story acting from complementary disciplinary perspectives. This book emerged from a Literacy Research Association symposium in Dallas 2013 which drew together a multidisciplinary team of academics from the international stage who were exploring the learning potential of Paley's storytelling and story-acting curriculum with particular focus on its contribution to young children's literacy development. Whilst the onset of an ice storm and the subsequent cancellation of flights prevented the whole team from presenting, synergies between members' studies, and interest in each other's research lenses, prompted discussion of a book proposal. A common desire was identified to share theorisations and analyses of Paley's child-centred approach in order to enrich the field and offer support to early years educators who often struggle to foreground creative approaches to learning, particularly given the professional tensions that result from the cultures of assessment and accountability that predominate in the UK and US education systems. The volume thus offers evidence and examples of the power and learning potential of children's dictated and dramatised stories from early years classrooms in England and across the USA.

In order to set the context for the book, the opening chapter by Cremin and Flewitt reviews the research literature with regard to the role of narrative in early learning. Recognising the prevalence of narrative and its potency as a tool for thinking, the authors indicate that through storytelling and imaginary play, young children seek to understand and make sense of their world. The authors examine early narratives in the home and studies of the development of autobiographical memory, these suggest not only that narrative begins to be established very early in life (e.g. Nelson, 1989), but that it also supports young children's capacity to make inferences, imagine and understand experience. Sociocultural research from many cultures is discussed, and this body of research highlights how children learn to talk about and organise their mental representations of past events through engaging in family conversations and through interaction in the wider communities that they experience (e.g. Nelson and Fivush, 2004). Studies of everyday narratives in the home and in preschool settings are drawn upon to argue that these practices support early socialisation and integration into the worlds of their families and peers, and are often collaboratively achieved (e.g. Gupta, 2009). Additionally, research which examines the role of imaginary play and its dynamic relationship to narrative is considered, and how, for instance, through play children explore notions of self via their engagement with narrative. Working in harmony, both these forms of socially situated symbolic action make a rich contribution to young children's social, emotional and cognitive development. The nature of this complementary contribution, the creativity inherent in children's stories and pretend play and their contribution to early literacy learning are core considerations in this chapter.

Finally the authors turn to evidence which suggests that despite the wealth of research attesting to the value of narrative in the early years, the opportunities for children to participate in storytelling and improvisational play in classroom contexts are gradually being reduced and even eroded. Perceiving that practitioners are tethered to the accountability agenda, the authors argue that teachers in many western societies are increasingly obliged to focus on measurable outcomes at the expense of creative approaches to early learning. In these contexts, teachers and other early years practitioners are positioned as little more than technicians, charged with the task of delivering a centralised curriculum and preparing children for standardised assessments. Stripped of their professional agency and autonomy, Cremin and Flewitt argue that many practitioners find it hard to align their understanding and experience of child development and literacy learning with the narrow, mandated curriculum and its accompanying programmes of formalised literacy instruction.

In response to this challenging context, Flewitt, Cremin and Mardell focus in Chapter 2 on an approach which has stood the test of time: Paley's storytelling and story acting. As detailed earlier, although the operationalisation of this approach varies slightly in different contexts, its main components remain the same. These are: children telling their teachers a story which is scribed for them (storytelling), and later that day children enacting their own and their peers' tales in the forum of the classroom (story acting). Chapter 2 examines research in the USA and more recently in England, which has specifically considered this approach, and its value both as a context for children's early learning, and as a practice which teachers can integrate effectively into the early years curriculum. In examining this focused research, the chapter thus locates Paley's approach within the wider empirical literature on children's stories discussed in Chapter 1. Whilst recognising the substantial body of work undertaken by Nicolopoulou and her colleagues, a thematic stance is adopted. Initially the focus is upon the research evidence to date regarding the contribution that storytelling and story acting can make to aspects of young children's learning. These include, for example, consideration of advances in children's narrative competence and cognitive abilities (e.g. Nicolopoulou, 2002); the nurturing of young children's oral language skills (e.g. Cooper, 2009; Typadi and Hayon, 2010); preparedness for school (e.g. McNamee et al., 1985; Nicolopoulou et al., 2015), borrowing of each other's story elements reworked from popular culture and story books (Nicolopoulou et al., 2014); and the development of cohesion and a common classroom culture (e.g. Nicolopoulou and Richner, 2004) which, research suggests, are supported by the multimodal and co-constructed nature of the practices of storytelling and story acting (e.g. Cremin, Flewitt, Swann, Faulkner and Kucirkova, forthcoming). Many of these topics are further advanced in the later empirical chapters in this volume.

Chapter 2 additionally examines the diverse routes that have enabled teachers in the USA and England to experience Paley's storytelling and story-acting curriculum, and the types of training and professional development they have been offered, as well as the perceived benefits. A résumé of the multiple initiatives in both countries is offered which demonstrates the legacy of Paley's work in the classroom. Finally, Flewitt, Cremin and Mardell present some background information on the methodologies employed by the scholars whose research studies are included in this volume.

Moving from reviews of the broader context and previous studies of Paley's story-based approach, Nicolopoulou, in our first empirical chapter in the volume, traces the development of young children's narrative abilities as they participated in this pedagogy over the course of a school year. Whilst valuing the contribution that adult–child interaction can make to children's early narrative abilities, Nicolopoulou argues that complementary educational practices are needed which are more 'child-centered, peer-oriented, and playful'. She considers storytelling and story acting one such approach and in detailing the context of her research underscores the voluntary nature of this activity. In this study, during 'choice time' the children (who were from 'disadvantaged' home backgrounds) were free to decide which activity to participate in, including storytelling. As she notes, almost all the children enthusiastically told stories during this time – between 9 and 21 stories each – and they all took part in acting out their own and their peers' stories. Most were not initially familiar with the basic conventions for telling free-standing stories, and many of their early tales were proto-narratives which encompassed little character action. However, through a thorough, systematic and detailed quantitative analysis of 118 spontaneously produced stories, Nicolopoulou reveals the presence of a clear and significant pattern of narrative development.

Her quantitative approach employed seven measures of narrative development, the first four of which captured the narrative complexity and sophistication of the children's storytelling, whilst the remaining three measures focused on the representation of characters in their narratives. The detailed results unequivocally indicate that the children's stories improved significantly on all seven measures of narrative quality between the autumn and spring semesters. Their stories included for example: more active characters with enhanced complexity and depth; higher proportions of narrative clauses; and a shift from the children's previous use of the present tense to the past tense when telling their tales. In discussing these findings, Nicolopoulou recognises that these shifts might be due simply to the children's maturation over time, but she draws on other evidence from related studies to further endorse the inference that the approach plays a significant role in promoting children's narrative skills. In reflecting upon why this apparently simple storytelling and story-acting activity is so influential, Nicolopoulou posits that the public, peer-oriented and peer-evaluated nature of this activity supports the 'narrative cross-fertilization and reciprocal influence' which was evidenced in the data. She argues convincingly that it is the interplay between storytelling (and its highly decontextualised use of language) and story acting (and its highly contextualised enactment of narrative scenarios) which both promotes and facilitates the children's narrative development.

Cremin, also examining the contribution of Paley's storytelling and story-acting practice in Chapter 4, focuses on children's early print awareness and their agentic development as authors. Working from a sociocultural stance to literacy and learning, she commences by discussing children's early authoring from different ontological perspectives, arguing, alongside others (e.g. Dyson, 2009; Rowe, 2008) that such authoring needs to be viewed as a socially situated act of meaning making, one which children become accustomed to and later adapt the available cultural resources. Cremin draws attention to children's close observation of the adult during storytelling as their spoken words are scribed, and to their later engagement in bringing written tales to life through enactment. Based on a study of the approach in the south-east of England, Cremin explains that some children (aged three to six years old), initiated their own related writing activities, authoring and co-authoring tales with friends and also scribing their peers' stories for later dramatisation (Cremin et al., 2013). In one classroom this child-initiated practice became so popular the teacher provided the class with two of their own storybooks for the purposes of child-initiated narrative composition and scribing.

The specific, local enactments of learning-to-write practices that were evidenced across the study are examined in detail here, with examples of children's stories – drawn, written and scribed for their peers. The analysis indicates that story scribing offered opportunities for children to become acquainted with the relationship between the spoken and the written word, the sequential nature of writing, the direction that writing unfolds in English, and the notion that stories have endings. In addition, and significantly, the whole-class enactment phase served to affirm the permanence of their written words and imbued the practice of telling and scribing with a genuine purpose. Cremin argues this sense of purpose may have served to motivate children to spend their free-play time writing and drawing their own stories and scribing their peers' tales. Connecting to Dyson and Dewayni (2013), she also suggests that the non-regulatory nature of this time and space acted as a potential 'textual playground' for young writers, and afforded new possibilities for exercising freedom. The children's early authoring comprised a naturally occurring individual and often collaborative activity, which not only served social-relational purposes, but also enabled them to creatively and intentionally position themselves as writers. On the basis of the evidence presented, Cremin asserts that the interdependence of the two strands of the approach combine to help apprentice young writers, creating a possibility space for learning both about writing and perhaps more significantly about being a writer and an author.

In Chapter 5, drawing upon the same study in England and also working from a sociocultural perspective, Faulkner explores young children's social and collective meaning making through focusing on the individual narratives children generated during the storytelling sessions. She highlights the presence of other children in 87 per cent of these sessions as children's tales were scribed by adults, yet acknowledges that these young people did not overtly intervene or contribute their own ideas to the storyteller's narrative. Faulkner sought to explore if there was a relationship between the nature and quality of children's involvement in these sessions and cultural transmission.

Through employing Robbins' (2007) analytic framework, she analysed the video data and transcripts of children's stories on the interpersonal and cultural level and includes aspects of the personal. Building on an earlier study by Nicolopoulou et al. (2014) in Pennsylvania, Faulkner also undertook a thematic analysis of the 350 teacher-scribed stories from the English study in order to identify common categories and the children's use of conventional narrative structures. In addition she sought to trace interrelationships between particular story themes and identifiable groups of children. On the basis of this work, Faulkner argues that the nature of children's involvement in storytelling and story acting is well aligned with Rogoff et al.'s construct of 'learning through keen observation and listening, in anticipation of participation' (2003: 176). She discusses how the partnership between the child telling the story and the adult scribing it guides the child's participation in the activity of storytelling at the personal level, and considers the nature of other children's intent participation in this, demonstrating that their participation takes different forms depending on their proximity to the storyteller and their involvement in activities peripheral to the storytelling activity. The thematic analysis of the stories revealed narrative fertilisation within and between storytelling sessions, with central narratives and certain recurring themes and expressions which Faulkner argues served to build local 'communities of mind' characterised by distinctive narrative traditions employed by particular groups of children. Faulkner therefore asserts that Paley's (1990) storytelling and story-acting approach involves learning both through guided and intent participation, in anticipation of the children's own later participation as storytellers and actors. These processes of participation not only develop children's narrative competence, but also facilitate the emergence of distinctive peer cultures and community mindsets.

Connecting to the social, creative and interactional aspects of storytelling and story acting, Swann in Chapter 6 focuses on the collaborative nature of both practices. Like Cremin and Faulkner, she draws on evidence from the south-east England study of MakeBelieve Arts' 'Helicopter Stories'. Swann draws on research from outside education to understand the collaboration evident in interactions between the young storytellers, their teachers and other children in this context. She argues that the analysis of conversational narratives (e.g. Norrick, 2000), while clearly focusing on very different types of stories, can shed light on storytelling practices in classrooms; and that the study of performance by linguistic anthropologists and folklorists (notably Bauman, 1986) may usefully inform the analysis of children's story acting.

Swann illustrates this argument in a close analysis of stories told by George, an initially reticent child who grew in confidence during his participation in storytelling and story acting. Detailed transcription and close analysis of the interactions between George, his teacher and a trainer during storytelling; and the interactions between the adults and children involved in story acting, illustrate the ways in which both written and performed narratives are co-constructed by all participants. The analysis makes evident, for instance, the subtle, moment-by-moment interactional support provided by an adult as George produces each narrative clause in storytelling, and the close negotiation between the adult narrator, child actors and sometimes members of the audience as they contribute to the performance of a character on stage. Storytelling and story acting are inherently creative, and Swann relates both practices to contemporary research on creativity that highlights its collaborative nature. She argues that such collaborative processes of co-creation both value and add value to children's stories.

Chapters 7 and 8 are written by two scholars and researchers who have studied storytelling and story acting as classroom teachers and teacher educators, helping others understand and implement the practice. In Chapter 7 McNamee introduces us to a specific classroom where storytelling and story acting thrives, and a theoretical perspective to understand how the practice promotes children's learning. The theoretical perspective is based on the ideas of the Soviet psychologist Lev Vygotsky, whose explanation of the social nature of learning includes the concept of the zone of proximal development. In a zone of proximal development children move from what they are able to do with the support of others to internalising thought and action and being able to act independently. Vygotsky believed that play provides young children with ideal conditions for learning through the rich zone of proximal development it creates. Among the many benefits of play, children take their first steps into reading and writing. McNamee makes the connection between storytelling and story acting and Vygotsky's theory of learning through play. She argues storytelling and story acting are natural extensions of play and thus create rich zones of proximal development that promote literacy development and other learning as well.

Then, in a storytelling style reminiscent of Paley, McNamee introduces us to Veronica Adams and her eighteen three- and four-year-old students in an early childhood classroom in an economically stressed neighbourhood of Chicago. In Mrs Adams' classroom we find an oasis of safety, a rich learning environment and a powerful illustration of storytelling and story acting in action. McNamee shares one morning's sessions in Mrs Adams' room. We meet Keisha, Zoe and their classmates, and see how, through careful listening and skilled teaching, this teacher implements storytelling and story acting. Like all teachers, Mrs Adams makes mistakes; ones that we can learn from. She also skillfully works with her students, eliciting a story from a shy child by first approaching his playmate, and protecting a child from sharing a private story involving domestic abuse. We see young children joyfully brought into the world of reading and writing.

In Chapter 8 Cooper also draws on Vygotskyan theory, again with play as the link between Vygotsky's ideas and Paley's storytelling and story acting. Along with Vygotsky, Cooper references the work of John Dewey to explain her characterisation of Paley's teaching as involving a 'pedagogy of meaning'; an intentional effort to foster children's imaginative thinking and problem solving. In Cooper's words, this pedagogy 'involves implementation of curricula that scaffold young children's investigations into or engagement with things, first, compatible with their *present* identity and knowledge base, and, second, the pull of new identities and knowledge'.

In the spirit of promoting an open attitude about the themes of the stories children often tell, Cooper also introduces a lens for understanding young children's narratives. Citing Paley, she explains that children's stories often involve the themes of fantasy, friendship, fairness and fear. For Cooper, fantasy does not necessarily mean not true, in the sense that true can be the most meaningful and reasonable explanation to a five-year-old. Using this lens, Cooper makes a case for embracing unrestricted and unoriginal content in the stories children tell. She recognises what many teachers find, that children often tell stories that are derivative from popular culture and are very much like the tales their peers tell. But that, according to Cooper, can be the point for children: to tell stories not to stand out but to fit in. Cooper and Paley both believe young children should have the right to use stories to create a sense of belonging. Cooper identifies sources that are placing this under threat by requiring children to write true stories (in the sense of abiding by an adult standard of reality): state and national curriculum standards and a popular writing curriculum that is often used in kindergarten. She offers a spirited critique of these threats.

Building on the theme of children's meaning making and interest in their own learning, in Chapter 9 Flewitt draws on data from a multicultural inner-city primary school in England, and explores how young children in the early stages of learning English express their thoughts and interests through combinations of spoken, embodied and enacted modes. The chapter begins by reviewing comparatively recent research in the field of multimodality, tracing this work back to its origins in social semiotic theory (Halliday, 1978), and discussing the radically new insights offered by a multimodal perspective into how children make meaning through the intentional interplay of multiple modes. The term 'multimodality' refers to the ways that meaning can be represented through different 'signs' (semiosis), such as gesture, gaze, facial expression, movement, vocalisations *and* language. It also refers to the range of modes used in spoken, handwritten, printed or on-screen texts, such as words, images and layout in printed texts, and wider modal combinations in digital media, including spoken and written words, still and moving images, screen design, sounds, music and so forth.

Flewitt illustrates the relevance of multimodality for understanding early literacy, its compatibility with sociocultural theories of learning and its potential for celebrating diversity and difference in the classroom. Through detailed analysis of the stories told by two boys aged three and five years, both from ethnic and linguistic minority families, the chapter argues that valuing the communicative potential of all modes in storytelling and acting, rather than always prioritising oral and written language, enables young children from diverse backgrounds, regardless of their English-language proficiency, to share their personal interests, perspectives, knowledge and expertise holistically, creatively and practically in ways that link with their imagination and promote their intellectual and social inclusion in the classroom.

In the penultimate chapter of the volume, Mardell and Kucirkova focus their attention on how children's sense of democratic responsibility can be promoted through this story-based approach. Connecting to Paley's own words and colleagues' observations, they highlight the essentially democratic nature of storytelling and story acting, including its child-initiated, voluntary, shared, collaborative and public nature. They argue that in the climate of curriculum pressure and direct instruction it is vital that practitioners employ practices that strengthen democracy. In particular these authors explore the ways in which the approach can nurture young children's own unique and individual voices and foster their agency as learners, as well as the ways in which it can support the development of learning communities within classrooms and early education settings. They highlight the trusting relationships that are built through the telling and enacting of stories – what they describe as 'the glue of democratic classroom communities' and the fact that by listening to the stories of others, children get to know each other. The authors also consider the way in which the scaffolding of storytelling represents an opportunity to either support or undermine children's agency and voice and, drawing on the work of Mardell in Boston, and the efforts to scale up the approach within Boston public schools, offer a strong theorisation of the professional development practices that will support teachers in preserving the democratic character of this approach.

In the Conclusion, Mardell and Swann review earlier chapters and identify important themes that emerge from the presented studies. These include the interdependence of spoken and written language: how a significant oral practice also provides pathways to literacy. Children's agency and creativity are also significant themes, as is the support provided by close collaboration between adults and other children in the production of individual children's narratives. Chapters take a holistic approach to children's development, pointing to the contribution of storytelling and story acting to children's cognitive, social and emotional development, and the essential links that exist between these. Chapters also illustrate the interplay between storytelling and story acting: critically, their interdependence is seen to underpin the potency of Paley's approach. Several chapters illustrate the contribution of visual communicative modes alongside verbal language. The multimodal lens adopted in these chapters adds to our understanding of the value of storytelling and story acting. Finally, chapters see storytelling and story acting as associated with equity and inclusion in individual classrooms whilst also promoting wider democratic ideals.

Whilst these themes demonstrate a degree of consensus between chapter authors, it is recognised that the storytelling and story-acting field is far from settled. Mardell and Swann identify new theoretical, empirical and practical questions that require further research and debate. These include the value of the approach for dual language learners and children with special educational needs, e.g. the potential of using two or more languages in storytelling and story acting. The pressure of time in early years classrooms raises the question of 'dosage': how much time needs to be devoted to this storytelling and story-acting practice in order to reap the full benefits of it? Proponents of storytelling and story acting also differ with respect to teacher intervention: should teachers simply transcribe a child's utterances, or may they intervene with 'gentle scaffolding' to support and guide the child? Should they accept any content or place restrictions on violence, or a reliance on popular culture? Mardell and Swann see differing views on these questions as part of healthy dialogue within the storytelling and story-acting community.

Mardell and Swann's review also looks towards the future of storytelling and story acting. The vibrancy of this approach, they argue, depends on a supportive educational environment, including continuing recognition of the value of play; valuing the professionalism of early years educators; and seeing children as contemporary citizens with independent rights. None of these principles is guaranteed, in particular in the light of the 'accountability' culture discussed in Chapter 1, which tends to reduce agency (teachers' and children's) in the classroom. This uncertain climate highlights what we see as the value of the present volume. We hope the evidence, ideas and arguments presented in these pages will support educators, researchers and others seeking to engage with story in the early years; that they will stimulate further dialogue and debate; and promote further critical enquiry.

References

Bauman, R. (1986) *Story, Performance, and Event: Contextual studies of oral narrative.* Cambridge: Cambridge University Press.

Booth, D. (2005) *Story Drama: Reading, writing and role playing across the curriculum* (2nd edn). Markham, Ontario: Pembroke.

Cooper, P. (1993) *When Stories Come to School: Telling, writing, and performing stories in the early childhood classroom.* New York, NY: Teachers & Writers Collaborative.

Cooper, P. M. (2005) Literacy learning and pedagogical purpose in Vivian Paley's storytelling curriculum. *Journal of Early Childhood Literacy,* 5(3): 229–251.

Cooper, P. M. (2009) *The Classrooms All Young Children Need: Lessons in teaching from Vivian Paley.* Chicago, IL: University of Chicago Press.

Craft, A. (2002) *Creativity and Early Years Education: A life wide foundation.* London: Continuum.

Cremin, T., Swann, J., Flewitt, R. S., Faulkner, D. and Kucirkova, N. (2013) *Evaluation Report of MakeBelieve Arts Helicopter Technique of Storytelling and Story Acting.* The Open University. Available at: http://www.makebelievearts.co.uk/docs/Helicopter-Technique-Evaluation.pdf

Cremin, T., Flewitt, R. S., Swann, J., Faulkner, D. and Kucirkova, N. (forthcoming) Storytelling and story-acting: Co-construction in action. *Journal of Early Childhood Research.*

Dyson, A. H. (2009) Writing in childhood worlds. In R. Beard, D. Myhill, M. Nystrand and J. Riley (eds), *Handbook of Writing Development* (pp. 232–245). London: Sage.

Dyson, A. H. and Dewayni, S. (2013) Writing in childhood cultures. In K. Hall, T. Cremin, B. Comber and L. Moll, *International Handbook of Research on Children's Literacy, Learning, and Culture* (pp. 258–274). Oxford: Wiley Blackwell.

Fox, C. (1993) *At the Very Edge of the Forest: The influence of literature on storytelling by children.* London: Continuum.

Gupta, A. (2009) Vygotskian perspectives on using dramatic play to enhance children's development and balance creativity with structure in the early childhood classroom. *Early Child Development and Care, 179*(8): 1041–1054.

Halliday, M. A. K. (1978) *Language as Social Semiotic.* London: Arnold.

Lee, T. (2015) *Princesses, Dragons and Helicopter Stories: Storytelling and story acting in the early years.* London: Routledge.

McNamee, G. D. (2015) *The High-Performing Preschool: Story acting in Head Start classrooms.* Chicago, IL: University of Chicago Press.

McNamee, G. D., McLane, J. B., Cooper, P. M. and Kerwin, S. M. (1985) Cognition and affect in early literacy development. *Early Child Development and Care, 20*: 229–244.

Nelson, K. (1989) *Narratives from the Crib.* Cambridge, MA: Harvard University Press.

Nelson, K. and Fivush, R. (2004) The emergence of autobiographical memory: A social cultural developmental theory. *Psychological Review, 111*: 486–511.

Nicolopoulou, A. (1997) Worldmaking and identity formation in children's narrative play-acting. In B. D. Cox and C. Lightfoot (eds), *Sociogenetic Perspectives on Internalization* (pp. 157–187). Mahwah, NJ: Erlbaum.

Nicolopoulou, A. (2002) Peer-group culture and narrative development. In S. Blum-Kulka and C. E. Snow (eds), *Talking to Adults: The contribution of multiparty discourse to language acquisition* (pp. 117–152). Mahwah, NJ: Erlbaum.

Nicolopoulou, A. (2005) Play and narrative in the process of development: Commonalities, differences and interrelations. *Cognitive Development, 20*, 495–502.

Nicolopoulou, A. and Richner, E. (2004) 'When your powers combine, I am Captain Planet': The developmental significance of individual- and group-authored stories by preschoolers. *Discourse Studies, 6*: 347–371.

Nicolopoulou, A., Brockmeyer Cates, C., de Sá, A. and Ilgaz, H. (2014) Narrative performance, peer-group culture, and narrative development in a preschool classroom. In A. Cekaite, S. Blum-Kulka, V. Aukrust and E. Teubal (eds), *Children's Peer Talk: Learning from each other* (pp. 42–62). New York, NY: Cambridge University Press.

Nicolopoulou, A., Cortina, K. S., Ilgaz, H., Cates, C. B. and de Sá, A. (2015) Using a narrative- and play-based activity to promote low-income preschoolers' oral language, emergent literacy, and social competence. *Early Childhood Research Quarterly, 31*: 147–162.

Norrick, N. R. (2000) *Conversational Narrative: Conversation in everyday talk.* Amsterdam: John Benjamins.

Paley, V. G. (1981) *Wally's Stories.* Cambridge, MA: Harvard University Press.

Paley, V. G. (1984) *Boys and Girls: Superheroes in the doll corner.* Chicago, IL: University of Chicago Press.

Paley, V. G. (1986) *Mollie is Three: Growing up in school.* Chicago: University of Chicago Press.

Paley, V. G. (1988) *Bad Guys Don't Have Birthdays: Fantasy play at four.* Chicago: University of Chicago Press.

Paley, V. G. (1990) *The Boy Who Would Be a Helicopter: The uses of storytelling in the classroom.* Cambridge, MA: Harvard University Press.

Paley, V. G. (1992) *You Can't Say You Can't Play.* Cambridge, MA: Harvard University Press.

Paley, V. G. (1997) *The Girl with the Brown Crayon*. Cambridge, MA: Harvard University Press.

Paley, V. G. (2001) *In Mrs. Tully's Room: A childcare portrait*. Cambridge, MA: Harvard University Press.

Paley, V. G. (2004) *A Child's Work: The importance of fantasy play*. Chicago, IL: University of Chicago Press.

Pound, L. and Lee, T. (2011) *Teaching Mathematics Creatively*. London and New York: Routledge.

Robbins, J. (2007) Young children thinking and talking: Using sociocultural theory for multi-layered analysis. *Learning and Socio-Cultural Theory: Exploring modern Vygotskian perspectives*, 1: 46–65.

Rogoff, B., Paradise, R., Arauiz, R. M., Correa-Chavez, M. and Angelillo, C. (2003) Firsthand learning through intent participation. *Annual Review of Psychology*, 54: 175–203.

Rowe, D. W. (2008) The social construction of intentionality: Two-year-olds' and adults' participation at a preschool writing center. *Research in the Teaching of English*, 42(4): 387–434.

Typadi, E. and Hayon, K. (2010) Storytelling and story acting: Putting the action into interaction. In F. Griffiths (ed.), *Supporting Children's Creativity through Music, Dance, Drama and Art: Creative conversations in the early years*. London: Routledge.

Whitebread, D. and Bingham, S. (2012) *TACTYC Occasional Paper No. 2, School Readiness: A critical review of perspectives and evidence*. TACTYC. http://tactyc.org.uk/occasional-paper/occasional-paper2.pdf

Whitehead, M. R. (2004) *Language and Literacy in the Early Years* (3rd edn). London: Sage.

Wood, E. and Attfield, J. (2005) *Play, Learning and the Early Childhood Curriculum* (2nd edn). London: Paul Chapman.

Wright, S. (2010) *Understanding Creativity in Early Childhood*. London: Sage.

1

LAYING THE FOUNDATIONS

Narrative and early learning

Teresa Cremin and Rosie Flewitt

In order to understand the developmental and educational significance of storytelling and story acting we locate this within the body of wider research on narrative. Nearly half a century ago, Moffett (1968: 121) claimed that 'young children must, for a long time, make narrative do for all'; from an early age children use narrative as a way of thinking, to construct stories and explanations. Through imaginary play and storytelling children seek to understand and make sense of their world. These significant forms of symbolic activity make a sustained impact upon children's social, emotional and language development, and influence their identity formation (see Engel, 1999, 2005; Fox, 1993; McCabe and Bliss, 2003). By considering the nature and role of narrative, its relationship to pretend play and to creativity, and its potential to influence and support children's early learning and literacy, this chapter seeks to lay the foundations of the book. Narrative is considered in terms of its developmental and cognitive elasticity, which render it instructive and rich across theory, curriculum, and the arts. Through examining research undertaken in homes, preschool settings and early years classrooms, the nature of children's playful and often self-initiated narrative practices is examined.

Following this conceptual focus, the chapter considers the challenge of retaining a strong place for storytelling and imaginary play in early years and early primary education by considering the contemporary context of literacy curricula with particular reference to the UK and USA. In these countries, where the empirical research upon which this book is based was undertaken, there has been an increased emphasis on standardised testing and school accountability. This highly performative (Ball, 1998) agenda is discussed and the pressure it places on teachers and children to focus on measurable outcomes, often at the expense of creative, playful and child-oriented approaches to literacy learning and teaching, is considered.

Narrative

The centrality of narrative as a critical aspect of human thought and development is widely recognised by scholars from many disciplines. Linguists and psychologists, for example, assert that narrative is a major 'organising device' (Langer, 1953) enabling us to order experience, and that it is 'a natural way of thinking' and 'a fundamental mode of thought' (Bruner, 1986, 1990) through which we construct meaning and make sense of experience and the world. Hardy's (1977) well-known assertion that narrative is a 'primary act of mind transferred to art from life' is further underlined when she states:

> we dream in narrative, daydream in narrative, remember, anticipate, hope, despair, believe, doubt, plan, revise, criticize, construct, gossip, learn, hate and love by narrative. In order really to live, we make up stories about ourselves and others, about the personal as well as the social past and future.
> *(Hardy, 1977: 12–13)*

Researchers from many disciplines also testify to the prevalence of narrative, with Barthes (1977), a literary theorist, claiming narrative is 'international, transhistorical and transcultural' and anthropologists, within this universality, documenting cultural diversity in oral and literary storytelling traditions and practices (e.g. Heath, 1983; Hymes, 2004 [1981], 2003). In considering conceptual definitions of narrative, the philosopher Rudrum (2005) notes that the most frequently recurring definition is of narrative as a representation of an event or sequence of events, although Kvernbekk (2003), adopting a broader definition, includes events, characters and plots, causal sequences, a unity through the beginning, middle and end and significance. The significance criterion links to the sociolinguist Labov's (1972) concept of evaluation. In analysing the naturalistic stories of inner-city adolescents, he positions evaluation at the heart of narrative structure and highlights the narrator's affective stance towards events. Researching early education, Wells (1986) claims that making sense, constructing stories and sharing them with others is 'an essential part of being human' (1986: 222). The educationalist Rosen (1984) further argues that story plays a profoundly important part in children's cognitive and emotional development and asserts the potency of narrative, claiming it 'is nothing if not a supreme means of rendering otherwise chaotic, shapeless events into a coherent whole saturated with meaning' (Rosen, 1988: 164). In relation to the practice of storytelling in early childhood, the symbolic potential of language and 'its power to create possible and imaginary worlds through words' (Bruner, 1986: 156) is widely recognised as significant.

However, narrative as an inherently human endeavour is not tied to purely linguistic forms. Narrative expression frequently transcends the spoken or written word and is embodied, as children and adult narrators communicate their narratives multimodally, using gestures, eye gaze, physical proximity and bodily movements, for example, as well as language (Ochs and Capps, 1996). Writing from a dance education research perspective, Chappell (2008) speculates that meaning gleaned from embodied narratives emerges and is felt, but is often difficult to put into words. In order to understand the felt and embodied nature of narrative, since feelings may be 'grasped and intuited only in their moment of experiencing' (Gibson quoted in Abbs, 1989: 58), Chappell (2008) suggests that there needs to be recognition of the aesthetic and affective qualities at play. Embodied narratives, she submits, use movement, dance and the dynamics of the physical human form to express these difficult meanings. Priddis and Howieson's (2010) work connects to this idea that emotional, felt and aesthetic elements are always at play within narrative, and Bruner (1986) too sees emotions, memory and imagination combined in narrative thinking. Links between the emotions, narrative and the imagination are also explored in the work of the educational philosopher Egan (1988, 2005) who maintains that the development of imagination occurs through narrative, and that children's pretend play offers an imaginative space (Vygotsky, 1978) in which story enables thinking about the world, people and relationships.

Early narratives in the home

Studies of the development of autobiographical memory suggest that narrative begins to be established early in life. In analysing the pre-sleep monologues of her daughter (between the ages of 21 and 36 months), Nelson (1989) found that she reproduced fragments of talk and narratives which played out both past and future events and routines. Nelson suggests that these narratives enabled her daughter to make inferences, to imagine and to understand her experiences and that this contributed to her self-regulation and development. Whitehead's (1977) work in early childhood indicates that from very early on, children begin to structure and sequence life experience into simple proto-narratives and later into more complex and layered sequences. Fivush and her colleagues, working from a sociocultural perspective, have established that in a number of cultures, from approximately two years of age, children learn how to talk about and organise their mental representations of past events and activities, often through participating in family conversations (Fivush and Hammond, 1989; Nelson and Fivush, 2004; Wang and Fivush, 2005). As children listen and contribute to the stories their families tell and retell about activities in their shared past, they internalise these as intrapersonal autobiographical memories. This socialising function allows mothers (and other caregivers) to help the young make sense of their world, ensure that their shared stories are aligned with their family's ways of organising life experience, and build a sense of the family's collective identity (Congleton and Rajaram, 2014). Smidt (2006) observes that 'there is no correct way of making stories; we learn the story grammars, discourses and patterns from our society and culture' (2006: 71), and arguably develop our sense of self by storying our lives, for 'we need stories as we need food, and we need stories most of all in childhood, as we need food then in order to grow' (Hollingdale, 1997: 70).

Pretend play and narrative

The relationships between narrative and play are multiple and complex. In the words of Vivian Gussin Paley, 'play … [is] story in action, just as storytelling is play put into narrative form' (1990: 4). Indeed she further asserts 'that this view of play makes play, along with its alter ego, storytelling and acting, the universal learning medium' (1990: 10). Not dissimilarly, Wilson (1998) claims that 'playing with anything to make something is always paralleled in cognition by the creation of a story' (1998: 195). In particular, imaginary play enables children to assume roles and engage in 'as-if' thinking and pretending to be someone or something else. In looking across numerous studies of imaginary play and narrative, Nicolopoulou (2005) suggests that these have established that children's developing story skills help them to own and use a wide variety of symbolic resources to construct possible worlds, and that as they do so, they draw upon the imaginative capacities expressed in and supported by their pretend play (e.g. Baumer et al., 2005; Dyson, 1993; Engel, 2005; Gupta, 2009; Rowe, 2000). Connecting to the work of Vygotsky (1978), Nicolopoulou (2005) also observes that narrative and play are both forms of socially situated symbolic action and that in children's play the enactment of narrative scenarios is key.

> Action in the imaginative sphere, in an imaginary situation, in the creation of voluntary intentions and the formation of life-like plans and volitional motives—all appear in play and make it the highest level of preschool development.
>
> *(Vygotsky, 1978: 102)*

Many scholars have studied the contribution of pretend play to children's narrative development (Pellegrini and Galda, 1982), to their logical reasoning (Amsel et al., 2005), to their language and cognition (Gupta, 2009), to their literacy (e.g. Mages, 2006; Nicolopoulou et al., 2015; Pelligrini, 1984; Roskos and Christie, 2000) and to their multilingual abilities (Long et al., 2007).

Both Engel (2005) and Ilgaz and Aksu-Koc (2005) stress that sociodramatic play prompts narrative thinking which is expressed through verbal narration. Engel (2005) gives the example of two children moving cars and making appropriate engine noises as they pretend to drive them. She describes this as pretence not narrative play. However, if one of the children voices narrative actions and undertakes these ('the car is skidding, it's going to crash' for example), then Engel (2005) suggests, this can be viewed as narrative play. (Although from a multimodal perspective, enacting skidding, a crash etc. is also a simple narrative action even if not voiced as such.) Engel argues that narrative play is a direct 'descendant of pretend play' and demonstrates that when preschoolers use language to weave their symbolic play into a narrative, this enables exploration in an alternative symbolic world, one which stimulates experimentation and speculation. Children's stories, which become quite complex by their fourth year, enable them, Engel (2005) claims, to move easily between 'what is' narratives (in which their play simulates everyday life), and 'what if' narratives (in which they play in an imaginary world of fictive possibilities). She suggests that children not only oscillate between these two domains of experience with ease, but also explore the boundaries between them.

Recognised as 'the serious and necessary occupation of children' (Dyson, 2009: 122), studies of young children as 'symbol weavers' (Dyson, 1990) reveal the significant role of imaginary play and show how through such play children explore notions of self through oral narrative. For example, Kendrick's (2005) study of a five-year-old's story, voiced as she played with her doll's house, shows how she engages in exploring who she is and who she might be, effectively authoring her own potential autobiography through play. Through her narrative play she not only explores her sense of self but also 'communicates her understanding of what it means to be a woman in her particular family and culture' (Kendrick, 2005: 22). In another study, eighteen four- and five-year-olds' learning was examined when they told and enacted their own stories (Gupta, 2009). Each child was enabled to tell their stories (which were scribed), create an impromptu 'play' and become personally involved in directing the dramatisation of this with their peers, often with costumes and props and scenery. In the process of exploring options and identifying solutions, the young learners engaged in peer discussions. Gupta (2009) argues that through their collective participation in this cultural activity, the children had the opportunity to develop cognitively, linguistically, interpersonally, intrapersonally, emotionally and artistically. Whilst recognising that the breadth of learning involved was shaped by the small class size and the innovative teacher, Gupta suggests this particular dramatic play curriculum evidenced Rogoff's (2003) conception of guided participation. In relation to classroom drama, which many scholars argue is closely linked to play (both make use of the imagination, narrative, emotions and dialogue), a meta-analysis of studies by Podlozny (2000) indicates that drama has a beneficial effect on young children's oral language development and facilitates both their narrative recall and their understanding. As Mages (2008) observes, however, it is unclear whether the language gains reported in the meta-analysis 'were due to drama, to tutoring, to peer interactions, or to a combination of these factors' (2008: 130).

Scholars have also investigated how children's improvisations and everyday creativity are encouraged and enhanced when they are able to bring to school ideas and resources from their out-of-school interests and activities, including their everyday practices with new media. Drawing on Pennycook's (2010) conceptualisation of 'relocalisation' as a term to describe how texts and text-making practices are creatively transformed as they are repeated and reused in new contexts, Collier (2013) observed in a longitudinal study how a young boy, Kyle, explored his interest in wrestling by watching it online, on television, by playing wrestling games on his PlayStation 2 and by enacting and narrating pretend wrestling matches with miniature wrestlers and Pokémon action figures. Over the course of this two-year study, as Kyle grew from eight to ten years of age, he repeatedly enacted his favourite professional wrestler, using invented props to populate his pretend play, and blurring the boundaries between real and imagined practices. In so doing, he creatively relocated the world of professional wrestling into his own life at home and in school. These practices allowed him to display his expertise through his enactments, to gain control and bring a topic of personal interest into his school work. As Collier explains, although expressions of any kind of violence were taboo in Kyle's school, wrestling *per se* was not, and Kyle's teachers acknowledged the importance for him of his interest in this form of popular culture which cut across his physical and digital play activities. Rather than ignoring or dismissing his interest, they recognised the pleasure and learning opportunities that popular culture practices and texts can offer to school learning (Buckingham, 1998).

Pretend play, like narrative play, can be solitary, but is often a collaborative endeavour, a socially shared phenomenon, which Rowe (2000: 20) observes 'allows children to walk around in story settings', to touch, feel and pretend 'otherwise'. Research into the everyday narratives of preschool classrooms suggests that these socialisation practices are also collaboratively achieved and support children's integration into the social world of their peers. Kyratziz and Green (1997), in documenting storying during drawing activities, reveal that even when children appear to retell their tales of lived experience these are often joint productions, involving several children. Puroila et al.'s (2012) work studying children's spontaneous narratives affirms this. They show that when 'space' is available for children to narrate together, then their stories, whilst fragmentary, are co-constructed. In the process, they co-construct their friendships, peer cultures and identities, further demonstrating the centrality of narrative in early learning.

Creativity and narrative

Like storytelling, dramatic play proceeds without a script and is a prime example of Sawyer's (2004) 'performance creativity' in which the creative process and the resulting product are co-occurring. There are a number of studies that explore the importance of narrative and play in fostering children's creativity *in* and *through* language (for a review see Cremin and Maybin, 2013). As noted above, scholars have shown that children naturally experiment with language sounds, structures and meanings (e.g. Whitehead, 1977; Nelson, 1989). This kind of spontaneous, often playful, creativity in language arguably contains the seeds of more prestigious poetic, literary and dramatic cultural forms (Cook, 2000; Tannen, 2007). Children also engage creatively through language, using it for the construction of alternative worlds, practising social roles, rational exploration and hypothetical thinking. For example, in studying the oral narratives of four- and five-year-olds, Fox (1993) reveals the generative nature of narrative and the complex ways in which children draw on their experience of literary stories read and told to them. Whilst she notes that 'the model for the children's stories was very obviously literary', Fox (1993: 84) also demonstrates that children combine these with stories about their own lives, since as Rosen (1984: 33) asserts 'any story presupposes the existence of other stories ... for both reader and listener (or teller and told) threads of connection exist, threads of many different kinds'. In the stories Fox (1993) collected, children combined real and fantasy events, producing complex narrative structures that motivated their exploration of physical laws and logical thought, as well as their social world.

Through examining preschool aged children's self-initiated play, the creativity inherent in their narratives has also been documented (Craft et al., 2012b). In this study, driven by a leading question or narrative, voiced by children and/or teachers, children's play demonstrated individual, collaborative and communal creativity. In related work, also focused on the conception of 'possibility thinking' at the heart of creativity, the foundational nature of narrative was revealed (Cremin et al., 2013). The concept of 'possibility thinking', developed by Craft (2001), refers to 'what if' and 'as if' thinking in children aged three to eleven. The 2013 paper examined three previously published empirical studies of possibility thinking (Chappell et al., 2008; Craft et al., 2012a; Craft et al., 2012b) and revealed that reciprocal relationships exist between questioning, imagination and narrative (Cremin et al., 2013). Leading questions voiced by practitioners or children appeared to create a possibility space in which children's imaginations and ongoing questioning contribute to the development of narratively framed 'sequences' of possibility thinking. Additionally, narrative itself provides the possibility space for children's questioning and imaginative engagement (Cremin et al., 2013). This connects to earlier work by Fox (1990) who asserted that:

> the practice of narrating stories, either invented or retold, helps young children to come to know what it is to think through problems, argue cases, see both sides of questions, find supporting evidence and make hypotheses, comparisons, definitions and generalizations.
>
> *(Fox, 1993: 121)*

It is clear that rich creative opportunities are afforded by the space to tell and dramatise stories; in narrating and enacting both 'what is' and potential 'what if' world narratives, young children's learning is enabled.

Narrative and early literacy learning

Research into narrative in early learning suggests that early narrative competence proffers a secure foundation for emergent literacy and long-term success in schooling (e.g. McCabe and Bliss, 2003; Tabors et al., 2001). In addition, some studies indicate that early narrative skills are linked to and predictive of reading comprehension in the later primary school years (e.g. Dickinson and Tabors, 2001; Griffin et al., 2004). Early literacy activity is often embedded in children's playful approach to early learning. Their deployment of narrative to organise and make sense of experience not only serves to promote academic learning and enhance their literacy skills, but also supports the development of the skills that are required for success in the twenty-first century – skills such as creativity, risk taking and coping with uncertainty (Fisher et al., 2011). Additionally, the roles children adopt during early pretend play and their use of cultural symbols and practices prepare the ground for their participation in literacy events (Gillen, 2002; Vygotsky, 1978).

When retelling and re-enacting stories in the early years (regardless of whether these are based on traditional oral stories, printed texts or life experiences), play enriches the language children use as they improvise and adopt perspectives (e.g. Rowe, 1998, 2000; Sawyer, 2003). Some scholars such as Gerrig (1993) argue that young children's ability to inhabit imaginary circumstances during pretend play is 'a basic aspect of narrative experience that endures through the lifespan' (1993: 195), and that this may later be seen in adults' engaged and absorbed mental states whilst reading (Harris, 2000). Meek (2002), too, suggests that the reading and experience of fiction is somewhat like play, in that it has the capacity to expand children's imaginations, building the imaginary 'what if' world, as well as enabling them to recognise elements of the world of 'what is'. Indeed, the use of 'life to text' and 'text to life' strategies (Cochran Smith, 1984, cited in Gregory, 1996: 81) are now widely accepted as essential aspects of the process of learning to read. It is precisely these strategies which young children stretch when narrating and enacting their own and others' stories.

However, children's early narrative competence, imaginative capacities and out-of-school interests do not always translate easily into schooled practices. In early years settings in England for example, due to the downward pressure of the primary curriculum and its attendant assessment regime, storytelling and socio-dramatic play are rarely given the attention they deserve. When the preschoolers that Fox (1993) studied entered formal education, their narrative capacity was unnoticed; one was never invited to tell a story and another was 'tested on suspicion of "language retardness" during the period when he was recording 29,000 words of narrative at home' (Fox, 2004: 193). In the US, the seminal work of the anthropologist Heath (1983) described how young children growing up in the highly oral environment of the Trackton community told stories in the same manner and style as their community, creating highly exaggerated and imaginative retellings of real events and making multiple metaphoric connections. Nonetheless, these skills were not transferred into the classroom where children were asked to label discrete features of objects and events; they were not given the space to share the texts of their lives or create imaginary tales and enact them with their peers. Unsurprisingly therefore, unable to draw on their language and cultural practices for learning, they were often perceived to have low literacy levels, and gradually became alienated from school.

Whilst both these studies were undertaken some years ago, there is little evidence that the situation has altered dramatically. Indeed, more recent research suggests that despite children's narrative capacities and wide recognition of the role of narrative in early learning, playful child-initiated and story-based activities are being pushed to one side in favour of structured literacy routines and practices (Dyson and Dewayni, 2013; Genishi and Dyson, 2009; Hirsh-Pasek et al., 2009). The challenge of integrating the creative practices of storytelling and enactment into the literacy curriculum, even in the early years of schooling should not be underestimated. These challenges are now examined in the light of recent developments in UK and USA early years literacy curricula, which in turn reflect global trends in early education policy and curricula.

Current trends in early years literacy curricula

Literacy has always been viewed as the cornerstone for learning, as essential for personal development and for the social, cultural and economic growth of communities and nations. For many decades, literacy has been central in national and international policy debates about making high-quality education accessible to all, and, along with numeracy, as having the potential to transform individual lives by offering pathways to overcome poverty, unemployment and poor health (Flewitt and Roberts-Holmes, 2015). Literacy levels have been assessed and compared as never before through the development of international comparative 'league tables' such as the Organisation for Economic Co-operation and Development's (OECD) Programme for International Student Assessment (PISA) and the National Center for Education Statistics' Progress in International Reading Literacy Study (PIRLS). International assessments such as these have been designed explicitly to influence national policy (Rizvi and Lingard, 2013), and have become defining features of the sustained political drive to improve national and global levels of literacy from the earliest years onwards.

Governments have responded variously to the pressures imposed on them by transnational organisations, such as the OECD and UNESCO, which hold national systems to account against international benchmarks and indicators. In the UK and the USA, policy-makers have committed to intervening directly in public education systems, and in the case of literacy, to raising literacy levels by applying new principles (Moss, 2009). The chosen principles for systemic reform in these contexts are based on the premise that 'standards' are an effective tool for improvement – that setting high standards with measurable goals can improve individual outcomes, that standards can be reliably assessed through the administration of national tests, and that improved standards will lead to higher performance in international education league tables. The standards agenda has therefore led to the development and implementation of highly prescriptive literacy curricula, standardised measures for child assessment and a new era of governance where schools and teachers are held to account for annual increases in test scores (see Ball, 2013; Moss, 2009).

Within a global culture of performativity (Ball, 1998), national tests have become the focus for policy-makers concerned with early years and primary education. In the USA, education policy was dominated from 2002–2010 by 'No Child Left Behind' (NCLB), which held schools responsible for year-on-year increases in the percentage of children who passed a series of national tests, and rated schools according to their level of success. When flaws in NCLB became apparent, the US government response was to increase the use of high-stakes testing (mandated in the Race to the Top law) and to strengthen the standards

(Snow, 2014). A significant policy led by the National Governors Association, and championed by the Obama administration, the 'Common Core State Standards' (CCSS; see http://www.corestandards.org/) was instituted. These standards work backwards from the skills that all students may ultimately need to enter university or employment, and set out what students need to learn at every grade level along the way, with profound 'trickle-down' consequences for early education in the USA.

Similar systems of testing national standards have dominated education in the UK, particularly since the 1990s through the introduction of Standard Assessment Tasks for seven-, eleven- and fourteen-year-olds in England. Following a series of critical reports and a fiasco over flaws in their marking, the tests for fourteen-year-olds in England were abandoned in 2008. However, tests for younger children have increased, with the introduction of a national Phonics Screening Check for five- and six-year-olds in 2012 (Flewitt and Roberts-Holmes, 2015), and a new national Spelling, Grammar and Punctuation test for seven-year-olds in 2016. Whilst the heavily critiqued plans for 'Baseline Assessment' of all four- and five-year-olds at the point of school entry from autumn 2016 (Bradbury and Roberts-Holmes, 2016) have been dropped, the profession expects an alternative assessment regime to be forthcoming.

These national tests carry high stakes not only for individual children, their teachers and schools but also for politicians, whose very political futures are dependent on providing a wavering electorate and competitive international markets with evidence of national success. Consequently over the past two decades, standardised test results with quantifiable outcomes have become the narrow benchmark against which the quality of early education is rated. As Mansell (2007) points out, whereas in the public mind 'raising standards' may have become synonymous with improving the quality of education, in schools 'raising standards' has the more tightly defined meaning of raising test scores, which are then measured against a set of narrow indicators that have been decided by policy-makers rather than educators.

Although 'raising standards' is by no means synonymous with 'improving quality', the political drive to raise literacy standards can yield positive gains. The question is, at what educational, professional and financial cost? The breadth of the curriculum on offer is inevitably affected, and children's access to rich and playful literacy learning opportunities has been diminished. Alexander (2011) argues that in England:

> The tests impoverished the curriculum; the national strategies and professional standards impoverished pedagogy in both conception and practice … in many primary schools a professional culture of excitement, inventiveness and healthy scepticism was supplanted by one of dependency, compliance and even fear; and the approach may in some cases have depressed both standards of learning and the quality of teaching.
>
> *(Alexander, 2011: 273)*

His observations also pertain to early years education contexts, where the downward pressure of assessment and the dubious concept of reading readiness combine to constrict the literacy curriculum and reduce opportunities for play, for storytelling and other creative early practices underpinned by narrative (Whitebread and Bingham, 2012). In the USA, Wohlwend and Peppler (2015) argue that:

> Play is losing to rigor in American classrooms as more and more structured reading and math replaces traditional playtime, thanks in large part to pressure to meet the Common Core State Standards. Young children, in particular, are losing out because this increasing standardization of the curriculum restricts the variety of ways they could and should be learning.
>
> *(Wohlwend and Pepper, 2015: 22)*

For young children and their educators, the outcomes of education performativity policies have intruded with ever greater insistence into the ways that classroom learning is framed. Rather than being encouraged by curriculum requirements to plan for educational experiences that engage children's interest and enthusiasm, and build on the narrative practices that they bring to school, teachers are statutorily obliged to observe measurable outcomes that are demonstrated through the successful completion (or not) of simple tasks. Many of these tasks involve routinised learning, and often have no identifiable purpose other than the achievement of a quantifiable measure, which is subsequently used for school and teacher accountability rather than for planning child learning. Arguably, this fosters 'a professional mindset characterised more by compliance and conformity than curiosity and creativity' (Cremin, 2016: 19) and shifts the professional role of teachers to being technocrats first and foremost and educators if and when they can find the time.

Conclusion

In early learning, narrative matters. From birth onwards young children make extensive use of imaginary play and storytelling in order to understand and make sense of their world. Over the past 25 years, a considerable body of research by sociolinguists and child psychologists has established the developmental significance of storytelling and imaginary play during early childhood. These activities benefit social, emotional and language development as well as children's understanding of their identities and their worlds. Educationalists, too, recognise the power of story and imaginary play and the value of both to young children's learning and literacy development.

Yet in many preschool classrooms, particularly in England and the USA, the narrative-driven world of the young who rely upon telling their own narratives and using imaginary play to make sense of their world, is all too often sidelined by the test-driven world of politicians. National mandates and state policies that are underpinned by narrow conceptualisations of literacy and learning position formalised literacy instruction and measurable outcomes frontstage – in the footlights. Almost inevitably therefore playful story-based approaches to early learning and literacy tend to be relegated backstage – in the shadows. It is in response to this contradictory and challenging context, that this book was written. Drawing on new research into Paley's (1990) storytelling and story-acting approach, it provides evidence from the USA and the UK that not only offers hope and possibility in this constraining context, but bears testament to the value of making spaces for children's stories and for nurturing and valuing these through Paley's (1990) storytelling and story-acting curriculum.

References

Abbs, P. (1989) *The Symbolic Order: A contemporary reader for the arts debate*. London: The Falmer Press.

Alexander, R. (2011) Evidence, rhetoric and collateral damage: The problematic pursuit of 'world class' standards. *Cambridge Journal of Education, 41*, 3: 265–286.

Amsel, E., Triofi, G. and Campbell, R. (2005) Reasoning about make-believe and hypothetical suppositions: Towards a theory of belief-contravening reasoning. *Cognitive Development, 20*(4): 545–575.

Ball, S. J. (1998) Performativity and fragmentation in 'postmodern schooling'. In J. Carter (ed.), *Postmodernity and Fragmentation of Welfare* (pp. 187–203). London: Routledge.

Ball, S. (2013) *The Education Debate: Politics and policy in the 21st century*. Bristol: Policy Press.

Barthes, R. (1977) *Image, Music, Text*. New York: Hill and Wang.

Baumer, S., Ferholt, B. and Lecusay, R. (2005) Promoting narrative competence through adult–child joint pretence. *Cognitive Development, 20*: 576–590.

Bradbury, A. and Roberts-Holmes, G. (2016) 'They are children not robots, not machines': The introduction of Reception Baseline Assessment. Report for National Union of Teachers. Available at: http://www.betterwithoutbaseline.org.uk/uploads/2/0/3/8/20381265/baseline_assessment_2.2.16-_10404.pdf

Bruner, J. S. (1986) *Actual Minds, Possible Worlds*. Cambridge, MA: Harvard University Press.

Bruner, J. (1990) *Acts of Meaning*. Cambridge, MA: Harvard University Press.

Buckingham, D. (1998) Media education in the UK: Moving beyond protectionism. *Journal of Communication, 48*(1): 33–43.

Chappell, K. (2008) Embodied narratives. In S. Parry, H. Nicholson and R. Levinson (eds), *Creative Encounters* (pp. 160–173). London: Wellcome Trust.

Chappell, K., Craft, A., Burnard, P. and Cremin, T. (2008) Question-posing and question-responding: The heart of possibility thinking in the early year. *Early Years, 283*: 267–286.

Collier, D. R. (2013) Relocalizing wrestler: Performing texts across time and space. *Language and Education, 27*(6): 481–497.

Congleton, A. R. and Rajaram, S. (2014) Collaboration changes both the content and the structure of memory. *Journal of Experimental Psychology: General, 143*(4): 1570–1584.

Cook, G. (2000) *Language Play, Language Learning*. Oxford: Oxford University Press.

Craft, A. (2001) Little c Creativity. In A. Craft, B. Jeffrey and M. Leibling, *Creativity in Education* (pp. 45–61). London: Continuum.

Craft, A., Cremin, T., Burnard, P., Dragovic, T. and Chappell, K. (2012a) Possibility thinking: Culminative studies of an evidence-based concept driving creativity? *Education, 3–13.* http://dx.doi.org/10.1080/03004279.2012.656671

Craft, A., McConnon, L. and Matthews, A. (2012b) Child-initiated play and professional creativity. *Thinking Skills and Creativity* 7(1): 48–61.

Cremin, T. (2016) Open Dialogue peer review: A response to Claxton and Lucas. *The Psychology of Education Review,* 40(1): 17–22.

Cremin, T. and Maybin, J. (2013) Language and creativity. In K. Hall, T. Cremin, B. Comber and L. Moll, *The Wiley Blackwell International Research Handbook of Children's Literacy, Learning and Culture* (pp. 275–290). Oxford: Wiley Blackwell.

Cremin, T., Chappell, K. and Craft, A. (2013) Reciprocity between narrative, questioning and imagination in the early and primary years: Examining the role of narrative in possibility thinking. *Thinking Skills and Creativity,* 9(3): 136–151.

Dickinson, D. K. and Tabors, P. O. (eds) (2001) *Beginning Literacy with Language: Young children learning at home and school.* Baltimore, MD: Paul H. Brookes.

Dyson, A. H. (1990) Research in review. Symbol makers, symbol weavers: How children link play, pictures and print. *Young Children, 45*(2): 50–57.

Dyson, A. H. (1993) *Social Worlds of Children's Learning to Write in an Urban Primary School.* New York: Teachers College Press.

Dyson, A. H. (2009) Writing in childhood worlds. In R. Beard, D. Myhill, M. Nystrand and J. Riley (eds), *Handbook of Writing Development* (pp. 232–245). London: Sage.

Dyson, A. H. and Dewayni, S. (2013) Writing in childhood cultures. In K. Hall, T. Cremin, B. Comber and L. Moll, *International Handbook of Research on Children's Literacy, Learning, and Culture* (pp. 258–274). Oxford: Wiley Blackwell.

Egan, K. (1988) *Teaching as Story Telling. An alternative approach to teaching and curriculum in the elementary school.* Chicaco, IL: University of Chicago Press.

Egan, K. (2005) *An Imaginative Approach to Teaching.* San Francisco: Jossey-Bass.

Engel, S. (1999) *The Stories Children Tell: Making sense of the narratives of childhood.* New York, NY: W. H. Freeman and Co.

Engel, S. (2005) The narrative worlds of what-is and what-if. *Cognitive Development, 20*: 514–525.

Fisher, K., Hirsh-Pasek, K., Golinkoff, R., Singer, D. and Berk, L. (2011) Playing around in school: Implications for learning and educational policy. In A. D. Pellifrini (ed.), *The Oxford Handbook of the Development of Play.* New York, NY: Oxford University Press.

Fivush, R. and Hammond, N. R. (1989) Time and again: The effects of repetition and retention interval on two year old's event recall. *Journal of Experimental Child Psychology,* 47: 259–273.

Flewitt, R. S. and Roberts-Holmes, G. (2015) Regulatory gaze and 'non-sense' phonics testing in early literacy. In M. Hamilton, R. Heydon, K. Hibbert and R. Stooke, *Multimodality and Governmentality: Negotiating spaces in literacy education* (pp. 95–113). London: Bloomsbury/Continuum Books.

Fox, C. (1993) *At the Very Edge of the Forest: The influence of literature on storytelling by children.* London: Continuum.

Fox, C. (2004) Playing the storyteller. In N. Hall, J. Larson and J. Marsh, *Handbook of Early Childhood Literacy* (pp. 189–198). London: Sage.

Genishi, C. and Dyson, A. Haas (2009) *Children, Language, and Literacy: Diverse learners in diverse times.* New York, NY and Washington, DC: Teachers College Press and The National Association for the Education of Young Children.

Gerrig, R. J. (1993) *Experiencing Narrative Worlds: On the psychological activities of reading.* New Haven, CT: Yale University Press.

Gillen, J. (2002) Moves in the territory of literacy? The telephone discourse of three and four year olds. *Journal of Early Childhood Literacy, 2*(1): 21–43.

Gregory, E. (1996) *Making Sense of a New World: Learning to read in a second language.* London: Paul Chapman.

Griffin, T. M., Hemphill, L., Camp, L. and Wolf, D. P. (2004) Oral discourse in the preschool years and later literacy skills. *First Language, 24*: 123–147.

Gupta, A. (2009) Vygotskian perspectives on using dramatic play to enhance children's development and balance creativity with structure in the early childhood classroom. *Early Child Development and Care, 179*(8): 1041–1054.

Hardy, B. (1977) Towards a poetics of fiction: An approach through narrative. In M. Meek, A. Warlow and G. Barton (eds), *The Cool Web.* London: Bodley Head.

Harris, P. L. (2000) *The Work of the Imagination.* Oxford: Blackwell Publishers.

Heath, S. B. (1983) *Ways with Words: Language, life and work in communities and classrooms.* Cambridge: Cambridge University Press.

Hirsh-Pasek, K., Golinkoff, R. M., Berk, L. E. and Singer, D. G. (2009) *A Mandate for Playful Learning in Preschool: Presenting the evidence.* New York, NY: Oxford University Press.

Hollingdale, P. (1997) *Signs of Childness in Children's Books.* Stroud: The Thimble Press.

Hymes, D. (2003) *'Now I Only Know So Far': Essays in ethnopoetics.* Lincoln, NE: University of Nebraska Press.

Hymes, D. (2004 [1981]) *'In Vain I Tried to Tell You': Essays in Native American ethnopoetics.* Lincoln, NE: University of Nebraska Press.

Ilgaz, H. and Aksu-Koc, A. (2005) Episodic development in preschool children's play-prompted and direct-elicited narrative. *Cognitive Development, 20*(4): 526–544.

Kendrick, M. (2005) Playing house: A 'sideways' glance at literacy and identity in early childhood. *Journal of Early Childhood Literacy, 5*(1): 5–28.

Kvernbekk, T. (2003) On identifying narrative studies. *Philosophy and Education, 22*: 267–279.

Kyratziz, A. and Green, J. (1997) Jointly constructed narratives in classrooms: Co-construction of friendship and community through language. *Teaching and Teacher Education, 13*(1): 17–37.

Labov, W. (1972) *Language in the Inner City.* Philadelphia, PA: University of Pennsylvania Press.

Langer, S. K. (1953) *Feeling and Form.* London: Routledge and Kegan Paul.

Long, S., Volk, D. and Gregory, E. (2007) Intentionality and expertise: Learning from observations of children at play in multilingual, multicultural contexts. *Anthropology and Education Quarterly, 38*(3): 239–259.

Mages, W. K. (2006) Drama and imagination: A cognitive theory of drama's effect on narrative comprehension and narrative production. *Research in Drama Education: The Journal of Applied Theatre and Performance, 11*(3): 329–340.

Mages, W. K. (2008) Does creative drama promote language development in early childhood? Review of the methods and measures employed in the empirical literature. *Review of Educational Research, 78*(1): 124–152.

Mansell, W. (2007) *Education by Numbers: The tyranny of testing.* London: Politico.

McCabe, A. and Bliss, L. S. (2003) *Patterns of Narrative Discourse.* Boston, MA: Allyn and Bacon.

Meek, M. (2002) What more needs saying about imagination? Address at the 19th International Reading Association World Congress on Reading, Edinburgh, Scotland.

Moffett, J. (1968) *Teaching the Universe of Discourse.* Boston, MA: Houghton Mifflin.

Moss, G. (2009) The politics of literacy in the context of large-scale education reform. *Research Papers in Education, 24*(2): 155–174.

Nelson, K. (1989) *Narratives from the Crib.* Cambridge, MA: Harvard University Press.

Nelson, K. and Fivush, R. (2004) The emergence of autobiographical memory: A social cultural developmental theory. *Psychological Review,* 111: 486–511.

Nicolopoulou, A. (2005) Play and narrative in the process of development: Commonalities, differences and interrelations. *Cognitive Development, 20*: 495–502.

Nicolopoulou, A., Cortina, K. S., Ilgaz, H., Cates, C. B. and de Sá, A. B. (2015) Using a narrative- and play-based activity to promote low-income preschoolers' oral language, emergent literacy and social competence. *Early Childhood Research Quarterly, 31*: 147–162.

Ochs, E. and Capps, I. (1996) Narrating the self. *Annual Review of Anthropology, 25:* 19–43.

Paley, V. G. (1990) *The Boy Who Would Be a Helicopter: The uses of storytelling in the classroom.* Cambridge, MA: Harvard University Press.

Pelligrini, A. D. (1984) The effect of dramatic play on children's generation of cohesive text. *Discourse Processes,* 7: 57–67.

Pellegrini, A. and Galda, L. (1982) The effects of thematic fantasy play training on the development of children's story comprehension. *American Educational Research Journal,* Fall, *19*(3): 443–452.

Pennycook, A. (2010) *Language as a Local Practice.* London: Routledge.

Podlozny, A. (2000) Strengthening verbal skills through the use of classroom drama: A clear link. *Journal of Aesthetic Education, 34*(3–4): 239–275.

Priddis, L. E. and Howieson, N. D. (2010) Narrative as a window to the inner mental world of young children: Attachment representations, affect and memory. *Journal of Early Childhood Research, 8*(2): 161–174.

Puroila, A-M., Estola, E. and Syrjälä, L. (2012) Does Santa exist? Children's everyday narratives as dynamic meeting places in a day care centre context. *Early Child Development and Care, 182*(2): 191–206.

Rizvi, F. and Lingard, B. (2013) *Globalizing Education Policy.* New York, NY: Routledge.

Rogoff, B. (2003) *The Cultural Nature of Human Development.* New York, NY: Oxford University Press.

Rosen, H. (1984) *Stories and Meanings.* Sheffield: National Association for the Teaching of English.

Rosen, H. (1988) The irrepressible genre. In M. Maclure, T. Phillips and A. Wilkinson (eds), *Oracy Matters.* Milton Keynes: Open University Press.

Roskos, K. A. and Christie, J. F. (eds) (2000) *Play and Literacy in Early Childhood: Research from multiple perspectives.* Mahwah, NJ: Lawrence Erlbaum Associates.

Rowe, D. (1998) The literate potentials of book-related dramatic play. *Reading Research Quarterly, 33*: 10–35.

Rowe, D. (2000) Bringing books to life. In K. A. Roskos and J. F. Christie (eds), *Play and Literacy in Early Childhood.* Mahwah, NJ: Lawrence Erlbaum.

Rudrum, D. (2005) Towards the limits of definition. *Narrative, 13*(2): 195–204.

Sawyer, K. (2003) Levels of analysis in pretend lay discourse: Metacommunication in conversational routines. In D. E. Lytle (ed.), *Play and Educational Theory and Practice* (pp. 137–157). Westport, CT: Praeger.

Sawyer, K. R. (2004) Creative teaching: Collaborative discussion as disciplined improvisation. *Educational Researcher, 33*(3): 12–20.

Smidt, S. (2006) *The Developing Child in the 21st Century: A global perspective on child development.* London: Routledge.

Snow, C. (2014) Language, literacy and the needs of the multilingual child. *Perspectives in Education, 32*(1): 7–16.

Tabors, P. O., Snow, C. E. and Dickinson, D. K. (2001) Homes and schools together. In D. K. Dickinson and P. O. Tabors (eds), *Beginning Literacy with Language* (pp. 313–334). Baltimore, MD: Brookes.

Tannen, D. (2007) *Talking Voices: Repetition, dialogue and imagery in conversational discourse* (2nd edn). Cambridge: Cambridge University Press.

Vygotsky, L. (1978) *Mind in Society: The development of higher psychological processes*. Cambridge, MA: Harvard University Press.

Wang, Q. and Fivush, R. (2005) Mother-child conversations of emotionally salient events. *Social Development, 14*: 473–495.

Wells, G. (1986) *The Meaning Makers*. Portsmouth, NH: Heinemann.

Whitebread, D. and Bingham, S. (2012) *TACTYC Occasional Paper No. 2, School Readiness: A critical review of perspectives and evidence*. TACTYC. http://tactyc.org.uk/occasional-paper/occasional-paper2.pdf

Whitehead, M. (1977) *Language and Literacy in the Early Years* (2nd edn). London: Paul Chapman.

Wilson, E. (1998) *Consilience: The unity of knowledge*. New York: Knopf.

Wohlwend, K. and Peppler, K. (2015) All rigor and no play is no way to improve learning. *Phi Delta Kappan, 96*(8): 22–26.

2

PALEY'S APPROACH TO STORYTELLING AND STORY ACTING

Research and practice

Rosie Flewitt, Teresa Cremin and Ben Mardell

Introduction

This chapter serves as an anchor for the book by presenting a focused examination of one of Vivian Gussin Paley's advocated practices in the early childhood classroom: teachers scribing children's stories (storytelling) and children enacting these later on the same day (story acting). We begin by tracing the approach back to its origins in the 1970s, where as an early childhood teacher in Chicago, Paley was seeking to offer routes into early education that appealed to children from diverse social and ethnic backgrounds, and with different learning needs. We discuss the affinity of her story-based practice with sociocultural theory, and consider key themes that have emerged from research evidence regarding the contribution of storytelling and story acting to young children's narrative competence, cognitive and oral language development, and their preparedness for school. We also summarise research findings regarding how children share story elements reworked from popular culture and story books, how the approach can promote a cohesive and shared classroom culture, and how meanings are jointly constructed during storytelling and story acting through embodied actions as well as through spoken and written language. We then present an overview of the different routes that have brought teachers in the USA and England to Paley's storytelling and story-acting curriculum, and the types of training and professional development they have been offered. Lastly, we provide background information on the diverse studies that are referred to across the chapters in this book, including their methodological and ethical stance towards the respectful conduct of research with young children.

Paley's storytelling and story-acting approach

The genesis of Paley's storytelling and story-acting approach can be traced back to her 1970s ethnically and socially diverse early childhood classroom. As described in her book *Wally's Stories* (and by McNamee in Chapter 7 and Cooper in Chapter 8 of this volume), Paley felt badly for Wally, a young boy who was often in trouble in school. One day, out of a sense of kindness, she scripted his story and then asked the other children in her class to help act it out (Paley, 1981). Eventually, Paley chose to make this a regular classroom practice. Each day Paley would take down the stories of any child who wanted to tell her one. Later the same day, all the children in the classroom would sit around an improvised stage that was delineated by masking tape on the classroom floor. Reading out the story, Paley would support children in acting it out without props. Over time this practice evolved. Initially, the storyteller chose which classmates would play each character. Later, in consideration of fairness, Paley began inviting children to come to act in turn, with the storyteller only choosing which character he or she would play. This feature of Paley's practice though has been differently developed over time, with some teachers offering the storytellers the option to choose who acts out each role in their story, whilst others invite each child in turn to enact the next character or object. What is key in this approach is that the two practices of story scribing and story dramatisation are offered, indeed Paley (2004: 5) asserts that 'the dictated story is but a half-told tale. To fulfil its destiny it is dramatised on a pretend stage with the help of the classmates as actors and audience and the teacher as narrator and director.'

A teacher at the University of Chicago Laboratory School (a historically progressive and private setting founded by John Dewey, offering education from kindergarten through to Grade 12), Paley sought to develop an inclusive classroom culture that could be 'an island of safety and sensibility for everyone' (Paley, 1990: xi). Paley's storytelling and story-acting curriculum formed part of her overall approach to teaching such that it focused on meaning and fairness (Cooper, 2009). Paley's text on this approach (Paley, 1990) and many of her other books (e.g. Paley, 1981, 1986, 2004) are underpinned by a child-centred, play-based philosophy, reflecting her view of children as creative thinkers and active meaning makers. She foregrounds the power of fantasy play and the potency of storytelling, dictation and dramatisation in the curriculum and argues that, in early childhood, 'fantasy play is the glue that binds together all other pursuits, including the early teaching of reading and writing skills' (Paley, 2004: 8). She has not however, sought to document this claim through conventional research and as Nicolopoulou and Cole (2010: 63) observe:

> Because these accounts focused on one teacher and her classroom, various questions arise concerning the generalizability and effectiveness of this programme. Moreover, Paley did not fully articulate the theoretical underpinnings of this activity or specify the conditions for its implementation in other classrooms.

Nonetheless her work, whilst unconventional, has made a rich contribution to the field of early education, both theoretically and practically, with many scholars recognising and endorsing her views and sensitive accounts of young children's playful, story-based learning. As Cooper (2009: 5) observes, Paley's work 'has touched a chord with a legion of educational philosophers, psychologists, cultural theorists and teacher educators'. However, perhaps due to the unusual nature of her books, written as they are in the first person from the perspective of a practitioner, without reference to the available literature, it could be argued that her insights have not been afforded their full value. Cooper (2009) explains why she perceives teachers in the USA have not made systematic use of Paley's ideas. Firstly, she notes that Paley herself does not engage in the kind of theoretical and methodological discussions that normally lend credence to new approaches to teaching and learning. Secondly, she posits that her books and articles usually focus on a single issue and this limits the application of her professional strategies. Finally, for many teachers and teacher educators, Paley's radical stance towards critical issues in childhood education can be challenging and uncomfortable. Cooper (2009: 8) argues that:

> Paley is at heart an activist, who urges us to embrace the privilege of teacher as pedagogue and moral authority inside the classroom. Her classroom studies ask us how far we are willing to go to defend young children against the somewhat pernicious realities of schooling.

As an unabashed advocate of the play-based curriculum, Paley's work challenges current pressures in the USA and the UK to introduce a skills-based early years curriculum and formal literacy instruction, and for this reason also her work may lack take-up as teachers struggle to find time for non-statutory aspects of early education. Furthermore, as noted in our introductory chapter, with the exception of the body of work by Nicolopoulou (e.g. Nicolopoulou et al., 2015), Cooper (e.g. 2009), McNamee (e.g. 2015), Cremin et al. (2013) and this volume, scholarly analyses of the value of the practice of Paley's storytelling and story-acting pedagogy are relatively sparse. Thus the education profession in many countries (with the exception of those teachers who have worked with proponents of the approach in the USA and more recently in England), are arguably unaware of the flexibility and potential of storytelling and story acting for fostering young children's learning. This is problematic in the current context where concerns are regularly voiced about a perceived decline in children's early language (e.g. Nelson et al., 2011) and where practitioners, due to the current structures of accountability, governance and assessment, are obliged to deliver an arguably inappropriately formal or functionalist curriculum. Additionally, it has been argued that children's social and cultural capital as informal story performers and artful language users remains somewhat unrecognised, underestimated and underdeveloped in educational settings (Maybin, 2005).

Considering the theoretical basis of Paley's approach, most commentators on her work (including Paley herself) agree that it is firmly grounded in Vygotsky's

(1978) sociocultural conceptualisation of play (e.g. Wright, 2007), although Nicolopoulou and Cole (2010) argue that her work sits within a particular 'take' on sociocultural learning theory called cultural-historical activity theory (CHAT). This theory, currently influential with educational researchers in the UK (e.g. Daniels, 2008), nonetheless draws on Vygotsky's views about the cultural nature of learning and his belief that development and learning depend on the ways pupils and teachers learn how to share 'cultural tools' (van Oers et al., 2008). According to this theory, social interactions and meaning-making activities combine to form complex interacting systems within distinctive 'learning ecologies'. For example, pretend play and storytelling are described as 'complementary expressions of children's symbolic imagination that draw from and reflect back the inter-related domains of emotional, intellectual and social life' (Nicolopoulou, 2005: 496). A core feature of Paley's pedagogical approach is her understanding that within the particular 'learning ecology' of her classroom, children's spontaneous imaginative activities, such as fantasy play, can be harnessed in a more formal way through story to support diverse areas of social and cognitive development. As Nicolopoulou and Cole (2010) explain in their studies, the storytelling and story-acting practice demonstrates the following characteristics of a learning ecology:

- It has tasks or problems that children are asked to, or want to, solve (e.g. make decisions about how the stories should be acted).
- It encourages particular kinds of discourse (as when children dictate their stories).
- It establishes particular norms of participation (e.g. turn-taking, the number of children on stage, active listening to other people's stories).
- It provides specific cultural tools and material means (e.g. the tools used to record the stories, the 'story stage').
- It offers teachers practical means to orchestrate relations among these elements.

Paley's storytelling and story-acting approach: Research evidence

In this section, we reflect on key themes that emerge from the research literature regarding the contribution of Paley's storytelling and story-acting pedagogy to young children's learning in early childhood education. Firstly, we discuss how storytelling and story acting support young children's narrative and cognitive development, drawing primarily on Nicolopoulou and colleagues' influential work in this domain. We then present empirical evidence on the contribution of the approach to children's oral language, and how children borrow and rework elements from each other's stories, popular culture and story books. We reflect on how these practices contribute to cohesion and a common culture in the classroom, and help to prepare young children for elementary education. We then consider the multimodal and co-constructed nature of young children's storytelling and story-acting practices, and finally we outline some key conditions that need to be in place for teachers' training and support, in order to ensure that the storytelling and story-acting practice works well in class.

Developing children's narrative and cognitive competence

Many scholars have acknowledged the contribution of Paley's story-based approach to young children's engagement with narrative (e.g. Bodrova and Leong, 2007; Booth, 2005; Fox, 1993; Gupta, 2009), which, it has been argued, is a key foundation for emergent literacy and longer term school success (e.g. McCabe and Bliss, 2003; Tabors et al., 2001). Scholarly investigation of Paley's work began in the 1980s, when Gillian McNamee and colleagues published data on storytelling and story acting from ten classrooms (McNamee et al., 1985). A former student teacher in Paley's classroom when Wally was in kindergarten, McNamee used controlled comparisons to investigate five classrooms' storytelling and story acting over a twelve-week period, and five classrooms' storytelling with no story acting. The study demonstrated that participation in Paley's story-based approach strongly promoted young children's narrative development, but only if both the storytelling and the story-acting components were included.

Nicolopoulou and her colleagues subsequently amassed an extensive body of evidence regarding the development of young children's narrative competence in a range of studies undertaken between 1993 and 2015 in California, Massachusetts and Pennsylvania, USA. These studies involved the collection of thousands of stories told and enacted by hundreds of preschool-aged children, mostly three- to four-year-olds, from a range of socio-economic groups. Nicolopoulou and colleagues' study methods have varied, but most have combined ethnographic observation of children's classroom interactions, friendships and meaning making, with systematic narrative analysis of the content of their stories, sometimes employing quantitative measures of learning outcomes such as controlled comparisons and standardised vocabulary tests, or coding scheme typologies (e.g. Nicolopoulou, 2002; Nicolopoulou and Richner, 2007, respectively).

Typically, Nicolopoulou and colleagues have worked with teachers over a sustained period of time to support the introduction of storytelling and story-acting practice into preschool classrooms. Their rigorous and extensive analyses of children's stories have provided compelling evidence of middle- to high-income and low-income children's engagement with storytelling and story-acting activities, and of tangible progress in their narrative skills and cognitive competence, with children's stories becoming increasingly complex and sophisticated as they become more familiar with this story-based activity (e.g. Nicolopoulou, 2002; Nicolopoulou et al., 2006; Nicolopoulou et al., 2015). Nicolopoulou et al. (2014) propose that combining storytelling with story acting provides a unique and highly motivating forum for young children to compose stories not only for adults but for each other, and to share them in a public space rather than in one-to-one interaction 'it seems clear that the public *performance* of the children's narratives plays a critical role in these processes. It does so in several ways, but above all by helping to generate and maintain a *shared public arena* for narrative performance, experimentation, collaboration, and cross-fertilization' (Nicolopoulou et al., 2014: 45; italic in original).

Throughout their studies, Nicolopoulou and her colleagues have drawn attention to the interwoven and mutually supportive nature of storytelling and pretend play, suggesting that both are forms of narrative activity – ranging from the discursive development of narrative in storytelling to their enactment in pretend play scenarios. They have also highlighted the considerable cognitive load of coordinating imagination and spontaneity on the one hand, and rule-governed action on the other during narrative activity and social pretend play, and have produced empirical evidence to support Vygotsky's proposal that 'what passes unnoticed by the child in real life becomes a rule of behavior in play' (Vygotsky, 1967: 9; see also Nicolopoulou et al., 2015). Indeed, a fundamental aspect of both pretend play and narrative is the mimicry, or subversion, of observed social rules. Nicolopoulou et al. (2015) argue that narrative activity – whether in pretend play or in storytelling – is one of the first activities where children self-consciously impose rules on themselves, rather than follow rules imposed on them by others. As in pretend play, participating in storytelling and story acting requires children to engage both cognitively and socially in terms of cooperation and self-regulation. Furthermore, research into Paley's approach has found that when stories are written with the intention of being shared, their narrative structure is richer, more ambitious and more illuminating than when told or written in isolation or in response to 'teacherly' agendas (Nicolopoulou, 1996, 2002).

Nurturing young children's oral language and emergent literacy

Children's oral language skills have long been recognised as an important foundation for emergent literacy and long-term school success (e.g. see Dickinson and Tabors, 2001; Reese et al., 2010; Whitehead, 2010). Key indicators for later school achievement include vocabulary development, abstract thinking, reflective reasoning and print awareness, and these characteristics are highly correlated with middle-class child-rearing practices in the first five years of life (Snow, Tabors and Dickinson, 2001). Arguably, an oral language approach to emergent literacy can help to bridge the gap between home and school, and there is a strong body of research evidence suggesting that participation in storytelling and story acting can significantly promote young children's oral and narrative development. This has been found for children from middle-class families (Nicolopoulou, 1996) and from low-income or otherwise disadvantaged backgrounds (Nicolopoulou, 2002), although there are noteworthy differences between these two groups in terms of children's familiarity with narrative when they first enter early education. Children in the former group have been found to apply their existing oral and narrative skills and hone their mastery of language and narrative conventions through telling and acting out their own stories in the classroom. By contrast, children in the latter group may have weaker oral language skills and less familiarity with narrative conventions, and so they begin storytelling and acting by building up basic language and narrative foundations (Nicolopoulou et al., 2015). (See also Nicolopoulou in Chapter 3 in this volume.)

Whatever a child's starting point may be, through their rigorous and systematic studies over more than two decades, Nicolopoulou and colleagues have consistently found that storytelling and story acting enable all children's oral language to flourish in the long run, particularly when combined with regular classroom book reading practices with adults (for more detail, see Nicolopoulou, 2002; Nicolopoulou et al., 2014; Nicolopoulou et al., 2015). For example, where teachers used the storytelling and story-acting practice in US Head Start preschool classrooms, children from low-income families developed a wider range of decontextualised, oral language skills compared to children in comparable classrooms in the same school that did not use the technique (Nicolopoulou et al., 2006). The children in this study also began to think actively about connections between thoughts, spoken words, marks on paper, the arrangement of text on the page and the transformations of spoken to written representation and back. Taking this further, in Chapter 4 in this volume Cremin examines the influence of the approach on young children's print awareness and documents the self-initiated story authoring observed in English settings.

From 25 years' experience of implementing a storytelling curriculum in her own classrooms and working with teachers in Atlanta, New York and Houston, Cooper has found that Paley's storytelling curriculum can have a positive impact on vocabulary development, oral narrative and the kind of literacy skills that support later reading. A key study in this regard is reported in Cooper et al. (2004), where 95 children from low and mixed-income families took part in Paley's storytelling curriculum over the course of one school year, some with recently qualified teachers and some with experienced teachers. Oral language pre- and post-tests were used to measure their language and early literacy development (Pearson Assessment of Expressive Vocabulary Test (EVT), Peabody Picture Vocabulary Test (PPVT) [3rd ed.] Form IIIA, and Whitehurst's Get Ready to Read!). The children's scores were compared with the performance of young children of the same age in the same or similar schools who had not participated in the storytelling curriculum. The findings showed that in comparison with their peers, children who had been immersed in Paley's story-based approach showed significant gains in oral language and literacy skills, suggesting this is a potent alternative to skills-dominant approaches to early literacy.

At the same time as Cooper's US-based study, Typadi and Hayon (Westminster Education Action Zone, 2005) introduced Paley's story-based approach to 22 practitioners in two mainstream school nurseries and two nursery schools in England. The aim of this study was to support the language and communication skills of young children who were learning English as an additional language and were struggling to meet the curriculum milestones for speaking and listening. Paley's curriculum was used in conjunction with a 'Talking Together' teacher training programme, which used video feedback and self-reflection to help practitioners develop effective scaffolding strategies to support children's talk.

These included: waiting for children to initiate conversations, following their lead, and using a variety of questioning and modelling strategies to extend children's language and vocabulary. Typadi and Hayon's analysis established that all children made measurable language gains when Paley's story-based approach was combined with 'Talking Together' teacher training.

Typadi and Hayon subsequently introduced Paley's (1990) story-based pedagogy into one preschool class and five reception classes in two private schools, and worked with these classes for varying lengths of time (between five months to two years), again focusing on children's language development and changes in teachers' interaction strategies over time. All participating children showed improved language ability, confidence, attention level and turn taking. Reflecting across these studies, Typadi and Hayon (2010) concluded that for children in the early stages of learning English, and those with specific language difficulties, complementary programmes should be used to build children's language skills and enable these children to tell and act out their stories. Overall, Typadi and Hayon (2010: 86) found that Paley's approach provided 'a practical and flexible framework, allowing both one-to-one and whole-class work. It compels adults truly to listen to children and accept their ideas within a large classroom.'

Preparing children for school

The development of oral language and literacy skills, the cognitive load of planning, telling and enacting a narrative (whether in the form of a narrated story or in pretend play) and the progress in young children's cognitive competence that result from their regular participation in Paley's story-based curriculum, all combine to indicate that the approach offers children rich preparation for school learning. These key areas are known to contribute to children's preparedness for success in formal education, along with social-emotional competence, self-regulation, and the ability and willingness to cooperate (for example, see Denham, 2006; Dickinson et al., 2006).

All these facets of learning are embedded explicitly and implicitly in Paley's approach. For example, the children's and teachers' involvement in story activities require their mutual adherence to certain ground rules: that a storyteller is entitled to the uninterrupted and focused attention of the teacher whilst the story is being told; that the stories will be scribed exactly as they are told (and this can be problematic for some teachers!); that the storyteller can choose which character they would like to act out; that all children must sit quietly and neatly around the improvised stage so that everyone has a 'front row' seat; that the roles will be allocated in strict rotation around the stage; that it's alright to choose not to act out a role; that all stories and enactments will be celebrated by the whole class clapping, and so forth. These may seem aspirational rules for young children to adhere to, yet their regular repetition during the rhythm of everyday classroom activity enable children to make sense of them, and over time, to promote important dimensions of their social competence such as cooperation, social understanding and self-regulation (Nicolopoulou et al., 2006). However, when working with large classes of disadvantaged, ethnically diverse children, Nicolopoulou's research has established that unless the storytelling and story-acting practice is incorporated as a regular activity (e.g. at least twice-weekly), the benefits to children's social competence, and to their language and literacy development, are unlikely to persist in the long term. The repetition and rhythm of the approach, and its embeddedness in the classroom culture are therefore key.

Sharing interests and developing a common classroom culture

Young children's lives unfold in overlapping sociocultural worlds: at the most immediate level these include their families, peer groups and classroom cultures. These intimate relationships are embedded in larger community and institutional structures, which in turn are enmeshed in broader cultural frameworks. Children's interactions are intertwined with these contextual layers, simultaneously constituting and maintaining the social contexts that can enable or constrain them, and that structure their nature and impact. Even if children's home cultures and languages vary, the symbolic play and learning spaces offered in early education can lead to a sharing of conceptual tools and systems of meaning making. As Nicolopoulou et al. (2014: 43) argue, 'an effective approach to understanding development requires that we pay systematic attention to the ongoing interplay between three dimensions of the human world that are at once analytically distinct and mutually interpenetrating: individual, interactional or relational, and collective'.

With Paley's approach, children's storytelling and acting becomes part of the classroom culture, but each child tells their story voluntarily and spontaneously. This rather unusual format for narrative in the classroom means children are free to choose their own characters, topics and plots, and their stories are told and acted out in a shared, public space. Each child's storytelling and acting is embedded in the ongoing context of the classroom culture and the child's relationships within that culture. The public nature of the story sharing, and the interpersonal relationships within that space, facilitate narrative cross-fertilisation: children pool their interests from within and beyond the classroom through the stories they tell, often sharing their interest in elements reworked from popular culture and story books, and borrowing characters and plots from each other's stories. Through their storytelling and acting, children form and sustain a shared culture of collaboration, experimentation and mutual cross-fertilisation of ideas that serves as a powerful matrix for their social, cognitive and linguistic development (for further discussion, see Nicolopoulou et al., 2014).

Unsurprisingly therefore, children have been found to use their stories as vehicles to affiliate themselves with sub-groups of other children within their classrooms, seeking and affirming both friendship and prestige (e.g. Nicolopoulou, 1996, 1997, 2002) and building up gendered subcultures within the classroom. This gendered polarisation in story themes and characters has been observed consistently in studies of middle-class children, and less so with children from low-income and otherwise disadvantaged families – an area identified as ripe for further investigation (Nicolopoulou, 2002; Nicolopoulou et al., 2014). Over a series of studies, Nicolopoulou and colleagues have found gendered differences in both the form and content of children's narratives, including different approaches to social relationships, the social world, and images of the self. For example, girls' stories typically (but by no means always) feature networks of stable and harmonious relationships, with activities located in specified physical settings, such as the family and home, whereas boys' stories have often featured conflict, movement, rivalry and disruption, with heroes and 'extravagant imagery' (Nicolopoulou et al., 2014: 47).

The educational and social significance of the storytelling and story-acting practice therefore intertwine. Participating in storytelling and story acting engages and mobilises children's interests and motivations through play, fantasy and friendship, and the public and peer-oriented facets of the activity help to create a community of storytellers and actors in the classroom, drawing on the power of peer-group processes to realise important social-relational developments for children. As McNamee (2005: 276) eloquently suggests:

> A central theme in Paley's work is finding a home for the homeless in school: the lost, the lonely, the excluded, the forgotten, the misunderstood, the rejected child (and his or her family). In creating a classroom each year as a place for the mind and heart of each child to grow and flourish, she studies the premises of fairness, friendship and kindness, and how they can and ought to work in the community of the classroom.

The multimodal and co-constructed nature of storytelling/story acting

Whilst past research into storytelling and story acting has documented the significance of the approach for children's cognitive, linguistic and social development, the focus of attention has been primarily on the analysis of language, with some discussion of how story enactment enhances the benefits of storytelling (e.g. Nicolopoulou et al., 2014). More recently, scholars have begun to consider the contribution that multimodal analysis can make to understanding the interactional processes through which children's narratives (as scribed by an adult and later dramatised by the class) are co-constructed by multiple players and through multiple modes (e.g. Cremin et al., forthcoming).

This work has made visible the complexity of how children's narratives are finely tuned multimodal co-constructions from start to finish (as discussed in Chapters 6 and 9 by Swann and Flewitt, respectively, in this volume), with often subtle support and encouragement expressed by peers and teachers through silent modes, including adopting open and attentive body postures towards storytellers and actors, fine-tuning gaze direction and gaze aversion in response to storytellers' hesitancy and need for time to reflect on how their story might develop, or how they might enact the challenging prospect, for example, of 'being an orange'

(Cremin at al., 2013). This multimodal strand of analysis offers scope for further investigation of the complexity of classroom interaction, and the layering of meanings as expressed between peers, and between teachers and children, through multiple modes.

The enduring need for teacher support

Nicolopoulou and Cole (2010) outline some key conditions that need to be in place in order for the storytelling and story-acting practice to work well. In her early studies, Nicolopoulou observed that many teachers found it difficult to relinquish control to the children during storytelling/story-acting activity, and to manage children's transition between story acting and other quieter, possibly less stimulating activities. This was resolved by creating a classroom environment where children were provided with a clear set of rules about how to move between activities. When working with disadvantaged children, teachers also found it difficult to make acting run smoothly with relatively large groups. In part this was because initially children had little knowledge and understanding of narrative structure and tended to include long lists of characters in their stories so that they could include all their friends. Providing ample opportunities to tell stories alongside other book reading practices allowed teachers to scaffold children's developing understanding of narrative structure and offered a solution to this problem.

Across many of the studies cited above, and indeed in the studies reported in this volume, many teachers expressed concern about the simplicity of children's initial stories. This has led to the realisation that it is important to provide professional development activities for teachers that could 'guide their understanding and appreciation of children's narrative development so that in turn they could guide children's narrative development in productive ways' (Nicolopoulou and Cole, 2010: 66).

Storytelling and story acting in US and UK classrooms

In this section we outline the spread of this approach to storytelling/story acting beyond Paley's own classroom, and how this has been taken up in geographic pockets of the USA and, to a lesser extent, in England. With the publication of Paley's first book, *White Teacher*, which appeared to critical acclaim in 1979, and *Wally's Stories* in 1981, educators were able to read about her story-based work with children. Paley continued to describe aspects of the approach in many of her subsequent books (e.g. *The Girl with the Brown Crayon* in 1997). In the 30-plus years of national and international speaking engagements that followed the publication of *White Teacher*, Paley would often arrange for a group of young children to join her on the stage to demonstrate storytelling/story acting. These speaking engagements have inspired several generations of American teachers, and an occasional policy-maker, to adopt the approach.

Storytelling and acting is embedded in the graduate programme and student teaching experiences of early childhood educators at Erikson Institute, Chicago, where McNamee is currently director of teacher education, and where online studies have helped to spread Paley's work nationally and internationally. Formerly a teacher in one of the experimental classrooms in McNamee's research, in the mid-1980s Cooper became director of the Trinity School for Young Children in Houston where she made storytelling/story acting a core part of the school's literacy programme. This work was further developed thanks to a grant to start the Teachers' Network for Early Literacy at Rice University, which has disseminated storytelling/story acting to classroom teachers throughout the Houston area (now renamed School Literacy and Culture (SLC), see http://literacy.rice.edu/). In the years since, close to 500 teachers have been introduced to Paley's work through an intense year-long residency programme in which teachers attend monthly seminars and receive in-class coaching from mentors. SLC staff also mentor approximately 250 public and private school teachers in storytelling/story acting each year through its summer institutes, writing camp and other professional development efforts, and provides a Vivian Paley scholarship for a year-long residency.

With time, the approach spread to Boston, after Jason Sachs, the head of Public School's (BPS) Early Childhood Department, was inspired by hearing Paley speak at the 2011 National Association for the Education of Young Children's annual conference. Paley was invited to speak at a BPS professional development conference for pre-kindergarten and kindergarten teachers, and later the same year, 25 teachers attended a seminar led by Marina Boni and Ben Mardell to learn more about the approach, and to help craft a guide for colleagues about storytelling/story acting (see http://bpsearlychildhood.weebly.com/storytelling.html). This was incorporated in the revised BPS kindergarten curriculum in 2013, and two years later in the revised pre-kindergarten curriculum. As a result, storytelling/story acting is now part of the mandatory curriculum in 250 kindergarten and 120 pre-kindergarten classrooms (serving 4,000 and 2,000 children respectively in the Boston area). The BPS Early Childhood Department is now working with 30 school districts in Massachusetts to help them implement their kindergarten curriculum, which includes storytelling and story acting.

The history of storytelling/story acting in the USA is one of organic, decentralised and episodic growth. Beyond Paley, there are others who speak and have written about the approach, including Cooper (1993), McNamee (2015) and Katch (2001), another graduate student of Paley. As champions retire, sometimes activity declines, but at the same time, new areas spring up. For example, in the winter of 2015/16 teachers from public school and community-based preschools signed up for a four-session seminar on storytelling/story acting in Somerville, Massachusetts.

In England, Paley's curriculum is less well-known, but it has received consistent promotion since 2002 through the work of Trisha Lee and the story-based programme of professional development offered by her London-based theatre and education company 'MakeBelieve Arts'. The UK instantiation of Paley's work led by this company, initially entitled 'the Helicopter Technique' and now known as 'Helicopter Stories', is self-evidently based on Paley's (1990) book *The Boy Who Would Be a Helicopter*. Lee, with a background in theatre and education, has worked with Isla Hill and other MakeBelieve Arts staff, to introduce the approach in several local authorities in England, including Tower Hamlets, Lewisham, Kent, Thurrock, Cheshire, Bristol, and Oxfordshire, among others. MakeBelieve Arts has developed a three-tiered approach to enabling schools to adopt the approach: 1) one-day training events; 2) modelling, supported by sustained in–class support; 3) a mixture of in–class support and training via intensive courses. Take-up following their annual conferences on creativity, which foreground children's play, has been substantial. They have also piloted work with parents, introducing them to the Helicopter Stories approach, and have worked with primary schools where older learners 'take story' for younger classes and support enactment (Lee, 2015). In addition, Lee has integrated the child-centred and creative nature of the approach into the teaching of primary mathematics (Pound and Lee, 2015), widening the reach of Paley's story-based pedagogy. Lee's (2015) most recent publication *Princesses, Dragons and Helicopter Stories* offers practical professional support for educators on how to implement storytelling and story acting in early years or early primary classrooms. Paley, who is the company's patron, fully endorses Lee's subtle development of the dramatisation element of the approach.

The MakeBelieve Arts story-based training programme was formally evaluated in 2012 by the Open University (discussed below), and has subsequently established four certified Centres of Excellence in Tower Hamlets, Gravesham, Sittingbourne and Thurrock. These teacher-led centres deliver introductory and full-day Helicopter Stories training sessions to support others in developing the approach within their own settings. The MakeBelieve Arts' website presents a rich repertoire of children's oral stories, often uploaded by teachers from the Centres of Excellence, demonstrating the diversity and difference of children's unique stories, as well as elements of commonality.

Methodological approaches to the study of Paley's approach to storytelling and story acting

Paley's studies of her story-based pedagogy gained validity through the rich perceptiveness of her accounts of young children's learning (e.g. 1979, 1981, 1986, 1990), but her work did not enter into the kinds of methodological or theoretical debate that is typical of academic research. Studies in the USA by McNamee (2015; McNamee et al., 1985), Nicolopoulou (e.g. 1997, 2002, 2005; Nicolopoulou et al., 2014, 2015) and Cooper (1993, 2009) have tended to blend detailed linguistic analysis of children's stories with ethnographic observations of their telling, scribing and acting over weeks or months. These investigations have often featured quantitative analysis of experimental test results, employing control groups and standardised assessment instruments in order to measure and compare the degree to which individual children's stories display certain attributes over time, such as vocabulary and narrative complexity. In this volume, Nicolopoulou reports on a study that comprised observations of children's storytelling and acting, with quantitative analysis of linguistic features in the story texts (Chapter 3), whereas the studies reported in Chapters 7 and 8, by McNamee and Cooper respectively, include observational accounts of storytelling and acting, with qualitative and thematic analysis.

Findings from the UK-based study reported in Chapters 4, 5, 6 and 9 arise from a year-long project to evaluate MakeBelieve Arts' Helicopter Stories training programme, a study funded by the Esmée Fairbairn Foundation (Cremin et al., 2013). The evaluation was conducted in six settings: three primary school Reception classes for children aged four to five years (two in inner London and one in a semi-rural setting), and three of their feeder preschool nurseries for children aged three to four years, which were located either in or near the primary school settings. During a six-week training period, MakeBelieve Arts' trainers worked closely with practitioners to establish the Helicopter Stories pedagogic principles. The trainers/mentors then returned once a week to observe the technique in action, and to reflect with teachers on the development of the approach in their setting.

Using a combination of ethnographic and multimodal methodologies for data collection and analysis (Flewitt, 2011), the researchers documented the delivery of the training programme in each setting, and returned to the settings in the following school year to assess its sustained use in the schools and nurseries. The methodological framework for the evaluation study is illustrated in Figure 2.1, and included: *ethnographic observations* of the children's storytelling and acting (video-recorded and described in field notes with accompanying photographs, resulting in seventeen hours of video recordings and 124 pages of field notes); *close scrutiny of the children's stories* as scribed by the teachers and trainers (six teacher-scribed storybooks and three child-scribed storybooks; total over 350 stories, told by 147 children); *teachers' structured observations of three case study children in each class* chosen by teachers as representative of the classroom's cohort: educators made weekly notes on any progress they observed in these children's language and communication, sociability and inclusion in classroom interaction (total eighteen detailed teacher logbooks); *scrutiny of school records* including student data and profiles; and *teachers' written evaluations* of the training programme. Furthermore, three rounds of *interviews were audio-recorded with the teachers/early years educators* in each class at the beginning and end of the training programme, and in the subsequent autumn term (total thirteen hours of audio-recorded interviews), and these insights were supplemented by *field notes* of impromptu conversations with staff during the ethnographic observations of the practice in action. Two rounds of *interviews were conducted with the MakeBelieve Arts Trainers* in each setting (total three hours of audio-recorded interviews). Finally *video-stimulated reflective review* was used with *classroom teachers and support staff,* and *children's perspectives* on the storytelling and story-acting episodes were reviewed using the 'Our Story'[1] picture-based storytelling application for iPads, to prompt children to reflect on their storytelling and acting experiences.

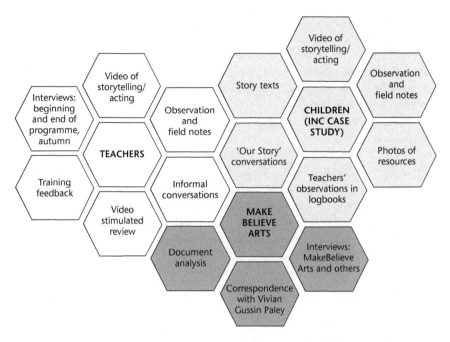

FIGURE 2.1   Sources of evidence for the MakeBelieve Arts' evaluation

Further *documentary material from the MakeBelieve Arts' archive* was analysed, including practitioner feedback and evaluations of previous training instantiations, observational accounts and in-house evaluations. Eight *interviews were conducted with educational advisors* who had long-term association with MakeBelieve Arts, and with the organisation's director, Trisha Lee.

The full data set outlined above was subjected initially to open-ended scrutiny. Audio-recorded interviews, teacher logs and field notes were transcribed and qualitative analytical software (Atlas-ti: Muhr, 2004) was employed to map axial themes across the data sets. Ethnographic analytic techniques helped to situate the children's sign making in the social practices of the classroom context, and this ethnographic lens informed the detailed multimodal analysis, making explicit how the children expressed their individual and collective funds of knowledge through interwoven semiotic modes when telling and acting out their stories. After coding and initial analysis, typical episodes were selected for detailed analysis, along with any episodes that ran counter to trends in the data and brought new issues to light. In-depth exploration of these data extracts combined interactional analysis (cf. Swann 2007, 2009) with multimodal analysis (cf. Flewitt, 2006, 2011, 2012). Interactional analysis focused on how the children interacted with practitioners and peers in telling and acting out their stories and any changes over time. Multimodality was employed to analyse the video data, both with and without sound, permitting in-depth scrutiny of the diverse modes used during storytelling and acting, focusing on gaze, action, the use of space and artefacts along with language, and how these modes were blended to create meanings in a 'multimodal ensemble'.

The highest ethical standards were maintained throughout the MakeBelieve Arts evaluation. Practitioners and parents received information and an explanatory letter about the research, with opportunities to discuss participation in the study, and their right to withdraw themselves, or in the case of parents their child, from the research process at any stage with no adverse effects. The project was explained verbally to children, and they were reassured that they were under no pressure at any stage to participate. The researchers and practitioners monitored participating children to ensure they did not appear uncomfortable. In the event, all children in each class participated and none withdrew. Principles of confidentiality were observed throughout: raw data were kept secure in password-protected files with access restricted to the research team, and pseudonyms were used to protect institutional and participant identity. Permission to use specific images was granted.

Conclusion

Empirical research investigating Paley's storytelling and story-acting practice, carried out over more than two decades and employing diverse methodological approaches in schools across the USA and in England, has produced compelling evidence of the contribution this practice can make to children's language development, narrative skills, cognitive abilities, and social and emotional competence, particularly when both storytelling and story acting are included regularly in classroom practice over lengthy periods of time, and when supplemented by other regular reading practices in the classroom. Narrative is known to play a crucial role in children's identity formation, and in their efforts to explore complex concepts that they encounter in their daily lives, particularly when offered in contexts that are genuinely meaningful, engaging and stimulating for the children themselves. Research presented in this and subsequent chapters suggests that Paley's approach offers rich insights into their developing understandings of the world, including their conceptions of themselves as effective learners in classrooms to which they feel they belong, regardless of their ethnicity, language, social or cultural background and learning support needs. Participating in storytelling and story acting engages and mobilises children's interests and motivations through play, fantasy and friendship, and helps children form and sustain a shared culture of peer-group collaboration, experimentation and mutual cross-fertilisation that serves as a powerful matrix for their learning and development.

However, empirical research has found that practitioners require training and mentoring in the approach – to understand its underpinning philosophy for social justice, to be reassured that it is okay to transcribe children's stories as they are told, to gain confidence in managing the sometimes excitable story enactments, and to resist the teacherly temptation to correct children's inventive uses of language and grammar. For some children, particularly those with additional learning needs, the technique appears to work well when supplemented by additional programmes of support, albeit in mastering the principal language of instruction used in a given classroom, or overcoming the social and cognitive challenges presented by specific learning impairments.

In contrast to the current curricula focus on specific literacy skills, as discussed in Chapter 1, and the increasing tendency to measure children against a set of one-size-fits-all standards of 'readiness' for school, Paley's story-based curriculum offers children and teachers a holistic experience of early language and literacy that has real purpose, and encourages interaction and collaboration between peers in a creative and expressive activity. In addition to laying important foundational skills and knowledge for young children's later schooling, the approach offers preschool and elementary educators the opportunity to get to know children, their strengths and interests, and enables teachers to plan for the individualised learning of children from a wide range of social and ethnic backgrounds, who bring with them an even wider range of skills and knowledge.

In examining the approach further and through drawing upon new empirical studies and analyses of previously collected data, this volume seeks to add to the evidence base regarding Paley's advocated practice of storytelling and story acting.

Note

1   Our Story is a free, picture-based, multimedia story creation app, available at http://itunes.apple.com/gb/app/our-story/id436758256?mt=8

References

Bodrova, E. and Leong, D. J. (2007) *Tools of the Mind: The Vygotskian approach to early childhood education.* Upper Saddle River, NJ: Pearson Merrill/Prentice Hall.

Booth, D. (2005) *Story Drama: Reading, writing and role playing across the curriculum* (2nd edn). Markham, Ontario: Pembroke.

Cooper, P. M. (1993) *When Stories Come to School: Telling, writing, and performing stories in the early childhood classroom.* New York, NY: Teachers and Writers Collaborative.

Cooper, P. M. (2009) *The Classrooms All Young Children Need: Lessons in teaching from Vivian Paley.* Chicago, IL: University of Chicago Press.

Cooper, P. M., Capo, K., Mathes, B. and Gray, L. (2004) One authentic early literacy practice and three standardized tests: Can a storytelling curriculum measure up? *Journal of Early Childhood Teacher Education, 28*(3): 251–275.

Cremin, T., Swann, J., Flewitt, R. S., Faulkner, D. and Kucirkova, N. (2013) *Evaluation Report of MakeBelieve Arts Helicopter Technique of Storytelling and Story Acting.* Available at: http://www.makebelievearts.co.uk/docs/Helicopter-Technique-Evaluation.pdf

Cremin, T., Flewitt, R., Swann, J., Faulkner, D. and Kucirkova, N. (forthcoming) Storytelling and story acting: Co-construction in action. *Journal of Early Childhood Research.*

Daniels, H. (2008) Reflections on points of departure in the development of sociocultural and activity theory. In B. van Oers, W. Wardekker, E. Elbers and R. van der Veer (eds), *The Transformation of Learning: Advances in cultural-historical activity theory.* Cambridge: Cambridge University Press.

Denham, S. A. (2006) Social-emotional competence as support for school readiness: What is it and how do we assess it? *Early Education and Development*, *17*(1): 57–89.

Dickinson, D. K. and Tabors, P. O. (2001) *Beginning Literacy with Language*. Baltimore, MD: Paul H. Brookes.

Dickinson, D. K., McCabe, A. and Essex, M. J. (2006) A window of opportunity we must open to all: The case for preschool with high-quality support for language and literacy. In D. K. Dickinson and S. B. Neumann (eds), *Handbook of Early Literacy Research* (Vol. 2) (pp. 11–28). New York, NY: Guilford Press.

Flewitt, R. S. (2006) Using video to investigate preschool classroom interaction: Education research assumptions and methodological practices. *Visual Communication*, *5*(1): 25–50.

Flewitt, R. S. (2011) Bringing ethnography to a multimodal investigation of early literacy in a digital age. *Qualitative Research*, *11*(3): 293–310.

Flewitt, R. S. (2012) Multimodal perspectives on early childhood literacies. In J. Larson and J. Marsh (eds), *The Sage Handbook of Early Childhood Literacy* (2nd edn) (pp. 295–309). London: Sage.

Fox, C. (1993) *At the Very Edge of the Forest: The influence of literature on storytelling by children*. London: Continuum.

Gupta, A. (2009) Vygotskian perspectives on using dramatic play to enhance children's development and balance creativity with structure in the early childhood classroom. *Early Child Development and Care*, *179*(8): 1041–1054.

Katch, J. (2001) *Under Deadman's Skin: Discovering the meaning of children's violent play*. Boston, MA: Beacon Press.

Lee, T. (2015) *Princesses, Dragons and Helicopter Stories: Storytelling and story acting in the early years*. London: Routledge.

Maybin, J. (2005) *Children's Voices: Talk, identity and text?* London and New York: Palgrave Macmillan.

McCabe, A. and Bliss, L. S. (2003) *Patterns of Narrative Discourse: A multicultural, life-span approach*. Boston, MA: Allyn and Bacon.

McNamee, G. D. (2005) 'The one who gathers children': The work of Vivian Gussin Paley and current debates about how we educate young children. *Journal of Early Childhood Teacher Education*, *25*(3): 275–296.

McNamee, G. D. (2015) *The High-Performing Preschool: Story acting in Head Start classrooms*. Chicago, IL: University of Chicago Press.

McNamee, G. D., McLane, J. B., Cooper, P. M. and Kerwin, S. M. (1985) Cognition and affect in early literacy development. *Early Childhood Development and Care*, *20*: 229–244.

Muhr, T. (2004) *Users' Manual for Atlas.ti 5.0*. Berlin: Atlas.ti. Scientific Software Development GmbH.

Nelson, K. E., Welsh, J. A., Vance Trup, E. M. and Greenberg, M. T. (2011) Language delays of impoverished preschool children in relation to early academic and emotion recognition skills. *First Language*, *31*(2): 164–194.

Nicolopoulou, A. (1996) Narrative development in social context. In D. Slobin, J. Gerhzudt, J. Guo and A. Kyratzis (eds), *Social Interaction, Social Context, and Language: Essays in honor of Susan Ervin-Tripp* (pp. 369–390). Mahwah, NJ: Erlbaum.

Nicolopoulou, A. (1997) Worldmaking and identity formation in children's narrative play-acting. In B. Cox and C. Lightfoot (eds), *Sociogenetic Perspectives on Internalization* (pp. 157–187). Mahwah, NJ: Erlbaum.

Nicolopoulou, A. (2002) Peer-group culture and narrative development. In S. Blum-Kulka and C. E. Snow (eds), *Talking to Adults* (pp. 117–152). Mahwah, NJ: Erlbaum.

Nicolopoulou, A. (2005) Play and narrative in the process of development: Commonalities, differences and interrelations. *Cognitive Development*, *20*: 495–502.

Nicolopoulou, A. and Richner, E. S. (2007) From actors to agents to persons: The development of character representations in young children's narratives. *Child Development*, 78(2): 412–429.

Nicolopoulou, A. and Cole, M. (2010) Design experimentation as a theoretical and empirical tool for developmental pedagogical research. *Pedagogies: An International Journal*, 17: 1–17.

Nicolopoulou, A., McDowell, J. and Brockmeyer, C. (2006) Narrative play and emergent literacy: Storytelling and story acting meet journal writing. In D. Singer, R. Golinkoff and K. Hirsh-Pasek (eds), *Play=Learning* (pp. 124–144). New York, NY: Oxford University Press.

Nicolopoulou, A., Brockmeyer Cates, C., de Sá, A. and llgaz, H. (2014) Narrative performance, peer group culture, and narrative development in a preschool classroom. In A. Cekaite, S. Blum-Kulka, V. Grover and E. Teubal (eds), *Children's Peer Talk: Learning from each other* (pp. 42–62). New York: Cambridge University Press.

Nicolopoulou, A., Cortina, K., Ilgaz, H., Cates, C. and de Sá, A. (2015) Using a narrative- and play-based activity to promote low-income preschoolers' oral language, emergent literacy, and social competence. *Early Research Childhood Quarterly*, 31: 147–162.

Paley, V. G. (1979/2000) *White Teacher*. Cambridge, MA: Harvard University Press.

Paley, V. G. (1981) *Wally's Stories: Conversations in the kindergarten*. Cambridge, MA: Harvard University Press.

Paley, V. G. (1986) *Mollie is Three: Growing up in school*. Chicago, IL: University of Chicago Press.

Paley, V. G. (1990) *The Boy Who Would Be a Helicopter: The uses of storytelling in the classroom*. Cambridge, MA: Harvard University Press.

Paley, V. G. (1997) *The Girl with the Brown Crayon*. Cambridge, MA: Harvard University Press.

Paley, V. G. (2004) *A Child's Work: The importance of fantasy play*. Chicago, IL: University of Chicago Press.

Pound, L. and Lee, T. (2015) *Teaching Mathematics Creatively* (2nd edn). London and New York: Routledge.

Reese, E., Suggate, S., Long, J. and Schaughency, E. (2010) Children's oral narrative and reading skills in the first 3 years of reading instruction. *Reading and Writing, 23*(6): 627–644.

Snow, C. E., Tabors, P. O. and Dickinson, D. K. (2001) Language development in the pre-school years. In D. Dickinson and P. Tabors (eds), *Young Children Learning at Home and School: Beginning with literacy and language* (pp. 1–26). Baltimore, MD: Brookes.

Swann, J. (2007) Designing 'educationally effective' discussion. *Language and Education*, 21(4): 342–359.

Swann, J. (2009) Doing gender against the odds: A sociolinguistic analysis of educational discourse. In E. Eppler and P. Pichler (eds), *Gender and Spoken Interaction*. Basingstoke, Hants: Palgrave Macmillan.

Tabors, P. O., Snow, C. E. and Dickinson, D. K. (2001) Homes and schools together: Supporting language and literacy development. In D. K. Dickinson and P. O. Tabors (eds), *Beginning Literacy with Language: Young children learning at home and school* (pp. 313–334). Baltimore, MD: Paul H. Brookes.

Typadi, E. and Hayon, K. (2010) Storytelling and story acting: Putting the action into interaction. In F. Griffiths (ed.), *Supporting Children's Creativity through Music, Dance, Drama and Art: Creative conversations in the early years*. New York and London: Routledge.

van Oers, B., Wardekker, W., Elbers, E. and van der Veer, R. (eds) (2008) *The Transformation of Learning: Advances in cultural-historical activity theory*. Cambridge: Cambridge University Press.

Vygotsky, L. S. (1967) Play and its role in the mental development of the child. *Soviet Psychology, 12*: 6–18 (translation of a lecture delivered in Russian in 1933).

Vygotsky, L. (1978) *Mind in Society: The development of higher psychological processes.* Cambridge, MA: Harvard University Press.

Westminster Education Action Zone (WEAZ) (2005) *WEAZ Evaluation 2005: The impact of working together.* Unpublished report. Available at MakeBelieve Arts: http://www. makebelievearts.co.uk

Whitehead, M. (2010) *Language and Literacy in the Early Years 0–7* (4th edn). London: Sage.

Wright, C., Bacigalupa, C., Black, T. and Burton, M. (2008) Windows into children's thinking: A guide to storytelling and dramatization. *Early Childhood Education Journal, 35*: 363–369.

Wright, S. (2007) Graphic-narrative play: Young children's authoring through drawing and telling. *International Journal of Education and the Arts, 8*(8): 1–27.

3

PROMOTING ORAL NARRATIVE SKILLS IN LOW-INCOME PRESCHOOLERS THROUGH STORYTELLING AND STORY ACTING

Ageliki Nicolopoulou

Introduction

Drawing on one of my studies of Vivian Gussin Paley's storytelling and story-acting practice, which I have observed and analysed in a range of preschool classrooms, this chapter traces the development of young children's narrative abilities as they participated in this activity over the course of a school year. Specifically, it analyses a body of 118 spontaneous stories generated through storytelling and story acting in a preschool classroom of children from low-income backgrounds in a semi-rural area in the northeastern United States. The results show significant improvements in the children's narrative skills, as measured by a range of criteria. The study reported here adds to increasing evidence that storytelling and story acting, in addition to its other valuable features, can help promote narrative development and the foundations of emergent literacy in young children from low-income and otherwise disadvantaged backgrounds.

The significance of narrative discourse

Narrative is a crucially important aspect of human thought, interaction, and development. It is a discourse genre that expresses culturally shaped ways of communicating with others about events that we have experienced, heard about, or invented. Narratives of various sorts are linguistic and cognitive tools that we use to represent and reflect on past happenings, to structure and evaluate present experience, and to make sense of the social world and ourselves (Bruner, 1990). Thus, developing the ability to construct and understand narratives, both factual and fictional, is critical for human development. It requires that the child learns to use complex language effectively to express their experiences and ideas while also taking the perspective of others, in terms of the characters and their social interactions depicted in the narrative and of the audience to whom the narration is directly or indirectly addressed (Boyd, 2009).

One manifestation of the significance of narrative for cognitive, linguistic, and socio-emotional development is accumulating evidence that early mastery of narrative discourse helps lay important foundations for literacy acquisition and success in formal education. While the full array of young children's oral language skills may help prepare them for literacy and schooling, research has pointed to distinctively *narrative* skills as being among the most significant in this regard. A number of studies have found that early narrative skills are predictive of reading comprehension during the elementary school years (e.g. Dickinson and Tabors, 2001; Griffin et al., 2004; Reese et al., 2010). For example, Dickinson and Tabors (2001) found that narrative production by low-income kindergarteners predicted reading comprehension in Grades 4 and 7.[1] Similarly, Griffin and colleagues (2004) found that length and quality of 32 middle-class five-year-olds' oral play narratives with structured materials predicted their reading abilities as eight-year-olds in Grade 3. More recently, Reese and colleagues (2010) found that the quality of 61 middle-class seven-year-olds' recall narratives, after listening to a story told by the experimenter with the aid of pictures, predicted their reading fluency concurrently at Grade 2 and longitudinally at Grade 3.

The reasons for these links between early narrative development and emergent literacy remain a subject of research and debate. One orienting hypothesis advanced by an extensive body of scholarship, with some differences of terminology and detail, is that the cognitive and language skills required and promoted by young children's narrative activity form part of an interconnected cluster of *decontextualized* oral language skills that play a critical role in facilitating children's achievement of literacy and their overall school success. Language use is 'decontextualized', in the technical sense used in this research (e.g. Snow, 1991; Westby, 1991), to the extent that it involves explicitly constructing, conveying, and comprehending information in ways that are not embedded in the supportive framework of conversational interaction and do not rely decisively on non-verbal cues and implicit shared background knowledge. Like written text, decontextualized oral discourse raises greater demands than conversational discourse for semantic clarity, planning, and linguistic self-monitoring. Examples of decontextualized language use include various forms of coherent extended discourse such as narratives, explanations, and other monologues, as well as metalinguistic operations such as giving formal definitions. There is evidence that 'skill at the decontextualized uses of language predict[s] literacy and school achievement better than skill at other challenging [oral language] tasks that are not specifically decontextualized' (Snow and Dickinson, 1991: 185).

For preschool children, stories are an especially important mode of decontextualized discourse in that they pose the challenge of explicitly building up a scenario or picture of the world using only words. And unlike many other forms of decontextualized language use, narrative is an important, engaging, and enjoyable activity for children from an early age. Furthermore, there is evidence that free-standing narratives encourage and enable the use of more complex language structures than conversational discourse (Berman and Slobin, 1994), and thus also help prepare children to master distinctive characteristics of written text and literate language.

How can we promote young children's narrative abilities?

Given the significance of early narrative abilities for literacy acquisition and later school success, among other benefits, the question arises how we can effectively promote young children's narrative abilities, especially among children from low-income and otherwise disadvantaged backgrounds who are disproportionately at risk for poor reading and writing proficiency (for the USA, see National Center for Education Statistics, 2013). Interactive bookreading (Pesco and Gagné, 2015) and certain other forms of adult–child interaction have been shown to promote early narrative abilities in valuable ways. But it is essential for early childhood education to complement practices focused on adult–child interaction with more child-centred, peer-oriented, and playful approaches (Nicolopoulou, 2002; Nicolopoulou et al., 2014, 2015). This chapter explores the promise offered by one activity that exemplifies such an approach, the storytelling and story-acting approach pioneered by Paley (1990), the teacher and writer.

This Paley-initiated practice of storytelling and story acting, sometimes also described as story dictation and dramatization, has been used, with variations, in classrooms across the USA and abroad (as the chapters in this book illustrate). Children are given the opportunity to compose stories and dictate them to their teachers, as a regular part of their self-chosen free play activities, and then to act them out later with their friends during a group-time activity that involves the entire class.

This is an apparently simple activity with complex and powerful effects. Several features of this practice are especially worth noting. Although this is a structured and teacher-facilitated activity, the children's storytelling is voluntary, typically self-initiated, and relatively spontaneous. Their stories are neither solicited directly by adults nor channelled by suggested topics or story props. Because this practice runs the entire school year and the children control their own participation in storytelling, it provides them with multiple opportunities to work over, refine, and elaborate their narratives and use them for their own purposes – cognitive, symbolic, and social-relational. Furthermore, the way that this practice combines story*telling* and story *acting* has several important implications. Children typically enjoy storytelling for its own sake, but the prospect of having their story acted out, together with other children whom they choose, offers them a powerful additional motivation to compose and dictate stories. And perhaps most critically, one result of having their stories read to and dramatized for the entire class at group time is that children tell their stories, not only to adults, but primarily to each other; they do so, not in one-to-one interaction, but in the shared public setting of the classroom peer culture. Children are therefore given opportunities to borrow elements from each other's stories and rework them, facilitating narrative cross-fertilization. When this practice is established as a regular part of the classroom activities, all children typically participate over time in three interrelated roles: (1) composing and dictating stories; (2) taking part in the group enactment of stories (their own and those of other children); and (3) listening and watching the performance of the stories of other children. Thus, the children's storytelling and story acting are embedded in the ongoing context of the classroom miniculture and the children's everyday group life. (For further elaboration, see Nicolopoulou, 2002; Nicolopoulou et al., 2014.)

Background and significance of this study

Paley's rich and perceptive ethnographic accounts of her preschool classrooms over the years (e.g. 1986, 1990) and other examinations of storytelling and story acting in action inspired by Paley provide evidence that it promotes children's narrative and emergent literacy skills as well as other cognitive and language abilities. These accounts of storytelling and story acting have mostly focused on preschool classrooms with predominantly middle-class children (exceptions include some of my own work, most recently Nicolopoulou et al., 2015, and McNamee, 2015). One reason is that those preschools are more likely to employ the sort of play-oriented, child-centred curriculum with which this practice dovetails easily. But there are good reasons to believe that practices of this type, if properly conducted, could be even more valuable for children from low-income and otherwise disadvantaged backgrounds than for middle-class children.

For the analysis reported here, I return to material collected in my first effort to study storytelling and story acting in a preschool class made up of children from low-income and otherwise disadvantaged backgrounds. The teacher of a Head Start class, who was planning to introduce this storytelling and story acting into her classroom for the 1997–1998 school year, invited me to help introduce it and to assess its operation and effects. (Head Start is a federally funded preschool programme in the USA serving children from poor families.) As it turned out, some features of this case still make it especially well-suited to illustrate the potential value and effectiveness of storytelling and story acting for promoting the narrative skills of disadvantaged preschoolers. The children in this Head Start class began the school year with exceptionally weak language skills in general and narrative competence in particular, even by comparison with children in other preschool programmes with low-income children that I have studied over the years. By comparison with children in middle-class preschools I have studied, these children faced the challenge of building up many of their basic narrative skills from scratch. If storytelling and story acting could work successfully in such difficult circumstances, it should be able to work anywhere. It is therefore illuminating to use the analysis of these children's stories to trace their patterns of narrative activity and narrative development over the course of the school year.

Evaluating storytelling and story acting in a low-income preschool classroom

The classroom and the children

The stories analyzed in this chapter were generated by eleven children attending one preschool class for the entire 1997–1998 school year (five girls, $M = 4;2$, and six boys, $M = 4;4$: ages calculated at the beginning of the school year).[2] This class was part of a Head Start programme serving children from low-income backgrounds in a small semi-rural New England town. In addition to low income, children's home environments almost all showed some degree of family difficulty or instability. More than two-thirds of the children lived with mothers who were divorced, separated, or single; and even those children who came from two-parent households had experienced various family difficulties. With regard to ethnic and racial background, 64 per cent of the children in the sample were non-Hispanic white, born and raised in the USA. The rest were Hispanic (one or both parents were immigrants from the Caribbean), but all of them spoke English as their dominant language. There were no non-Hispanic African-Americans.[3]

Implementation and data collection

The storytelling and story-acting practice was introduced in the classroom in early October and remained in operation throughout the school year until early May. We trained the teacher to conduct the activity and provided her with a booklet containing detailed guidance. (A research assistant and I provided further input and training during our monthly visits to the classroom.) The teacher was encouraged to use the activity as often as possible, but at least twice per week.

The storytelling part of the practice took place during 'choice time', when children were free to participate in different activities available to them. After the children had settled down into choice-time activities, the teacher made herself available to take children's stories. The number of stories she took down ranged from one to two up to four to five stories each time. If there were several more children who wanted to tell a story, a waiting list was established so that the waiting children could go on with other activities. The storytelling events were voluntary and largely self-initiated; no child was required to compose a story, though some of the more reticent ones were occasionally encouraged to do so. Furthermore, children were allowed to tell any kind of story they wished. In practice, the great majority were fictional stories. The teacher usually took the story down with minimal intervention (though during the first few months she sometimes found that she had to support some children's storytelling because of their limited language and narrative abilities).

The story-acting portion of the practice took place during 'group time', with the entire class assembled. All the stories dictated during that day were acted out in the order dictated. The teacher read the story aloud, after which the child/author first chose which character he or she wanted to play and then picked other children to act out other roles. After all the characters were selected, the teacher read the story aloud once again. As she was reading it, the child-actors acted out the story, while the rest of the children watched attentively. This process was repeated until all the stories dictated during that day were acted out.

This activity took place an average of two days per week (59 days out of 120 for the school year). The eleven children in the sample composed and dictated a total of 151 stories, of which 118 (comprising all their stories through the end of March) were included in the analysis. The reason for this restriction was that at the very end of March, the teacher introduced a rule limiting the number of characters a child could include in each story. While this rule was soon lifted, it had the unintended side-effect of distorting certain features of children's narratives that were significant for our measures of narrative development; thus, stories from April and May were excluded from the analysis.

Overall, the children found this activity highly engaging. As soon as it was initiated, most of them were immediately eager to tell stories and all were eager to participate in acting them out. Within a short time, almost all the children were participating enthusiastically in both components of this activity, and their enthusiasm remained undiminished throughout the year. During a storytelling session, there were always several children gathered around the story table, waiting their turns fairly patiently while other children dictated. Almost all the children in this class participated in telling stories, and most told between nine and twenty-one stories apiece during the year. Furthermore, all the children acted in other children's stories, and all acted in more stories than they told, as is usually the case. When characters were being chosen, many children vigorously expressed their desire to be picked, even waving their hands and shouting 'me, me!' to request desired roles.

The teacher wrote all the stories down in a single 'storybook' as they were dictated, also indicating who the author was and when the story was told. At the time of the story performance she indicated which children acted which roles. The storybook thus provided a record of how often the activity was carried out and how many children participated in it as tellers and/or actors. The storybook was given to us by the end of the year for analysis. (All the parents had signed consent forms to make the stories of their children available to us.)

The children's narratives and their development

Despite the children's enthusiasm for telling and acting in stories, at the beginning of the school year their enthusiasm often outran the limits of their narrative abilities. Most of them also did not display effective familiarity with some basic conventions and requirements for constructing coherent, free-standing, self-contextualizing stories. In their earliest storytelling efforts, several children named a few characters and assigned them no actions or minimal actions, with little or no effort to describe interaction between characters or to suggest a plot. In some cases, they simply listed characters and left it at that. To illustrate, here is the second story told by one of the older girls in the class, whom we will call Deena:[4]

> A book, a circle, a triangle, a longneck, and a snake.
>
> *(Deena, 4:6; 10/29/97)*

When Deena and the other child-actors were assembled in the story-acting circle for their performance, the teacher read out what Deena had dictated and then invited the audience to applaud. Deena became upset and complained to the teacher that 'we didn't do it!' It's clear that Deena did not yet fully grasp the need to spell out a complete narrative scenario explicitly when she told her story.

For some children, this initial phase of protonarrative groping lasted as long as two months. On the other hand, about three weeks after the initiation of storytelling and story acting, one of the girls, April, produced a story that for the first time met the minimal standards for a free-standing story.

> Wedding girl and wedding boy, and then there was a baby. And then there was the person that brought out the flowers. And then there was some animal that wrecked the house, the church house that people were getting married in. And a person was listening to a wedding tape. And that's all.
>
> *(April, 5:1; 10/29/97)*

Clearly, this story was not yet very polished or sophisticated. However, it did construct a relatively coherent and explicit scenario, presenting a set of interrelated characters and integrating them within a sketchy but readily discernible plot. It also introduced and combined a set of organizing themes that were to prove powerfully appealing to other children in the class: first, a wedding, featuring the two linked characters of Wedding Boy (WB) and Wedding Girl (WG); and second, animal aggression.

This story paradigm was gradually taken up, with various modifications and additions, by other children in the class, until it became pervasive in the children's storytelling. But this process took a little while to take off. About three weeks after April's first story, Anton, a boy who had been given the role of WB in acting April's story, told a brief story about a WG and WB getting married and having children (11/19/97). It was not until the day after Anton's story (11/20/97), following this recognition and appropriation of the storyline by a classroom peer, that April told a second story based, with variations, on the WG/WB + animal aggression model. The next week (11/26/97) Anton told a longer story that took up and elaborated this model, adding a dinosaur to the aggressive animals. Starting that day there was also a flurry of similar stories by other children, including a new story by April and this one by Deena:

> Wedding girl and wedding boy and an animal who knocked the house down and took a bite out of the wedding girl. And in the house that people were getting married in.
>
> *(Deena, 4:7; 11/26/97)*

Stories drawing on this cluster of themes, including the element of dinosaur aggression introduced by Anton, became increasingly popular as the year went on. This story paradigm thus became the common property of the classroom peer group. By the end of the fall semester, it had become a broadly influential model for the children's storytelling, and a shared point of reference even for stories that used different themes wholly or in part. By the spring semester, all children in the sample had used versions of this model, or at least some of its elements, in a number of their stories; and the overall proportion of stories that incorporated this model and/or drew on its central themes, in various configurations, during the school year was quite high (see Table 3.1). In short, after April introduced this narrative paradigm into the classroom miniculture, other children took major roles in its diffusion and elaboration, and it became a cultural tool that was shared and developed by the classroom peer group as a whole. This narrative sharing and cross-fertilization is one example of the ways in which storytelling and story acting helped create a shared body of publicly available narrative resources from which different children could draw, and to which in turn they could contribute, in the course of their participation.

Furthermore, within a short time following the group's exposure to this paradigm, the children largely ceased to dictate protostories consisting of simple strings of inactive characters. And with very few exceptions, all their stories improved in quality and sophistication over the course of the school year – becoming longer, more complex, and generally more coherent – even when they used other storylines. Here is April's last story of the school year, which had a more poetic and romantic tone than her earliest stories.

> A wedding girl and a wedding boy, the flowers the boyfriend gives her, and a moon. It was dark, and then it was sunny out. Then the sun went down, and the moon came up, and the sun went to China. Then the sun and moon fall in love, then they kiss, then they fall in love again. Then they don't fall in love anymore, and they were mad at each other, and then they fall in love again.
>
> *(April 5;7; 5/8/98)*

Of course, the developmental trajectories of individual children were far from simple, uniform, or unilinear. But systematic analysis of the children's stories demonstrates a clear and significant overall pattern of narrative development.

TABLE 3.1 Mean proportions of common overlapping themes in stories told by children in this sample

	Girls	Boys
Wedding Girl and Wedding Boy	.80	.51
WG and WB + aggression	.68	.49
Dinosaur aggression	.52	.62

Analysis of children's spontaneous narratives

The 118 stories generated by the eleven children in the sample through their participation in storytelling and story acting were coded using seven measures of narrative development developed for this study. The first four measures captured the *narrative complexity and sophistication* of the children's storytelling; these were loosely adapted from work in functional linguistics and sociolinguistics (particularly Berman and Slobin, 1994; Labov and Waletzky, 1997). The next three measures focused on the *representation of characters* in the children's narratives; these were derived from my own ongoing work on assessing young children's narrative development (Nicolopoulou, 2002; Nicolopoulou and Richner, 2007).

Because children differed in the number of stories they told, for comparisons we calculated mean proportions for the number and types of clauses as well as types of characters. For all other measures, children's scores were based on the highest level achieved in at least *two* stories each semester. Two coders (the author and a graduate student) independently coded the entire corpus of stories, and interrater agreement ranged from 89 per cent to 99 per cent. Repeated-measure Analyses of Variance (ANOVAS) were performed on these scores: one-way, when the measure yielded one score (e.g. number of clauses, temporality, connectivity), with semester as the within factor; and two-way, when the measure yielded more than one score (e.g. narrative vs. non-narrative clauses; active vs. passive vs. inactive characters), with that measure as one within factor and semester as the other. The results indicated that the children's stories improved significantly on all seven measures of narrative quality between fall and spring semester (see Table 3.2).

TABLE 3.2 Means (standard deviations), F and p values for dimensions of narrative development in stories told by children in this sample

	Fall (N = 46)	Spring (N = 72)	F	p
Narrative complexity and sophistication				
Number of clauses	4.13 (2.30)	7.50 (2.84)	17.19	.002
Types of clauses:				
% narrative	63 (31)	84 (9)	5.60	.04
% non-narrative	37 (31)	16 (9)	5.55	.04
Temporality	1.55 (1.92)	3.73 (1.25)	14.69	.003
	(Level 2)	(Level 4)		
Connectivity	.91 (.83)	2.73 (1.27)	26.67	<.0004
	(Level 1)	(Level 3)		
Representation of characters				
Types of characters				
% active	43 (24)	63 (11)	8.55	.01
% passive	11 (12)	22 (7)	2.44	.13
% inactive	45 (27)	15 (11)	19.88	.0002
Depth and complexity	1.68 (1.12)	2.91 (.54)	14.82	<.003
	(Level 2)	(Level 3)		
Interaction and coordination	2.00 (1.13)	3.18 (.60)	6.50	.02
	(Level 2)	(Level 3)		

Narrative complexity and sophistication

Number of clauses. One dimension of narrative development is that children should be able to handle an increasing *number* of clauses effectively within a single story. For young children's spontaneous stories, the increasing mean length of stories, as measured by the number of clauses each contains, can be treated as a rough baseline indicator of increasing narrative competence. To test this hypothesis, each story was broken down into *clauses* (following Berman and Slobin, 1994), each containing a subject and a verb. Statements external to the story, such as stage directions, were not included. The results indicate that the number of clauses per story increased significantly during the year ($p = .002$).

Types of clauses: Narrative vs. non-narrative. This measure examined the *types* of clauses that children used in their stories: whether these were *narrative* or *non-narrative* clauses, following the distinction introduced by Labov and Waletzky (1997). *Narrative clauses* are ones that move the narrative ahead by depicting a series of events in temporal sequence ('*The elephant went in town and found a store*'). *Non-narrative clauses* may be of several types. Some may be of the type Labov and Waletzky call *evaluative*, which signal the point or significance of the story; a well-formed story needs to include a certain proportion of evaluative clauses. Other types of non-narrative clauses are used to introduce or describe the characters and the setting; such clauses are also necessary, but in well-formed stories one would expect them to be less numerous than narrative clauses.

In these children's narratives, the non-narrative clauses consisted overwhelmingly of simple descriptions and introductions, with very few evaluative clauses. Thus, as an indication of narrative development, we expected an increasing proportion of narrative clauses per story. The results indicated that this did occur. Whereas the mean proportions of narrative vs. non-narrative clauses in the fall were 63 per cent vs. 37 per cent (a difference that was not statistically significant, $p = .07$), in the spring the corresponding proportions were 83 per cent vs. 16 per cent (a difference that was statistically significant, $p < .0001$). In addition, the increase in the proportion of narrative clauses from fall to spring was statistically significant ($p = .04$) as was the decrease in the proportion of non-narrative clauses ($p = .04$).

Temporality. This measure, loosely adapted from Berman and Slobin (1994), examined the tense children used in their stories (past or present) as well as their degree of temporal anchoring (i.e. consistent or inconsistent use of tense). Telling stories consistently in the past tense is the preferred narrative mode in English (Berman and Slobin, 1994: ch. IIIA). However, young children often start out telling stories in the present tense; and even when they begin to use the past tense, they often require some time before their use of past tense is fully consistent. To capture this developmental trajectory, a scale of six levels (scored from 0 to 5) was constructed: No Verb or Only One Verb Used; Consistent Present; Predominant Present (two-thirds of clauses); Mixed Uses of Past and Present (about half and half); Predominant Past (two-thirds of clauses); Consistent Past.

This measure indicated a clear pattern of development from fall to spring that was statistically significant ($p < .003$). In the fall, the mean level of temporality achieved by this sample was between Levels 1 and 2 ($M = 1.55$), with four children scoring at Level 0 and four at Level 2 (predominant present). By contrast, in the spring, the mean level of optimal temporality was Level 4 ($M = 3.73$), with three children achieving Level 3 (mixed), four children achieving Level 4 (predominant past), and another three achieving Level 5 (consistent past).

Connectivity. This measure examined how children connected clauses to each other and what kinds of connectors they used to do this. A scale of four broad levels with sublevels (0 to 6) was constructed: *Level 0*: no connectors; *Levels 1–2: Logical Connectors* (Level 1: 'and' only; Level 2: 'and' and 'but'); *Levels 3–4: Temporal Connectors* (Level 3: 'then' or 'and then'; Level 4: 'when' or 'and when'); *Levels 5–6: Causal–Temporal Connectors* (Level 5: temporal connectors used together with 'because' or 'so'; Level 6: temporal connectors used together with 'because' and 'so'). These levels are cumulative: each level indicates that the child used new connectors in addition to the ones already used in previous levels, thus achieving more complex modes of cohesion in the story as a whole.

This measure showed a clear pattern of development from fall to spring that was statistically significant ($p < .0004$). In the fall, the mean level of connectivity achieved by this sample was Level 1 ($M = .91$), with seven children scoring at Level 1 (conjoining logical connectors: 'and' only). In contrast, in the spring the mean level of optimal connectivity was Level 3 ($M = 2.73$), with six children having achieved this level.

Representation of characters

The next three measures addressed the depiction and use of *characters* in children's stories. Constructing narratives involves not only the depiction of sequences of events, but also the selection, portrayal, and coordination of characters.

Types of characters: Active vs. passive vs. inactive. In well-formed narratives, one would expect no inactive characters (character is named, but given no action), and a higher proportion of active characters (character is the agent of actions) than of passive characters (character is the recipient of action). Once again, the shifts in the relative proportions of character types per story from fall to spring showed a clear pattern of narrative development that was statistically significant.

The mean proportion of inactive characters decreased dramatically (fall $M =$ 45 per cent, spring $M = 15$ perc ent), and this difference was statistically significant ($p = .0002$); the proportion of active characters increased as well (fall $M =$ 43 per cent, spring $M = 63$ per cent), and this difference was statistically significant ($p = .01$). The mean proportion of passive characters per story also increased, from 11 per cent in the fall to 22 per cent in the spring, but this change was not statistically significant ($p = .13$). To describe these changes from a slightly different direction, in the fall the mean proportions of active and inactive characters were almost equal (43 per cent vs. 45 per cent), whereas in the spring the mean proportion of active characters was much higher than the mean proportions of either passive or inactive characters, and these differences were statistically significant: 63 per cent active vs. 15 per cent inactive (p <.0001); and 63 per cent active vs. 22 per cent passive (p <.0001).

Character depth and complexity. This measure focused on the depth and complexity with which children portrayed characters in their stories; it drew, in part, on research dealing with children's social understanding and their 'theories of mind'. A scale with eight levels (scored from 0 to 7) was constructed, with Levels 1 through 7 ranging from purely external depictions to increasingly explicit and sophisticated depictions of characters' internal states and motivations (see Nicolopoulou and Richner, 2007).

Level 0: No story (just lists of characters with no actions); *Level 1:* Actions only (e.g. '*A dragon came and then Batman came. They had a battle*'); *Level 2:* Actions plus external descriptions ('*There was a big clown who had a pet mouse and a dog and he lived in a castle*'); *Level 3:* Plus perception, communication, physiological states, and/or actions with implied intentions ('*A little girl was looking for her dog. She met a bear. The bear talked*'); *Level 4:* Plus reactive evaluations, emotions, and/or actions ('*There was a princess, a queen, a king, and a baby. A wolf came and ate the baby. And the queen was very sad*'); *Level 5:* Plus explicit intentions and desires ('*One night a woman offered the prince a rose. But he didn't want the rose. [...] Gaston wanted to kill the beast*'); *Level 6:* Plus desire–belief psychology (explicit desires and knowledge states, but knowledge does not mediate the character's actions); *Level 7:* Plus belief–desire psychology (explicit desires and knowledge states that mediate characters' actions).

The results indicated that the children significantly improved the depth and complexity of their character representation from fall to spring, and this increase was statistically significant (p < .003). In the fall, the mean level of optimal character representation was between Levels 1 and 2 ($M = 1.68$), with three children scoring Level 1 and five children scoring Level 2. In the spring, by contrast, the mean level of optimal character representation was Level 3 ($M = 2.91$), with eight children having reached Level 3 and one child Level 4. In other words, from fall to spring the mean level of optimal character representation improved from pure actions (Level 1) and simple external descriptions (Level 2) to depictions in which characters began to exhibit a perspective on the world and intentional actions (Level 3).

Character interaction and coordination. This measure addressed one dimension of structural complexity (as distinguished from linguistic complexity, discussed earlier) and coherence of the children's narratives, by examining the children's ability to *coordinate* characters in an effective way. A scale of seven levels was constructed (scored from 0 to 6). *Level 0: No Story:* just lists of characters with no actions; *Level 1: No Interaction:* one or more active characters, each of whom performs one or more actions, but the action or actions are not explicitly directed toward other characters; *Levels 2–4: Character Interaction (Level 2: Low Interaction:* interactions between isolated pairs of characters; *Level 3: Medium Interaction:* characters' actions directed towards other characters, and some overlap of characters between interacting pairs, so some reciprocal actions and chains of character interactions are presented; *Level 4: High*

Interaction: greater overlap between characters in interacting pairs, so that one or more characters emerge as stable throughout the story); *Levels 5–6: Character Coordination (Level 5: Simple Coordination*: most characters interact with other characters, and an overall theme or topic connects these interacting characters in a coherent plot; *Level 6: Complex Coordination*: characters' interactions are coordinated through the use of multiple themes and subthemes).

The results indicated that the children significantly improved their abilities to depict character interaction from fall to spring semester, and this increase was statistically significant (p = .02). In the fall, the mean level of character interaction achieved by these children was Level 2, low interaction between characters (M = 2.00), with about half of the children (five out of eleven) scoring at this level. By the spring, the mean level achieved was Level 3, medium interaction (M = 3.18), with ten children having achieved either medium interaction (Level 3: seven children) or high interaction (Level 4: three children).

Summary

Over the course of the year the narrative abilities of the children in this class improved consistently and significantly along all seven dimensions just discussed. Whereas these children's initial storytelling efforts consisted mainly of proto-narrative lists of inactive characters, their stories increasingly portrayed more active characters with improved depth and complexity as well as interaction and coordination between characters. Furthermore, whereas the children began by telling stories in the present tense (used also in pretend play), they gradually shifted to past tense, which is the preferred narrative tense in English. Their stories included more clauses and higher proportions of narrative clauses, and their levels of connectivity improved, i.e. they shifted from either not connecting clauses (and events) to each other or simply linking them with 'and' to also indicating temporal connections.

However, it is also necessary to add a cautionary note. In terms of the narrative competence and sophistication they displayed, the stories told by the children in this class in the spring were still considerably less advanced than the stories I have collected from children of equivalent ages in middle-class preschools (e.g. Nicolopoulou, 1996, 1997; Nicolopoulou et al., 1994; Nicolopoulou and Richner, 2007; Richner and Nicolopoulou, 2001) or even in other (urban) preschools serving disadvantaged children (e.g. Nicolopoulou et al., 2006, 2010, 2015). Despite the progress these children made in developing their narrative skills during the year, they still had a substantial amount of catching-up to do. But for purposes of the present study, the key point is that the children in this class did show a clear and significant pattern of narrative development.

Discussion and conclusion

This analysis traced the development of the stories composed and told by children in this preschool class while participating in storytelling and story acting over the course of the school year. We found clear and significant improvement on all seven measures of narrative development we used. By themselves, these results would not necessarily demonstrate a causal link between children's participation in storytelling and story acting and the development of their narrative skills. Those changes might simply be due to children's maturation over time, perhaps reinforced by a range of enriched language stimulations to which they were exposed in their preschool classroom. However, there is also further evidence to support the inference that storytelling and story acting, in particular, plays a significant role in promoting children's narrative skills.

In addition to the analysis of the children's stories discussed in this chapter, the study reported here collected and analysed two other types of data. This preschool class was matched with a control class in the same Head Start programme that did not use storytelling and story acting but continued its usual curriculum. Two tasks were administered to children in both the intervention and the control class at the beginning and end of the school year (i.e. prior to the introduction of storytelling and story acting and after the last time it was carried out): a narrative production task and the Expressive Vocabulary Test (EVT). Results from this controlled comparison confirmed that participation in storytelling and story acting significantly enhanced the development of children's narrative skills, as measured by the narrative task, and other decontextualized oral language skills, as measured by the EVT (for more details, see Nicolopoulou, 2002, in preparation). While these results from a study using only one intervention and one control classroom were promising but not necessarily conclusive, further evidence of the value of storytelling and story acting for promoting low-income preschoolers' narrative abilities was provided by a more large-scale study I subsequently conducted in a different preschool programme serving low-income children, comparing six intervention with seven control classes and using a wider range of outcome measures (see Nicolopoulou et al., 2010, 2015). Results from that study indicated that children's participation in storytelling and story acting was associated with improvements in their narrative abilities – as well as other oral language, emergent literacy, and social competence skills (though not expressive vocabulary).

The next questions to address are *how* and *why* storytelling and story acting can help promote children's narrative development. The kinds of mechanisms usually emphasized in the context of expert–novice interaction, such as scaffolding, expert guidance, or conversational fine-tuning, do not seem to play a key role here. (At the very beginning of this intervention the teacher sometimes tried to support some children's story dictation to help the activity get off the ground, but such assistance was transitory and lasted for only a brief period.) So how should the developmental benefits of children's participation in this practice be explained? Let me close by offering a brief and partial response (for more extensive discussions, from which some formulations below are drawn, see Nicolopoulou, 2002; Nicolopoulou, et al., 2010, 2014).

Peer-group culture and the dynamics of narrative collaboration

The heart of the matter, I submit, is that this storytelling and story-acting practice provides the framework for an ongoing, socially structured, and collectively constituted field of shared symbolic activity. Although teachers play a necessary and crucial role in structuring, facilitating, and sometimes guiding storytelling and story acting, the children themselves help to generate and sustain this activity system through their participation in storytelling and story acting and it serves, in turn, as a sociocultural context that shapes their participation and offers them opportunities, resources, and motivations for narrative development. In this respect, several (interconnected) features of storytelling and story acting, some of which were noted earlier, seem especially worth emphasizing.

One is the public, peer-oriented, and peer-evaluated character of the children's narrative activity. Each child freely composes his or her own stories (or, in other classrooms, a few children may sometimes cooperate to produce multi-authored stories), but then the stories are presented to the class as a whole, and at one point or another all the children also participate in acting out their own stories and each other's. As a result, this activity engages the children and creates a public arena for narrative communication, appropriation, experimentation, cross-fertilization, and collaboration. Even in a small class of children from similar backgrounds, different children come with distinctive experiences, knowledge, skills, concerns, and temperamental styles. The storytelling and story-acting approach allows these individual skills and perspectives to be transformed into shared and publicly available narrative resources, so that each child can benefit from the variety of resources that other children bring with them. In the classroom discussed in this chapter, these processes of narrative cross-fertilization and reciprocal influence were strikingly illustrated by the children's adoption and elaboration of the WG/ WB + animal aggression model and the circulation and use, with variations, of the cluster of themes associated with that narrative paradigm. To borrow a phrase from Paley (1986: xv), this public arena offers children an 'experimental theater' in which they can reciprocally try out, elaborate, and refine their own narrative efforts while getting the responses of an engaged and emotionally significant peer-group audience. Thus, storytelling and story acting can effectively integrate individual spontaneity and self-expression with peer-group collaboration and mutual support.

The public arena of storytelling and story acting is itself enmeshed in the sociocultural framework of the children's peer relations and group life, with their emotional importance for children and their significance for children's experience, socialization, and development. A mutually reinforcing dynamic is involved here. Children's participation in storytelling and story acting helps to form and sustain a common culture in the classroom (while also facilitating the expression and articulation of differences within this common culture); and, simultaneously, this storytelling and story acting is shaped, supported, and energized by its embeddedness in that peer-group culture.

Furthermore, the way that the storytelling and story-acting approach combines story*telling* with story *acting* integrates elements of narrative discourse and of pretend play – and utilizes the interplay between them in a manner that can promote and facilitate narrative development. To frame this slightly differently, the storytelling and story acting portions of this practice represent two dimensions of narrative activity that involve complementary cognitive and linguistic skills: (1) the highly *decontextualized* use of language in composing and dictating the stories; and (2) highly *contextualized* enactment of narrative scenarios, which is characteristically a central feature of children's pretend play. The contribution of this practice lies in the way that it links these two dimensions. On the one hand, the storytelling component of the practice poses for the child an exceptionally challenging demand for decontextualized discourse, since the child is called on to construct a complete, self-contextualizing fictional narrative using only words. The child's storytelling is not embedded in the immediate framework of conversational interaction and response (which means that in certain respects the demand for decontextualized use of language here is greater than, for example, in the conversational elicitation and construction of narratives of past experience), and the composition of the story is typically several hours removed from its enactment. On the other hand, my analyses of this storytelling and story-acting practice indicate that the reading-out and enactment of the children's stories not only helps to motivate the children's storytelling, but also serves some important educative functions. In particular, it helps bring home to the child in a vivid way what is required for a narrative scenario to be effectively complete, self-contextualizing, and satisfying.

In combination, these features of the storytelling and story-acting approach help explain why it can serve as a powerful context for promoting narrative development in young children, including those from poor and disadvantaged backgrounds. For these and other reasons, both research and educational practice should recognize it as a developmental matrix of rich complexity and great potential that can play a valuable role in early childhood education.

Notes

1 On average, children in the USA begin kindergarten at age five, Grade 1 at age six, Grade 2 at age seven, Grade 3 at age eight, Grade 4 at age nine, and Grade 7 at age twelve. Preschool children are three to five years of age.

2 The class began and ended the school year with seventeen students, but the sample used for the analysis included only children present the entire year. Three full-year children were excluded for various reasons: one suffered from microcephalia and had minimal language skills; one was Spanish monolingual; and one was mistrustful of adults in general and refused to participate in other tests used for the study.

3 It may be worth noting that in most studies of the storytelling and story acting in US preschools with low-income children, the preschools have been located in urban areas and the participants have included African-American children.

4 Pseudonyms are used for all children quoted or otherwise discussed.

References

Berman, R. A. and Slobin, D. I. (1994) *Relating Events in Narrative: A crosslinguistic developmental study*. Hillsdale, NJ: Erlbaum.

Boyd, B. (2009) *On the Origins of Stories: Evolution, cognition, and fiction*. Cambridge, MA: Harvard University Press.

Bruner, J. S. (1990) *Acts of Meaning*. Cambridge, MA: Harvard University Press.

Dickinson, D. K. and Tabors, P. O. (eds) (2001) *Beginning Literacy with Language: Young children learning at home and school*. Baltimore, MD: Paul H. Brookes.

Griffin, T. M., Hemphill, L., Camp, L. and Wolf, D. P. (2004) Oral discourse in the preschool years and later literacy skills. *First Language*, 24: 123–147.

Labov, W. and Waletzky, J. (1997) Narrative analysis: Oral versions of personal experience. *Journal of Narrative and Life History*, 7: 3–38 (Original work published 1967).

McNamee, G. D. (2015) *The High-Performing Preschool: Story-acting in Head Start classrooms*. Chicago, IL: University of Chicago Press.

National Center for Education Statistics (2013) *National Assessment of Educational Progress (NAEP), 1998, 2000, 2003, 2005, 2007, 2009, 2011, and 2013 Reading Assessments*. Retrieved from http://nces.ed.gov/nationsreportcard/neapdata

Nicolopoulou, A. (1996) Narrative development in social context. In D. I. Slobin, J. Gerhardt, J. Guo and A. Kyratzis (eds), *Social Interaction, Social Context and Language: Essays in honor of Susan Ervin-Tripp* (pp. 369–390). Mahwah, NJ: Erlbaum.

Nicolopoulou, A. (1997) Worldmaking and identity formation in children's narrative play-acting. In B. D. Cox and C. Lightfoot (eds), *Sociogenetic Perspectives on Internalization* (pp. 157–187). Mahwah, NJ: Erlbaum.

Nicolopoulou, A. (2002) Peer-group culture and narrative development. In S. Blum-Kulka and C. E. Snow (eds), *Talking to Adults: The contribution of multiparty discourse to language acquisition* (pp. 117–152). Mahwah, NJ: Erlbaum.

Nicolopoulou, A. (forthcoming) Using a storytelling/story-acting practice to promote narrative and other decontextualized language skills in disadvantaged children. In E. Veneziano and A. Nicolopoulou (eds), *Narrative, Literacy, and Other Skills: Studies in intervention*. Studies in Narrative [SiN] Series: John Benjamin Press.

Nicolopoulou, A. and Richner, E. S. (2007) From actors to agents to persons: The development of character representation in young children's narratives. *Child Development*, 78: 412–429.

Nicolopoulou, A., Brockmeyer Cates, C., de Sá, A. and Ilgaz, H. (2014) Narrative performance, peer-group culture, and narrative development in a preschool classroom. In A. Cekaite, S. Blum-Kulka, V. Aukrust and E. Teubal (eds), *Children's Peer Talk: Learning from each other* (pp. 42–62). New York. NY: Cambridge University Press.

Nicolopoulou, A., Cortina, K. S., Ilgaz, H., Cates, C. B. and de Sá, A. (2015) Using a narrative- and play-based activity to promote low-income preschoolers' oral language, emergent literacy, and social competence. *Early Childhood Research Quarterly*, 31: 147–162.

Nicolopoulou, A., de Sá, A., Ilgaz, H. and Brockmeyer, C. (2010) Using the transformative power of play to educate hearts and minds: From Vygotsky to Vivian Paley. *Mind, Culture, and Activity*, 5: 61–71.

Nicolopoulou, A., McDowell, J. and Brockmeyer, C. (2006) Narrative play and emergent literacy: Storytelling and story-acting meet journal writing. In D. Singer, R. Golinkoff and K. Hirsh-Pasek (eds), *Play = Learning* (pp. 124–144). New York, NY: Oxford University Press.

Nicolopoulou, A., Scales, B. and Weintraub, J. (1994) Gender differences and symbolic imagination in the stories of four-year-olds. In A. H. Dyson and C. Genishi (eds), *The Need for Story: Cultural diversity in classroom and community* (pp. 102–123). Urbana, IL: NCTE.

Paley, V. G. (1986) *Mollie is Three: Growing up in school.* Chicago, IL: University of Chicago Press.

Paley, V. G. (1990) *The Boy Who Would Be a Helicopter: The uses of storytelling in the classroom.* Cambridge, MA: Harvard University Press.

Pesco, D. and Gagné, A. (2015) Scaffolding narrative skills. A meta-analysis of instruction in early childhood settings. *Early Education and Development,* online. DOI: 10.1080/10409289.2015.1060800

Reese, E., Suggate, S., Long, J. and Schaughency, E. (2010) Children's oral narrative and reading skills in the first 3 years of reading instruction. *Reading and Writing, 23*: 627–644.

Richner, E. S. and Nicolopoulou, A. (2001) The narrative construction of differing conceptions of the person in the development of young children's social understanding. *Early Education & Development, 12*: 393–432.

Snow, C. E. (1991) The theoretical basis for relationships between language and literacy in development. *Journal of Research in Childhood Education, 6*: 5–10.

Snow, C. E. and Dickinson, D. K. (1991) Skills that aren't basic in a new conception of literacy. In E. M. Jennings and A. C. Purves (eds), *Literate Systems and Individual Lives: Perspectives on literacy and schooling* (pp. 179–191). Albany: State University of New York Press.

Westby, C. E. (1991) Learning to talk—Talking to learn: Oral-literate language differences. In C. S. Simon (ed.), *Communication Skills and Classroom Success: Assessment and therapy methodologies for language and learning disabled students* (pp. 334–355). Eau Claire, WI: Thinking Publications.

4

APPRENTICE STORY WRITERS

Exploring young children's print awareness and agency in early story authoring

Teresa Cremin

Introduction

This chapter examines the contribution of Vivian Gussin Paley's (1990, 1992) storytelling and story-acting pedagogy to young children's growing word and print awareness and their agency in early story authoring. Whilst many scholars have asserted and documented the value of Paley's approach for children's oral development and narrative comprehension (e.g. Cooper, 2009; Nicolopoulou et al., 2006; Nicolopoulou et al., 2014), considerably less attention has been paid to its potential contribution to children's early writing and their development as authors. In telling their tales to an adult, children watch as the adult scribes their spoken words and later they participate in bringing their own and others' written tales to life through enactment. This close observation of adults' writing, coupled with their active participation in the acting out of their peers' stories, were salient features of children's participation in a recent UK-based study of the approach upon which this chapter draws. In half the settings, children (aged three to six years old) initiated their own writing activities, authoring and co-authoring their own tales with friends and scribing their peers' stories for later dramatisation (Cremin et al., 2013). The agency and intentionality shown by these young authors was marked; they seized opportunities to write their own narratives and to scribe others' tales and in the process learnt about writing through their authorial engagement.

Anchoring the work within a sociocultural approach to learning (Lave and Wenger, 1991; Vygotsky, 1978) and literacy (Barton et al., 2000) the chapter begins by discussing children's early authoring and the concepts of intentionality and agency from different ontological perspectives. It argues that children's early authoring needs to be viewed as a socially situated act of meaning making, and recognises that reading, writing and oral language develop simultaneously, not as discrete entities (Bloome et al., 2005; Rowe, 2003). Related research on the writing practices associated with Paley's (1990) storytelling and story-acting approach is also considered. The chapter then details the ethnographic data collection tools which enabled close documentation of the writing experiences of the children who participated in the UK instantiation of this approach (see Chapter 2 for more detail on the methodological approach). Data are drawn predominantly from two of the six settings involved in the study: a primary school and one of its feeder preschools, located within half a mile of each other in a semi-rural, suburban context in southern England. One class in each setting was involved, with children aged three to four, and four to five respectively. Specific, local enactments of learning-to-write practices that were evidenced during the use of Helicopter Stories in these settings are examined. The chapter explores the ways in which storytelling and story acting enabled children to learn about writing and prompted some to scribe others' tales spontaneously as well as author their own. Importantly, it argues that this playful pedagogic approach creates a possibility space for young apprentice writers, one which not only draws attention to the written word enabling children to observe its use in a meaningful context, but which may, in some settings, also serve to motivate their engagement in self-initiated and purposeful writing activities and become authors.

Early authoring

The nature of young children's authoring is viewed from different ontological standpoints: research from cognitive and psycholinguistic perspectives locates authoring in the mind of the child as an individual mental act, whilst research from sociocultural and situated cognition perspectives locates it as occurring collectively between children and others. Working from an emergent literacy perspective, cognitive and sociocognitive scholars have tended to describe early authoring in relation to young children's intentionality (their understanding that written marks have cultural meanings), and children's cognitive hypotheses about print, which it is perceived shapes early authoring (e.g. Clay, 1975; Ferrreiro and Teberosky, 1982). As a consequence scholars have examined and described patterns and perceived progressions in children's early texts, focusing for example, on speech–print links, directionality and depiction of word units. They argue these are signs of emergent literacy which precede and develop into conventional literacy.

Sociocultural researchers have shifted this focus on cognitive intentionality to examine children's participation and the social construction of their understandings when engaged in joint social activity (Dyson, 2001; Gee, 2001; Rowe, 2008). From this standpoint, how children's hypotheses and texts are shaped by the cultural practices in the classroom (and their communities), and how these practices shape what it is to be an author in these contexts becomes central to understanding early authoring. The social construction of intentionality is specifically examined by Rowe (2008) in her study of two- to four-year-olds engaging in writing practices at an officially designated classroom 'writing centre'. In this context she found adult talk focused mainly on: understanding the children's literate intentions; guiding their participation in writing; drawing attention to the adult's own activity (by authoring/co-authoring at the table); and simultaneously explaining the thinking behind their actions. Other studies have also shown that teachers' conceptualisations of writing and their roles in guiding young children's participation as writers, frame and shape the authorial identity positions offered to children, as do the official learning-to-write practices on offer (Bourne, 2002; Fisher, 2010). Additionally, research reveals that children actively work to take up or reject the roles on offer and seek to exercise agency as authors, thus contributing to the shaping of literacy practices in classrooms (Dyson, 2009; Rowe and Nietzel, 2010). But how children exercise their agency varies as a result of their perceived degree of freedom and independence, and as Rowe and Nietzel (2010) have shown, children's underlying interests and orientations also influence their play and writing choices.

The study upon which this chapter draws, acknowledged the complex, contextual nature of early literacy, and the active role that children play as meaning makers. Recognising that young children author as they play, and that language is not the only or even the central semiotic mode they draw upon to do so, the study also viewed early authoring as multimodal (Flewitt, 2012). (See Chapter 10 for an examination of children's multimodal meaning making.) Research has additionally demonstrated that young children use the language practices of childhood as they write and that they appropriate, remix and recontextualise familiar cultural material in the world of school (Dyson, 1997, 2001, 2009). This body of work affirms that even in highly structured writing activities, writing is socially rooted in playful peer dialogues often of an unofficial nature. Pahl's (2007) work, too, shows that children playfully draw upon multiple modes, events and practices at home and at school to convey their meanings, which, she suggests, reveals the creativity and intertextuality involved. Early authoring can be seen therefore as 'a material and embodied process through which children adapt and transform cultural resources' (Rowe, 2003: 266). This underscores the inadequacy of locating authoring in the mind of the child and as uniquely expressed through words, since as Lancaster argues, early symbolic activity is 'a process in which bodily experience, living environments and culture are linked through semiosis' (2013: 30).

Despite the wealth of research into early authoring and the multiple assertions made about the potential of storytelling and story acting in supporting young writers (e.g. Paley, 1990; Cooper, 2009; Nicolopoulou et al., 2006; Nicolopoulou et al., 2014), there are only two known studies which include particular attention to the relationship between Paley's (1990) approach and writing in the early years (Nicolopoulou et al., 2006; Nicolopoulou et al., 2015). The first study highlighted that fourteen of the nineteen children in one pre-school class who participated regularly in this story-based practice increased their engagement with their journal writing activities (dictated and drawn); they began to narratise entries and the length and complexity of these increased substantially over the year (2003–2004). The second research study sought to examine the developmental and educational value of the approach for preschool children from low-income homes. It involved a randomised waitlist design, with half the classes randomly assigned to receive the intervention early and half randomly assigned to receive it later over a two-year period (2005–2007). A total of 149 preschoolers (almost all three- and four-year-olds) participated in the study. During the intervention, storytelling and story acting were used as part of a regular component of the preschool curriculum. Pre- and post-tests of eleven measures were administered to capture skills deemed relevant to 'school readiness', focusing on three domains: narrative and other oral-language skills, social competence and emergent literacy. Whilst the concept of 'school readiness', which is linked to cognitive perspectives on emergent literacy, has international currency, its use is contentious, and it is differently employed by policy-makers, practitioners and academics (Whitebread and Bingham, 2012).

In Nicolopoulou et al.'s (2015) study three items of the children's emergent literacy skills were assessed: beginning sound awareness, rhyme awareness, and print and word awareness (subscales from the Phonological Awareness Literacy Screening: PreK; Invernizzi et al., 2004). Through hierarchical linear modelling analysis, the research found that engagement in storytelling and story acting was significantly associated with increased print and word awareness and that within the intervention classes, the number of stories told by children was a significant predictor of this enhanced awareness (Nicolopoulou et al., 2015). As the researchers acknowledge, this is perhaps not surprising since the approach provides children 'with a range of engaging literacy-related experiences that concretely demonstrate the uses and mechanics of writing, reading and print' (Nicolopoulou et al., 2015: 159). Nonetheless, the nature of this large-scale study and the demands placed upon the team to ensure practitioner fidelity to the specific intervention programme, is likely to have reduced their documentation of the children's lived experience of both story scribing and dramatisation, and the nature of their interaction around writing during these activities. No mention is made of the practice of children scribing their own or their peers' stories which, as noted earlier, was an observed feature in half of the six settings in the UK study.

Methodology

This present study was not only much smaller scale, it also adopted a different ontological orientation and methodological approach. Whilst similarly naturalistic in nature, the design was not experimental, and ethnographic tools (Green and Bloome, 1997) were used to document the social practices of storytelling and story acting in the UK classrooms. The present study thus offers a complementary, closely observed data set. This is drawn upon to examine the contribution of the Helicopter Stories approach to children's growing word and print awareness and to their unprompted agentic participation as writers in the early years classroom.

The study was undertaken to evaluate a training programme offered by a theatre and education company who have developed Paley's (1990) approach in the UK. See Chapter 2 for further details of this programme entitled 'Helicopter

Stories', which in essence encompassed an eight-week programme of provision for practitioners through both professional development and in-class support in six early years settings. The university research team collected a wide range of data from the Helicopter Stories theatre art trainers, teachers, classroom support staff and child participants. The adult-focused data collection methods included: observations of the pre-programme training sessions; interviews with the key practitioners and trainers in each setting throughout (early, middle and late phase); and video-stimulated review at the end of the project with the education practitioners. The child-focused ethnographic data collection methods encompassed: observation and video recording of a sample of the programme's implementation (again early, middle and late phase), and the collection and photocopying of the children's stories, both those scribed by practitioners, theatre arts trainers and those that the children themselves wrote, as well as those that children scribed for other children. Both teachers and researchers documented the involvement of three case study children in each classroom. Two researchers visited each setting three times: one made detailed field notes on both observations and informal conversations with adults or children, whilst the other researcher video-recorded the storytelling and story-acting activities initiated by adults or children. The nature of this set of data collection methods enabled the research team to document the children's close attentive engagement in their teachers' scribing and their own self-initiated writing practices, although data collection was constrained to 'Helicopter' days.

The data set outlined was collated: audio-recorded interviews were transcribed, detailed logs were made of video recordings and the analytical software Atlas.ti was used. In line with the qualitative approach, the data set was subject to scrutiny, and open and later axial codes were identified. A sub-set of the data were checked to ensure consistency in coding both across the data and between the five coders. The axial themes identified included: children's agency; confidence; sense of belonging and identity; communication, language and literacy; and creativity in children's stories and performance. The data presented in this chapter connect to the axial themes of agency, and language and literacy. In relation to print awareness the data are drawn from all six settings, in relation to children scribing their own and others' stories, the data are drawn from two of the six settings. These were a Reception class in a school referred to as St Aidan's Primary School, with a class from one of its feeder preschools referred to as Eager Beavers. As children scribing their own and others' stories became a distinct and well-developed feature in these classrooms, and as they were located in the same catchment area (a semi-rural suburban area in the south of England), they were purposively selected for re-examination.

St Aidan's was a small primary school with less than 150 children on roll at the time of the study. The head teacher and staff had been stable for several years. The school catchment was diverse, with children coming from local farms, nearby villages and the local low-cost housing estate: 'It looks middle class when you drive through it, but I'd say it's mixed' (Reception teacher, 19 April 2012). In its last two Ofsted[1] reports, provision for children in Reception was seen as 'good', in particular the care provided and progress made. Good links with preschool provision were noted. The Reception class comprised twenty children aged four to five years old.

Eager Beavers was a preschool setting which provided full day and sessional care for children between one and four years old, with 82 children on roll at the time of the study. In its most recent Ofsted report the overall quality of the provision was judged as 'outstanding'. The environment was described as relaxed and nurturing; tailored to meet children's individual needs. The key strengths of the setting were reported as the drive for continual improvement, the organisation of transitions and the influence that children's interests and ideas had on planning. The preschool morning class that participated in the 'Helicopter Stories' programme included nineteen three- to four-year-olds. None of the children in the two participating classes at St Aidan's or Eager Beavers were identified as having special educational needs and none spoke English as an additional language. The study, which followed the BERA (2011) ethical guidelines, offered information to practitioners and parents, made clear that withdrawal was possible at any stage, and ensured principles of confidentiality, including the use of pseudonyms, were applied. Data were secured in password-protected files with restricted access.

In what follows, initially the practice of adults' scribing the children's stories and its inherent learning potential in relation to print awareness is considered. The teachers' observations included here are drawn from across the six settings to demonstrate the recognition and value afforded by all teachers of the approach's contribution to apprenticing storywriters. Then examples of children exercising their agency as authors and scribing their own and each other's stories are presented, first from the focus class in St Aidan's and then from Eager Beavers. The children who were observed undertaking these spontaneous writing practices were not those who were the focus of the project's case studies. Since the practice of self-authoring and scribing was child-initiated, data were collected opportunistically in the three extended visits to each of these two classrooms. The time spent in each classroom varied in response to the practitioners' own time frames; it was never less than an hour and a half and was frequently between two and three hours.

In the Reception class the teacher, in response to the children's observed practice of writing and scribing their own and others' stories, provided them with two 'non-school' 'Story Books' (lined and blank exercise books which had colourful covers) for this purpose. These were in addition to the conventional exercise book (with a plain cover) in which adults scribed children's tales. The Reception children frequently made use of their 'own' class Story Books; they drew and wrote their own tales in them and recorded stories dictated by their peers, both on 'Helicopter days' and in free-play sessions on other days. Two entries from the Reception books are examined: one drawn, one written. Such books were not offered in the preschool, but the practitioners noticed that one girl, three-year-old Fiona, began to scribe stories for her peers on 'Helicopter days'. In the example examined, Fiona took up the mantle of the scribe for her friend Will.

Enhancing children's awareness of written language

The observational data from all six settings evidenced the children's intense engagement in the adult scribing of their narratives (see Chapter 7). The adults in both St Aidan's and the Eager Beavers classes positioned themselves carefully to ensure that the young tellers who sat alongside them were able to see the lined page of the Helicopter story book. Tellers and scribes either sat together at tables or on the floor, sometimes leaning against a wall. Four salient print-related conventions appertained to story-scribing practice. The first was that the adult began by writing the child's name at the top of the page, often, though not always, speaking their name aloud as they did so. The second was voiced by the adult at the outset, this was so that the child's story could be as short or as long as they wanted, but could not extend beyond the page. In response to this, children sometimes pointed to where they wanted their story to end and if it looked as if a story might run over, the Reception teacher suggested the child's narrative might become a chapter in a longer story, to be continued another day. The third print-related convention, which was arguably for the adult's benefit, was the adult underlining nouns in the child's text in order to support the adult reader when allocating roles during the story's enactment. As the story was read aloud in story acting, the adult invited children, individually or in groups, to become the 'castle', the 'dragon' or the 'bin' for example; the underlining served to prepare the ground for the later telling. The final print-related convention at the close of the tale involved the adult asking the storyteller who they wanted to be in the story acting. This object or character was then encircled. Again, this drew children's attention to the teacher's writing; specifically to the selected word which the storyteller would later embody and enact.

During the process of scribing and without exception, as the children in the two classes became familiar with the storytelling process, they (like their counterparts in the other settings) paused as they told their story to allow the adult sufficient time to transcribe the words they had voiced. Most, if not all, watched very carefully as their words became pencil marks on a page, arranged on the lines from top left to bottom right. Joint attention between adults and children on the story text, both as the adult transcribed and later as the adult read the story back to the child, was a common characteristic of the practice observed. Sometimes children were seen to lean over the page as the adult scribed, looking intently at the marks being made as if they were studying them, and sometimes they pointed to particular words (not necessarily the right ones), if they thought the adult might have misheard what they had said, or if they wanted to act out a specific role.

Practitioners from all the settings and the researchers noted that the children were highly attentive as adults scribed. They also noticed that the gaze of other children present often focused on the text as it was being transcribed; they too were potentially developing print awareness through observation and attention. One practitioner commented that a story listener in the Reception class 'definitely wanted to know what happened in the end, and wanted a longer ending you know, pointing out where you could fit in more words'. Additionally, children sometimes commented upon their adult-scribed stories, for instance a practitioner from the preschool observed 'often at the end she'll look at it [the scribed story] and point to long words and ask what they say – she never asks about short ones!' Another practitioner noted that one boy 'was saying that "I filled a whole page" and looking at the words and he was so proud'. Some practitioners also referred to the significance of this for individual learners. One noted for instance about a boy that 'he wouldn't be a child who would sit and look at the book with you, and doesn't really show much interest in the written word at all'. In this context however, as their stories were committed to paper, such interest on the part of the young children was demonstrated frequently.

The children's stories were meant to be transcribed verbatim by the adult, including any use of non-standard grammar which might be expected as this age, since children aged between two and four years often engage in spontaneous language-creating attempts (Whitehead, 2003). Whilst the transcription of non-standard grammar was accepted by the preschool practitioner, the Reception teacher expressed a degree of uncertainty about this practice. She perceived tension between the power of Helicopter Stories to support children's self-expression and her assumed professional responsibility to improve the accuracy of children's language. She felt strongly that the 'teacher should model the correct language ... should model always if possible how to do things properly', and occasionally repeated children's words using standard grammar. As a consequence she re-voiced and wrote down the 'corrected' version of the child's text. The extent to which this influenced the children's understanding in this context is not known.

At the end of the scribing, the adults read the whole tale back expressively to each child; this arguably endowed increased significance to their story and demonstrated that their words were available for re-reading. It can be argued therefore that the process of telling stories to adults who scribed these before the children's eyes, offered the young writers multiple different opportunities to become acquainted with the relationship between the spoken and the written word, the sequential nature of writing, the direction that writing unfolds in English, and the notion that stories have endings which must be planned for in terms of overall story length. In addition, and significantly, the fact that this writing was used later the same day as the 'script' for whole-class enactment of their tale, not only served to affirm that their written words had permanence, but gave real purpose to telling and scribing.

Self-initiated authoring in Reception

This sense of purpose is likely to have motivated children in the Reception class at St Aidan's who began to spend their free-play time writing and drawing their own stories and scribing peers' tales. This child-initiated practice comprised a naturally occurring individual and often collaborative, shared activity. Their stories were committed to paper in various ways: in the class's two Story Books dedicated to this purpose, in 'instant books' (made from folded A4 paper) at the writing table, and on paper in the 'office' role-play area. The Reception teacher was enthusiastic about the children's self-directed engagement with writing. She commented that 'writing each other's stories and making books to write stories' became 'one of the main activities of the classroom'. As she noted:

> One of the things that has really fascinated me is the way the children have extended it, and put themselves into the roles of story taker and storyteller, and have actually wanted to be Caroline [trainer] or myself and do what we do, and they've done that both at the sessions and independently outside the sessions as well.

The motivational power of the approach was also commented upon by the teaching assistant who perceived it encouraged the boys to write:

> The thing that has had the real impact is the fact they want to write their own, so do what we've been doing themselves ... It's been getting the boys more into mark making. It almost seems to give them permission to do it, because the mark making table can be quite a girl-heavy area ... this seems to have given them [the boys] a purpose to put to their mark making and to have something to link it to.

The researchers observed some of this child-initiated story writing, and opportunistically filmed children scribing each other's stories and writing and drawing their own. The class's Story Books were packed with entries which were potentially ripe for analysis. However, the books were also used on 'non-Helicopter days' (when researchers were not present), entries were mostly undated and unnamed, and it was difficult to ascertain whether an entry had been authored, co-authored or dictated. This inevitably hampered the systematic data collection of this spontaneously occurring writing practice. Nonetheless, an examination of the Story Books revealed considerable diversity. All entries, which were made in felt tips, pencil and pens, were no longer than a page, and variously included: drawings, with and without accompanying writing (by an adult or a child); long strings of letters spread across the page; mixtures of letters, lines and dots, with and without drawings; and some short written tales. It was apparent that the books afforded space for child-directed authorial experimentation and exploration, and that in committing to paper in this context the young authors were not only ascribing meaning to their mark making, they were drawing upon the cultural practices inherent within the storytelling and story-acting approach that their teacher had adopted.

For example, observational field notes of one afternoon's Helicopter session during the middle of the eight-week programme, show that in 40 minutes of 'free-choice' time, six children (who had volunteered previously) told their stories to adult scribes, whilst at least five others were involved in writing and drawing their own and each other's stories. As soon as the teacher announced free-choice time, children quickly gathered around the two class Story Books, and five-year-old Joy, perhaps conscious it would not be easy to share, offered to 'take story'. Holding one Story Book like a prized possession, she was eagerly followed by two children, one of whom immediately asked Joy, 'Are we going to act them?' The remaining book was seized by Ellie. The last child, looking disappointed, initially went to the outdoor area and then to the office where he wrote a story on a piece of paper. Standing at a table, Ellie (also aged five) chose to write her name at the top of the page and then wrote a tale using visuals to represent parts of the narrative. She depicted these on a single page, starting at the top and working from left to right across the page and down (see Figure 4.1). As she did so she muttered subvocally, gesturing back to her first drawings (a godmother, princess and rain) almost every time she came to draw another element, as if she were re-reading at the point of composition. When the page was nearly full, she sought an adult and retold her tale thus far, pointing to her drawings as she did so. 'Once upon a time there was a fairy godmother, then the bad fairy/bad princess came along and then it started raining and the fairy godmother went to her house, but the bad fairy broke the house down.' The characters and the rain and the house can be seen in Figure 4.1, alongside other visuals, which remained key elements of the narrative when Ellie read it for the class to enact later that morning.

FIGURE 4.1 Ellie writing her story

Another example, which was not observed during the composition, but was found in a Story Book and connected to its author, is Isabelle's tale of the little bird (see Figure 4.2). Here she uses writing for an expressive and perhaps metaphorical purpose; the practitioner commented that this five-year-old was moving house and perceived her tale may have been alluding to this. Isabelle employed two

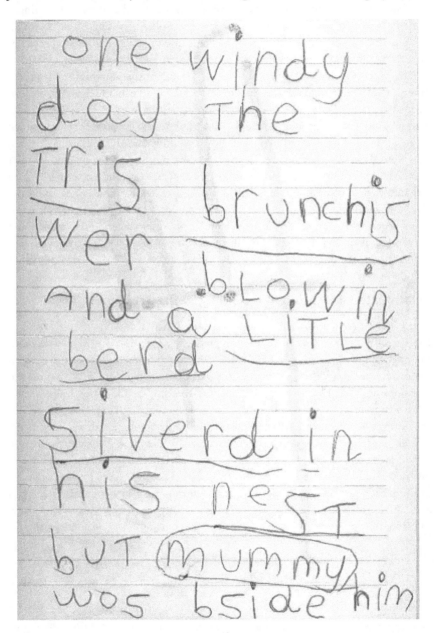

FIGURE 4.2 Isabelle's tale

conventions used by the adult scribes. She underlined a number of words, mirroring the convention to highlight roles for later enactment; these were mainly, although not exclusively, nouns: 'tree branches', 'little bird', 'nest' and 'shivering'. In addition, Isabelle encircled the word 'mummy', making use of the convention to encircle the character the author would 'like to be' in the dramatisation. In these ways she mirrored the adult scribes' written practices and engaged in writing a story – a kind of playscript – in the manner she had observed. The extent to which Isabelle's use of underlining and encircling was intentional in that she expected or hoped her tale would later be enacted is not known, but it seems likely.

The video footage and observational notes indicate that children who scribed others' stories or created their own tales during the designated Helicopter sessions frequently sought to 'read' these for peer dramatisation during story-acting time. The Reception teacher only assigned acting time on Helicopter days and tended to prioritise the tales scribed by adults, but sometimes the children's self-initiated tales were also enacted, giving real purpose to their writing and making public their narratives. Furthermore, on two occasions, small groups of children were observed enacting their written or scribed stories during free-choice time, once using the class's 'stage' denoted by white tape for this purpose, and once placing chairs to denote their own 'stage'. This further demonstrates their agentic participation and appropriation of resources enabling them to follow through from authoring and scribing to enactment.

Self-initiated authoring and scribing in the preschool

The Eager Beavers preschool practitioners noted that two children committed to paper for the first time when 'writing' their own stories, also that four weeks into the programme, three-year-old Fiona took this a step further and began to take up the mantle of the scribe for her peers on 'Helicopter days'. She did so on several occasions and was observed and filmed one morning as she scribed Will's tale. With a large sheet of paper in front of her, Fiona, leaning on her elbow, looked up at Will expectantly, crayon in hand. Due to the classroom noise only some elements of their interchange were captured; it was clear however, that she was adopting the role of scribe and seeking faithfully to commit Will's tale to paper. She had written his name in the top left corner and had half encircled/underlined this, reminiscent of the adult's recording of children's names in the class's Helicopter book. Fiona and Will both took the telling and scribing seriously. Initially he was unsure how to begin, but supported by Fiona in 'teacher role', he found his way forward.[2]

> Fiona: What does your story start with?
> Will: Don't know (pause) Once upon a time (pause) there ...?
> Fiona: Do you want to say 'Once upon a time there lived?'

Will appeared to agree with Fiona's suggestion and she committed this opening to paper, making a series of capitals Fs on the page, one for each word. She voiced each word aloud as she wrote it, in a similar manner to an adult taking down a story, although Fiona scribed each 'word' more slowly with considerable focused intent. Will waited until this was written before he continued his tale:

> Will: (indistinct utterance) …
> Fiona: (writing) There- lived- a li-ttle- doggy- that?[3]
> Will: Had a wolf in his belly
> Fiona: A wolf in his belly?
> Will: Yes
> Fiona: (writing) That- had- a- wolf- in- his- bell- y-
> Fiona: What happened next?
> Will: (indistinct utterance) … the wolf came out and he smashed the wolf in his window
> Fiona: (writing) The- wolf- came- (looks up at Will to check and mouths 'out')
> Will: Out
> Fiona: (writing) out-
> Will: And the wolf
> Fiona: (writing) And- he-
> Will: Smashed it out … (indistinct)
> Fiona: (writing) He smashed a
> Will: (indistinct utterance) … wolf
> Fiona: (writing) The- wolf- out- his- win- dow- (looks up at Will)
> Will: (indistinct utterance) …
> Fiona: (writing) And- the wolf- was- born-
> Will: (indistinct utterance) …
> Fiona: (writing) He- then- he- smashed- a- eye- ball- from- the- wolf-
> Will: (indistinct utterance)… belly
> Fiona: (writing) He-smashed- in- his- bell- ly-

Fiona continued to scribe Will's tale, which also involved a knife, the wolf dying and being born in a tree; the order and nature of events are hard to ascertain with any certainty. What is clearly audible is that after 4 minutes and 28 seconds of assiduously committing his tale to paper, Fiona advised Will, 'I think it should be the end now', whilst offering him the smallest smile. Will consented with a nod of his head and Fiona voiced 'the end' as she wrote two Fs at the bottom of the page with strong strokes. The pair then got up and set off together across the classroom. A practitioner commented as they passed, 'Have you written a story together? How exciting!' Fiona showed her the story (see Figure 4.3) observing 'It's very long!' Another practitioner, who had been scribing children's stories, asked Will if he wanted to tell her a story (that morning he had asked to be placed on the day's list), but he shook his head, informing her he had already told his tale to Fiona; he recognised her as a story scribe. Initially Fiona went to Will's tray to place the story there, but then held onto the story until the story acting began five minutes later.

FIGURE 4.3   Fiona scribing Will's story

In this extract Fiona can be seen to bodily engage in the beginnings of alphabetic writing as she represents sounds in abstracted symbols, in this case mostly using the single demarcated upper-case letter 'F' (she used a lower-case 'b' for ball and some Ps are evident although they may be indistinct Fs). As Kress observes, in such early writing the body is 'orientated towards regular repetition of similar simple units' (1997: 84). Each letter F represents a single word which Fiona repeats aloud following Will carefully as she records them, separating each letter from the others. Initially she commits these to paper in two rows from left to right, then returns to the top of the page and places the next Fs in an available space there, again working within the cultural convention of directionality from left to right. When this space is full she works from right to left back across the page, adding further Fs for each word she voices. Interestingly, she records two slightly shorter Fs to represent three multisyllabic words: 'li-ttle' 'bell-y', and 'win-dow', demonstrating an implicit awareness both of the complexity of written language and of syllabic beat. Her use of the upper-case 'F' is likely to be connected to her name; research indicates that children move more quickly towards conventional use of the letter forms in their own names than in other words (e.g. Levin et al., 2005).

Later, when Fiona was invited to read the tale for dramatisation, the practitioner offered to help, but Fiona, seeking to retain ownership of the telling space, replied firmly, 'I know how it goes'. She voiced various elements of Will's tale and later accepted the practitioner's support as Will and the class enacted it. The processes of telling, scribing and story acting appeared to serve social–relational purposes for Fiona and Will, who were friends outside school. As they returned to the class circle after the acting they were smiling broadly.

Discussion

The storytelling and story-acting approach adopted in the Reception and preschool classes at St Aidan's and Eager Beavers prompted the children to engage enthusiastically in these complementary classroom-based social practices. Their oral stories were respected, scribed by interested adults and later enacted by their peers. This not only supported their literate participation, but also afforded opportunities for these young apprentice writers to engage purposefully in writing. The children's commitment and interest in their own and each other's stories encouraged considerable self-directed learning and engagement with writing. It can be argued therefore that the approach has the potential to increase children's awareness of written language and the cultural practices associated with writing. It indicates the transformation of spoken to written representation, demonstrates that mark making can and should be read as linguistic messages and that the written word can be used for collaborative enactment. Nicolopoulou et al. (2015) suggest that Paley's approach opens up an opportunity space that supports children's learning and narrative development. This chapter, in examining the opportunities that some children seized to engage authentically and agentically as authors and scribes, significantly extends this to argue that the approach also affords a possibility space for learning about writing *and* becoming a writer. It reveals that the process of storytelling and its attendant scribing and later story acting represent not only rich and specific local enactments of learning-to-write practices, but also that the process can enable children to adopt the position of being-a-writer, a young, apprentice writer.

Some children imagined and identified themselves as authors or scribes in this possibility space for writing and became involved with other children in the production of meaningful narratives. They not only creatively and intentionally positioned themselves as writers; they were recognised as such by the practitioners who from the outset positioned all children as authors with oral stories to tell. The young people's adoption of the roles of tellers, writers, scribes and readers was accepted and valued in both classes and the resultant child-initiated writing was often shared through enactment. In this way Ellie, Isabelle, Fiona and Will experienced writing as a social and relational process, not only in the construction of the texts, but in their later enactment. Their texts were shaped by the cultural practices inherent within the approach (the print-related conventions for example and the later enactment) and these practices shaped what being an author comprised in these classrooms, at least during free-choice time.

The children's self-initiated practice of scribing and writing their own and others' stories was observed both on 'Helicopter days' and on other days during free-choice time. In the two classrooms this time involved open access to multiple areas (e.g. the role-play area, the outdoor area) and to resources (e.g. the construction equipment, dressing-up clothes); during these unstructured periods children made their own decisions and chose activities in which to engage. The non-regulatory nature of this time and space appeared to act as a potential 'textual playground' (Dyson and Dewayani, 2013: 258) for the young writers. Motivated by the newly introduced practice of storytelling and story acting, the playground afforded new possibilities for exercising their freedom. Indeed as Dyson (1997: 166) argues:

> For children, as for adults, freedom is a verb, a becoming; it is experienced as an expanded sense of agency, of possibility for choice and action.

Significantly, there was evidence of a desire and determination on the part of the young writers to follow through their texts (or those they scribed) to story acting, whether on the communal class stage or on a smaller group-created one, as seen in the Reception class. In the preschool it is likely that Fiona expected or hoped that her scribing of Will's tale would be used for later dramatisation; she chose to keep it with her until the acting time commenced. Her written text, which functioned as a vehicle for communication, and the sharing of Will's narrative, highlights the critical interdependence of the two strands of the approach in relation to apprenticing young writers. The telling establishes that each child has a story to tell, which by being committed to paper is ascribed value, and the enactment affords an opportunity to demonstrate the purposeful and social use of children's written stories. Thus the enactment, a communal social activity which involved the whole class, may represent the driver of the self-initiated practice of children authoring their own or scribing others' stories. Indeed, it is possible that the eventual peer-oriented enactment arouses an 'intrinsic need' (Vygotsky, 1978: 118) in children and that this prompts them to compose and share their stories, fostering their volitional involvement as young apprentice writers.

With the downward pressure of performative cultures, the focused early learning of letters, sounds and spelling and the evidence that many practitioners make use of copying (Dyson, 2010) in order to ensure that young writers learn 'the basics', Paley's (1990) story-based approach offers a richly conceived and complementary way forward. Few communal practices in the early years classroom offer as much scope and potential for young children to learn about writing *and* to position themselves as writers, apprenticed to the craft.

Notes

1   The inspection of publicly funded schools in England is carried out by the Office for Standards in Education, Children's Services and Skills (Ofsted), a non-ministerial department of the government.
2   The opening three lines of this conversation come from field notes; the remainder from the transcribed video.
3   Each mark made by Fiona, where visible in the footage, is demarcated by a line, e.g. The- wolf- .

References

Barton, D., Hamilton, M. and Ivanič, R. (eds) (2000) *Situated Literacies: Reading and writing in context*. London: Routledge.

BERA (2011) *Revised Ethical Guidelines for Educational Research (2011)*. British Educational Research Association; www.bera.ac.uk

Bloome, D., Carter, S. R., Christian, B. M., Otto, S. and Shuart-Faris, N. (2005) *Discourse Analysis and the Study of Classroom Language and Literacy Events: A microethnographic perspective*. Mahwah, NJ: Erlbaum.

Bourne, J. (2002) 'Oh, what will miss say!': Constructing texts and identities in the discursive processes of classroom writing. *Language and Education*, 16(4): 241–259.

Clay, M. (1975) *What did I Write?* Auckland, New Zealand: Heinemann.

Cooper, P. M. (2009) *The Classrooms All Young Children Need: Lessons in teaching from Vivian Paley*. Chicago, IL: University of Chicago Press.

Cremin, T., Swann, J., Flewitt, R. S., Faulkner, D. and Kucirkova, N. (2013) *Evaluation Report of MakeBelieve Arts Helicopter Technique of Storytelling and Story Acting*. The Open University. Available at: http://www.makebelievearts.co.uk/docs/Helicopter-Technique-Evaluation.pdf

Dyson, A. H. (1997) *Writing Superheroes: Contemporary childhood, popular culture and classroom literacy*. Columbia, SC: Teachers College Press.

Dyson, A. H. (2001) Where are the childhoods in childhood literacy? An exploration in outer (school) space. *Journal of Early Childhood Literacy*, 1(1): 9–38.

Dyson, A. H. (2009) Writing in childhood worlds. In R. Beard, D. Myhill, M. Nystrand and J. Riley (eds), *Handbook of Writing Development* (pp. 232–245). London: Sage.

Dyson, A. H. (2010) Writing childhoods under construction: Re-visioning 'copying' in early childhood. *Journal of Early Childhood Literacy*, 10(1): 7–31.

Dyson, A. H. and Dewayni, S. (2013) Writing in childhood cultures. In K. Hall, T. Cremin, B. Comber and L. Moll, *International Handbook of Research on Children's Literacy, Learning, and Culture* (pp. 258–274). Oxford: Wiley Blackwell.

Ferreiro, E. and Teberosky, A. (1982) *Literacy before Schooling*. Oxford: Heinemann.

Fisher, R. (2010) Young writers' construction of agency. *Journal of Early Childhood Literacy*, 10(4): 410–429.

Flewitt, R. S. (2012) Multimodal perspectives on early childhood literacies. In J. Larson and J. Marsh (eds), *The Sage Handbook of Early Childhood Literacy* (2nd edn) (pp. 295–309). London: Sage.

Gee, I. P. (2001) Foreword. In C. Lewis (ed.), *Literacy Practices as Social Acts: Power, status, and cultural norms in the classroom* (pp. xixiv). Mahwah, NJ: Erlbaum.

Green, J. and Bloome, D. (1997) Ethnography and ethnographers of and in education: A situated perspective. In J. Flood, S. B. Heath and D. Lapp (eds), *A Handbook for Literacy Educators: Research on teaching the communicative and visual arts* (pp.1–12). New York, NY: Macmillan.

Invernizzi, M., Sullivan, A., Meier, J. and Swank, L. (2004) *Phonological Awareness Literacy Screening: PreK teacher's manual*. Richmond, VA: University of Virginia Press.

Kress, G. (1997) *Before Writing – Rethinking the Paths to Literacy*. London: Routledge.

Lancaster, L. (2013) The emergence of symbolic principles: The distribution of mind in early sign making. *Biosemiotics*. DOI: 10.1007/s12304-013-9195-3

Lave, J. and Wenger, E. (1990) *Situated Learning: Legitimate peripheral participation*. Cambridge, UK: Cambridge University Press.

Levin, I., Both-De-Vries, A., Aram, D. and Bus, A. G. (2005) Writing starts with own name writing. *Applied Psycholinguistics*, 26: 463–477.

Nicolopoulou, A., McDowell, J. and Brockmeyer, C. (2006) Narrative play and emergent literacy: Storytelling and story acting meet journal writing. In D. Singer, R. Golinkoff and K. Hirsh-Pasek (eds), *Play=Learning* (pp. 124–144). New York, NY: Oxford University Press.

Nicolopoulou, A., Brockmeyer Cates, C., de Sá, A. and llgaz, H. (2014) Narrative performance, peer group culture, and narrative development in a preschool classroom. In A. Cekaite, S. Blum-Kulka, V. Grover and E. Teubal (eds), *Children's Peer Talk: Learning from each other* (pp. 42–62). New York, NY: Cambridge University Press.

Nicolopoulou, A., Cortina, K. S., Ilgaz, H., Cates, C. B. and de Sá, A. (2015) Using a narrative- and play-based activity to promote low-income preschoolers' oral language, emergent literacy, and social competence. *Early Research Childhood Quarterly, 31*: 147–162.

Pahl, K. (2007) Creativity in events and practices: A lens for understanding children's multimodal texts. *Literacy, 41*(2): 81–87.

Paley, V. G. (1990) *The Boy Who Would Be a Helicopter: The uses of storytelling in the classroom.* Cambridge, MA: Harvard University Press.

Paley, V. G. (1992) *You Can't Say You Can't Play.* Cambridge, MA: Harvard University Press.

Rowe, D. W. (2003) The nature of young children's authoring. In N. Hall, J. Larson and J. Marsh (eds), *Handbook of Early Childhood Literacy* (pp. 258–270). London: Sage.

Rowe, D. W. (2008) The social construction of intentionality: Two-year-olds' and adults' participation at a preschool writing center. *Research in the Teaching of English, 42*(4): 387–434.

Rowe, D. W. and Neitzel, C. (2010) Interest and agency in 2- and 3- year olds' participation in emergent writing. *Reading Research Quarterly, 45*(2): 169–195.

Vygotsky, L. S. (1978) *Mind and Society: The development of higher mental processes.* Cambridge, MA: Harvard University Press.

Whitebread, D. and Bingham, S. (2012) *TACTYC Occasional Paper No. 2, School Readiness: A critical review of perspectives and evidence.* TACTYC. http://tactyc.org.uk/occasional-paper/occasional-paper2.pdf

Whitehead, M. (2003) *Developing Language and Literacy with Young Children.* London: Sage.

5

YOUNG CHILDREN AS STORYTELLERS

Collective meaning making and sociocultural transmission

Dorothy Faulkner

Introduction

This chapter draws on sociocultural theories to explore young children's collective meaning making when they tell, listen to and act out each other's stories. The data for this study were collected from six research sites taking part in a London-based evaluation of Helicopter Stories, an eight-week in-service training programme for early years practitioners (Cremin et al., 2013). As described in Chapter 2, this programme was based on Vivian Gussin Paley's account of her storytelling/story-acting pedagogy in her book, *The Boy Who Would Be a Helicopter* (Paley, 1990). As I have a keen interest in young children's collective meaning making and the narratives they develop during play, it seemed to me that Helicopter Stories might provide an equally rich context for children's narrative co-creation. The copies of the storybooks, containing all the stories told during Helicopter Stories sessions, were available for analysis, as were videos of individual children telling their stories in each of the research sites. Over the eight-week period, multiple storytelling sessions were captured on video (comprising 17 hours of recording), and over 350 stories from 147 children were collected. These provided a rich source of data that could be used to test this prediction.

As the story-acting sessions were clearly designed to foster collective meaning making through drama and pretence, I decided to focus on the individual narratives children generated during the storytelling sessions. This was because, although these sessions ostensibly involved a single adult/child duo, the videos revealed that there was usually at least one other child watching and listening as the story unfolded, and often there were as many as five to six children present. This extract from my observational notes of one nursery classroom is typical:

Arthur is telling his story to Mandy (one of the MakeBelieve trainers). They are sitting on the floor in the main classroom. There are no other children to start with; then Lucy appears and sits next to Arthur. Both Arthur and Lucy watch Mandy as she writes. Lucy moves to sit directly in front of Mandy. Jake approaches, followed by Tina, as Mandy starts to read through Arthur's story. Mark and the teacher join the group. It is Mark's turn to tell a story to the teacher. Jake sits in front of the teacher, and Lucy sits right next to her. Mark sits on her other side opposite Jake and starts to tell his story. Jake moves off. A boy playing with blocks nearby turns round from time to time and appears to be listening to Mark's story.

Over all of the storytelling sessions captured on video, other children were present on 87 per cent of occasions.[1] While these children did not appear to be passive listeners (indeed in many cases they were monitoring the session closely), they did not overtly intervene in the session or contribute their own ideas to the storyteller's narrative. On the face of it, therefore, there was scant evidence of the peer collaboration observed in my previous studies of children's storytelling (e.g. Faulkner and Miell, 2005; Faulkner, 2011). This presented something of a theoretical challenge: if these children were not actively contributing to the story, apart from its simple entertainment value, what was the nature and purpose of their obvious interest in this activity? The written versions of the stories (recorded sequentially each day in class storybooks) suggested a partial explanation. There appeared to be evidence of sociocultural transmission, that is, evidence of children establishing and transmitting a shared understanding of story content and structure, where the same characters, actions, dramatic events (and in some cases verbatim excerpts of direct speech), appeared in the stories told by different individuals both within and between sessions. This is very much in accord with Paley's (1990: 21) observation that:

> Our kind of storytelling is a social phenomenon, intended to flow through all other activities and provide the widest opportunity for a communal response. Stories are not private affairs; the individual imagination plays host to all the stimulation in the environment and causes ripples of ideas to encircle the listeners.

Although Paley's observation can account for some aspects of sociocultural transmission, it does not explain other aspects of children's involvement in Helicopter sessions. As the video evidence shows, some children (like Lucy in the notes above), were clearly fascinated by the writing process, others like Jake and Tina were interested in hearing the final story, whilst some, although physically present and listening intermittently, were simultaneously engaged in another activity. I wished to establish, therefore, if there was a relationship between the nature and quality of children's involvement in these sessions and cultural transmission. As storytelling in this context appears to be social and communal rather than private and individual, it seemed appropriate to take a sociocultural approach to the analysis and interpretation of the available evidence.

In this chapter, therefore, I present an analysis of the video and story data to argue that the nature of children's involvement in Helicopter Stories fits Rogoff's construct of 'learning through keen observation and listening, in anticipation of participation' (Rogoff et al., 2003: 176). I also argue that it is possible to identify what children are learning from each other through a content analysis of the stories they produce. There is now considerable evidence that the practice of storytelling/ story acting promotes the development of oral narrative skills and enables preschool children individually and collectively to begin to master basic narrative structure and literary conventions (see Nicolopoulou et al. 2014, and Chapter 3 in this volume). As well as aiding narrative development, however, it is clear that storytelling/story acting has an important social function: it engenders the development of symbolic 'communities of minds' (Nelson, 2007, 2010). The evidence presented here suggests that learning through keen observation and listening facilitates this process by providing easy access to the local cultural knowledge and narrative conventions of the peer group. Thus particular popular themes and distinctive, local storytelling traditions can be seen to emerge in each classroom community. I propose, therefore, that what children appear to be learning is how to construct narratives that will prove popular with their immediate peer group. In the next section I outline the analytic strategy used to establish whether the video and story data supported this interpretation.

Analytic strategy

Robbins' (2007) multi-layered analytic framework informed my analysis of the video data and transcripts of children's stories in the class storybooks. Unlike developmental theories which adopt a deficit model and describe young children's thinking as immature, erroneous or untutored, Robbins has shown in a study of three- to eight-year-old children how a sociocultural analysis can offer a more sophisticated understanding of the complex, dynamic, collaborative and contextualised nature evident in their thinking. This framework employs Vygotskyan theory and Rogoff's three analytic foci (or lenses) to understand children's thinking as mediated through speech, gaze, gesture and other modes of communication such as the deliberate creation of physical proximity or distance between the speaker and his/her social partners. The three analytic foci as applied to the current study are as follows:

• **The personal**
   This refers to the participation of the child within an activity (the storytelling session), and how this changes during the course of the activity, in this case both within and between successive storytelling and acting sessions.

- **The interpersonal**

  Typically, this level of analysis examines how the presence of proximal others (the adults and peers also present in the activity) and their relationship with the child influences her/his participation in the activity. It also traces the influence of the beliefs she or he shares with distal others (e.g. parents, siblings and other relatives and friends in the home environment). Here, however, I was mainly interested in tracing whether the storyteller influenced the stories subsequently narrated by the children present as proximal others.

- **The cultural**

  This identifies the influence of cultural, institutional or community resources that the child and proximal others draw on during the activity (e.g. popular cultural and media texts; class texts and cultural artefacts and tools, institutional factors such as the 'rules' associated with Helicopter Stories and home and community resources). The analysis of story content was the main focus here.

In practice, as Robbins (2007) and Nicolopoulou (2002, Nicolopoulou et al., 2014) point out, analyses that concentrate on a single focus at the expense of the other two foci, risk losing sight of the multiple factors and influences that are constituted within the child's thinking. In order to examine the involvement of other children in the activity, therefore, the analysis here focused on the interpersonal and cultural, although this inevitably involved aspects of the personal as well, as children could be either storyteller, or proximal other. Detailed observational notes of the storytelling videos recorded the number of children present in addition to the storyteller, and the nature of their involvement. These notes also documented overt verbal and non-verbal interactions between the storyteller, the adult scribing the story and other children in the immediate vicinity as well as the apparent locus of children's attention and any other activities they were engaged in. The findings from this analysis are discussed in the section 'Learning through guided and intent participation'.

From their analysis of the stories told by children in Pennsylvanian preschool classrooms over the course of a year, Nicolopoulou and colleagues demonstrated that narrative cross-fertilisation is relatively common and that the stories children tell reflect the cultural, institutional and community resources they have in common. Their research also indicates that the practice of storytelling/story acting mediates the emergence of distinctive, gender-related narrative styles associated with peer-group subcultures (Nicolopoulou et al., 2014). To explore whether similar subcultures were evident in our study, I undertook a detailed thematic analysis (Braun and Clarke, 2006) of the 350 stories from the class storybooks, to identify common thematic categories appearing in children's narratives (e.g. fantasy, superhero, sociodramatic or domestic, novel and original). I recorded use of conventional narrative structures, and other structural features commonly found in young children's stories (e.g. Nicolopoulou et al., 2014; Stein, 1988). Next, I attempted to trace interrelationships between particular story themes and identifiable groups of children. Where it was possible to identify apparent clusters of stories with the same theme within a session, and where that session had also been video-recorded, it was possible to cross-reference the video recordings with the classroom storybooks to ascertain, as far as possible, whether the children appearing in the videos were also those who had generated the stories subsequently recorded in the storybook for that session. Finally, I attempted to identify local, cultural differences in children's narrative thinking across the six settings. The outcome of this analysis is discussed in the section 'Entering a community of minds'.

Learning through guided and intent participation

In her extensive review of the diverse ways different societies organise the socialisation, language learning and education of babies and children, Rogoff (2003) highlights major differences between communities that organise children's learning through age segregation and formal instruction in highly structured child-focused settings (common to the middle-class European-American families she studied), and those where, from an early age, children are expected to participate in community activities alongside adults (as in the Mayan communities of Guatemala she also studied). In both types of community, however, families support children's learning, understanding and mastery of key skills through 'guided participation'; a particular form of dyadic interaction that takes place usually between a child and his/her primary caregiver or an older sibling. During these interactions, communication between the partners is largely non-verbal and is aided by considerable social referencing (e.g. monitoring each other's expressions and gaze, timing and pauses, and the use of pointing and other gestures). This creates the conditions for the 'mutual bridging of meaning' and 'mutual structuring of participation' that enable young children to contribute to, and begin to master elements of the ongoing activity of interest (Rogoff, 2003: 285–286).

While guided participation is common to both European-American and indigenous-heritage Central American communities, in the latter children also learn through third-party attention to and close observation of the activities of adults (Rogoff, 2003). A significant body of ethnographic research has established that in these indigenous communities, adults expect children to learn by watching, and listening-in to adults' activities and conversations rather than by direct instruction, questioning or discussion (see de Haan, 1999 for a review). Furthermore, even when ostensibly engaged in play and activities of their own, children continuously monitor the activities of adjacent adults and remain alert to potentially important conversations and information. Rogoff et al. (2003: 176) describe this kind of learning as 'intent participation' and argue that:

> Children everywhere learn by observing and listening in on activities of
> adults and other children. Learning through keen observation and listening
> in anticipation of participation seems to be especially valued and emphasised
> in communities where children have access to learning from informal
> community involvement. They observe and listen with intent concentration

and initiative, and their collaborative participation is expected when they are ready to help in shared endeavours.

In such communities, children understand from an early age that ultimately they will be expected to become fully involved in 'grown-up' activities. They are thus highly motivated to attend closely to what adults and older children are doing and saying. In terms of young children's involvement in their own learning, Rogoff et al. found there was a profound contrast between the intent community participation practised in Guatemalan communities with 'child-centred' pedagogies of European-American communities that employ 'developmentally appropriate' curriculum materials. Nevertheless, Rogoff (2003) maintains that learning by observation and listening-in on adult activities is important for all children, and is likely to be present to some degree in most settings and communities.

Although Paley's storytelling and story acting typically occurs in formal educational contexts, I would argue that as a cultural practice it shares many of the features of guided and intent participation. In the following sections I discuss firstly how the partnership between the child telling the story and the adult scribe guides his/her participation in the activity of storytelling at the personal level. Secondly, I outline the nature of other children's intent participation in this activity and demonstrate how this takes different forms depending on proximity and children's involvement in activities peripheral to the storytelling activity. Finally, drawing on the thematic analysis of the stories, I argue that in this context, learning through keen observation and listening in anticipation of their own later participation as storytellers and actors, not only develops children's narrative competence, it also facilitates the emergence of distinctive peer cultures and community mindsets.

Learning through guided participation

Research on guided participation (e.g. Rogoff, 1990) typically focuses on the non-verbal communication characteristic of informal learning in routine domestic contexts where caregivers encourage children to acquire culturally valued skills. Although Paley's storytelling and story-acting pedagogy takes place in the formal educational setting of the classroom, in the hands of a skilled practitioner it shares many features of guided participation. For example, although practitioners are trained to respect the child's words as spoken, and not to 'correct' or improve upon these, the video data shows that as each child told his/her story, the scribes often took advantage of natural pauses in the child's train of thought to check back with the child that his/her words were recorded correctly. They also read the story back to the child, pointing to the words and repeating these slowly. When children hesitated or dried up, practitioners gave verbal prompts such as, 'What happened next'? 'Did anything else happen in your story'? 'Is that the end'? More often than not, however, their use of expectant gaze and questioning facial expression was sufficient to encourage further contribution. Non-verbal communication in the form of exaggerated facial expressions, changes of emphasis and tone of voice added drama to the story, and also created the conditions for the mutual bridging of meaning and structured the child's participation in the activity.

Further bridging and structuring were observed when the child indicated that the story was finished. Practitioners encouraged children to identify their preferred character and other acting roles. Under the watchful eye of the storyteller, practitioners carefully circled the character to be played by the story narrator and underlined the animate and inanimate nouns signifying these roles, as well as key objects and actions. These 'stage directions' contributed to the later dramatisation of the story. Finally, again using intonation and timing to amplify meaning and emotional tone, practitioners read the story once more, usually drawing the child's attention to the written words by pointing. For all children, but perhaps more noticeably those with English as an additional language, or with speech and language difficulties, this mutual bridging and structuring played an important role in establishing a story's meaning. In this way, at a highly personal level, narrators and 'scribes' co-constructed a written version of the story and reached preliminary agreement on its dramatisation, although this could change as other children made their own contribution to its later dramatic reconstruction.

First-, second- and third-party intent participation

In addition to the child/practitioner storytelling duo, however, there were usually at least one or two other children present as proximal others during storytelling sessions. Of the 90 storytelling sessions captured on video, there were only twelve sessions with no other children present. On 28 occasions there were at least four and sometimes as many as five or six children listening and watching with varying degrees of attention, not all of it 'keen'. As differing degrees of participation were evident depending on the proximity of these 'others' to the storytelling duo and the nature of their more peripheral activities, it was necessary to extend Rogoff et al.'s (2003) original definition of 'intent participation'.

For example, at least one child was frequently observed immediately on one side of, or directly in front of, the storytelling duo. Typically, there was no direct interaction, eye contact or facial expression monitoring between this child, the storyteller and the practitioner. Instead both children could be observed watching and paying close attention as the spoken narrative appeared as written words on the page (see Figure 5.1). Although most of these children were not yet readers, nevertheless they appeared keenly interested, firstly in how speech is represented by marks on a page, and secondly how this enables speech to be reproduced accurately by another person. In their role as watchers, therefore, both children can be said to be 'first-party' intent participants in the storytelling activity. The child generating the story, however, is also a direct participant.

Usually, as in Figure 5.2, we observed other children in the immediate vicinity of the storytelling session. These children could be described as 'second-party' indirect or incidental participants. Although they were listening in for part of the time, their attention was clearly divided between the storytelling activity and

Keen observation by story teller

Keen observation, listening and anticipating participation

FIGURE 5.1 Intent and direct first-party participation

Intent participation

Direct participation

Peripheral participation

Incidental participation

FIGURE 5.2 Second- and third-party incidental and peripheral participation

simultaneous engagement in another activity. Later, when the adult began to underline the acting parts, they would shift from indirect to intent participants, paying close attention to the identification of characters and potential acting parts. It was also possible to identify distal others, children on the periphery who were seen to repeatedly enter and leave the vicinity, stopping to 'listen in' briefly before moving away. These 'third-party' peripheral participants would also reappear in time to listen to the final read through of the story, indicating that they too had been watching and monitoring the progress of the session, albeit at some distance.

Finally, the videos also showed proximal others who, although physically present, were non-participants. These children were either completely engrossed in a parallel activity, or were attempting to interrupt the storytelling session in order to gain the attention of the practitioner.

With the exception of the children who were centrally involved either as direct or intent first-party participants, it was not immediately clear what the second- and third-party participants might be learning, apart from how the storytelling sessions were structured. Overt interpersonal interaction between the storyteller and his or her peers was infrequent, and although they usually paid close attention to the story, these peers did not overtly contribute to the evolving narrative. The class storybooks, however, provided clear evidence of narrative fertilisation within and between storytelling sessions, with certain themes and expressions achieving popularity through frequent repetition or elaboration by identifiable groups of children. It is likely that fertilisation between sessions was further enhanced by participation in story acting and informal play and conversation between peers (although the available data does not capture this) as much as participation in storytelling. Nevertheless, it was clear that over the eight-week period of the study, in each setting, children's participation in Helicopter Stories sessions led to the emergence of two or three central narratives. Some of these were imaginative variations of traditional fairy or superhero stories, popular television programmes or video games. In other instances, one child told a highly original story that clearly captured his/her classmates' imagination and enjoyment, resulting in different children relating their own variations on this story time and time again. Finally, there were clusters of 'stories' shared by groups of children that had a common theme but lacked both plot and action. Instead these stories had a common cast of characters that increased with each retelling. These central narratives and story clusters suggest that collective participation in storytelling and story acting gives rise to local 'communities of mind' characterised by distinctive narrative traditions employed by particular groups of children. Alongside Rogoff's account of intent participation, therefore, the next section draws on Nelson's account of children's language development and the emergence of narrative consciousness over the first five years. This offers a useful theoretical framework for understanding how Paley's classroom practices give rise to these communities and local narrative traditions (Nelson, 2007, 2010).

Entering a community of minds

Over the past 25 years, Nelson's studies of language and memory development have culminated in a bio-sociocultural account of children's development. In brief, she draws on developmental psychology and biological evolutionary theories to argue that both internal (biological) and external (sociocultural) influences must be taken into account if we are to understand the complexity and individuality of the developmental changes that result from children's everyday experiences and interactions (Nelson, 2007, 2010). Her theory relies on twin premises: firstly, human beings have a universal disposition to share knowledge through speech and language. Secondly, in collaboration with social guides and companions, the experiential child is constantly searching for meaning in his/her encounters with the social, cultural and physical world. Speech and language play a mediating role by bridging the gap between private consciousness (one's own thoughts and feelings) and public awareness of the thoughts and feelings of others (Nelson, 2010: 45). Language thus enables the 'sharing of minds'. In early childhood, one way in which this emerges is when parents encourage young children to join in with reflective conversations about past and future events. Nelson argues that these reflective conversations enable children to master the basic narrative structure needed for reporting and sharing personal stories. They also allow children to begin to construct an autobiographical identity and understand their role in the evolving family narrative (Hudson and Nelson, 1986; Nelson and Fivush, 2004).

As children become sufficiently well practised in constructing and reflecting on their own personal narratives, which Nelson suggests usually occurs at around four years of age, they acquire a more advanced level of narrative consciousness. Nelson (2010: 45) describes this as:

> a wonderful achievement in its own right. Through this new experiential mode – of personal narratives of the past or future or fictional narratives of other times and places – the child begins to achieve the more advanced level of *narrative consciousness*, a level that integrates knowledge of people's actions and motivations, and of situations in time and place detached from the present.

The achievement of narrative consciousness facilitates children's intent participation in adult 'communities of minds', where knowledge is shared, experiences are given meaning, and community and cultural traditions evolve through discourse and joint action. Intent participation in storytelling, coupled with later observation of audience reaction when the stories are enacted, appears to draw on this more advanced level of narrative consciousness, allowing children to understand that some stories or themes are more likely to capture and hold the attention of their peers than others.

The evidence from the London-based project suggests that Helicopter Stories enable four- to six-year-olds to develop local narrative traditions and create their own 'communities of minds' based on their shared knowledge of popular culture. Applying Robbins' (2007) third cultural analytic focus to an analysis of the children's stories revealed few obviously personal narratives recorded in the class storybooks. While the older children's productions had more sophisticated narrative structures than those of the younger children, as in the studies by Marsh and Millard (2000) and Nicolopoulou et al. (2014), popular culture proved to have had a significant influence on the majority of stories told by these young narrators. As outlined above, the thematic analyses of the class storybooks cross-referenced with the video data revealed interrelationships between particular story themes and identifiable groups of children as well as local, cultural differences in children's narrative thinking across the six settings. As discussed in the next section, there was considerable evidence of borrowing, repetition, re-use and re-versioning of popular narrative themes amongst identifiable groups of children. Also, over the eight-week duration of the study, distinctive themes and cultural conventions emerged that were specific to each setting, suggesting that intent participation in storytelling sessions did result in the formation of 'communities of minds' or mindsets.

Socially constructed narratives and community mindsets

This section offers a commentary on story themes and devices that achieved considerable salience amongst groups of children in the various settings, as in Alan's story – the first story recorded at Eager Beavers nursery:

> There was a dragon flying and he fell in the bin. And a big orange splatted on his head. Andy came and took him to the dungeon.

Slapstick elements such as falling into a bin and being 'splatted' clearly captured the imagination of Alan's peers. During the first storytelling session, seven out of the eight stories featured one or both actions. For some children it was evident that Alan's story offered an opportunity to engage in language play and humour. Words like 'splatted' and 'squished' had onomatopoeic and dramatic potential that were particularly attractive to some children. As Crystal (2001) has demonstrated, playing with language in this way is important for all learners and may be particularly important for second language learners, adding to the enjoyment of learning another language, especially if there is an appreciative audience to share the joke (e.g. Bell et al., 2014).

The following week, several children appropriated the slapstick elements from Andy's original story, introducing additional elements of their own, as in Lewis's tale:

> A orange fell on the bin and then the orange splat on his head and an apple squished the orange and the banana splatted the apple and he went to the hospital all of them.

The video of Lewis shows the next storyteller, Eden, and a little girl watching and listening as Lewis started to tell his story. The class storybook indicates that another boy, Barney, told a story containing a donkey falling on (and later driving) a car immediately before Lewis, although this was not captured on video. Eden wandered off briefly but knowing it was his turn next, returned as Lewis's story concluded. Eden's story went like this:

> Once there was a donkey and a orange splat on his head and then an apple splatted on the orange and then he ran away into his cars and drove away home. The End.

Here Eden draws on the orange and the apple splatting each other from Lewis's story along with Barney's donkey and cars suggesting that he had been a second-party participant during both of the previous two sessions. As Eden started telling his story six other children were present, including Robin and Carol, the next two storytellers. The observational notes for the video of Robin's story record the presence of four other children as first-party (Eden), second-party (boy in white and black) and third-party participants (Carol) and one non-participant:

> Boy in orange [Robin] and Eden are on either side of Julie [the practitioner] while she takes Robin's story. There is a boy in white and black also watching, first standing then sitting on the block behind Robin. Both watch Julie writing, especially during the recap. The boy in white and black wanders off, but stays close by playing with blocks. A little girl in blue [Carol] reappears towards the end of the story, also watching. Another little girl in an Eager Beavers T-shirt appears and climbs over the boys to sit next to Julie and puts her arm round her, waiting and trying to get Julie's attention.

Both Robin and Carol incorporated the orange, splatting and falling into a bin in their stories, although they introduced other novel elements as well. Over the course of eight weeks, 16 of the 23 children in this class included some variant on 'falling into the bin' and 13 told stories involving an orange splatting another character on the head. These stories were acted out with a great deal of enthusiasm later each day. The Eager Beavers storytelling videos provide clear evidence that as first-, second- and third-party participants these nursery school children developed a communal mindset that action-based stories containing word play made good theatre. In this particular setting, the core elements of the narrative detailed above acquired the status of a local, cultural resource that children could draw on in their own stories.

Socially constructed narratives were also evident in the other five settings. Many of these were imaginative adaptations of familiar fairy and superhero tales, reflecting the cultural resources the children had in common both within and beyond the classroom. For example, of the 24 children at Bournehill nursery, nine were registered with English as an additional language (EAL) and four with special educational needs (SEN). Rather than rely on their own linguistic skills when invited to tell a story, these children developed a strategy that involved re-combining elements of traditional fairy tales. Characters such as Goldilocks (with or without the three bears), Little Red Riding Hood and the Three Little Pigs made frequent appearances alongside a big bad wolf, which appeared on seventeen occasions. These characters feature in collections of fairy tales recommended for use in nursery classes[2] and their content, structure and language offer a readily available and highly familiar cultural resource that many children drew on for inspiration. Overall, 40 per cent of the Bournehill nursery's stories mentioned fairy-tale characters. For example, in the fifth week of the study, three-year-old Earl based his story on the classic tale, 'The Three Little Pigs and the Big Bad Wolf':

Big bad wolf have little piggies. They blow the house away. They run away and now back to the house. Now run. Finished.

Dalton took up this theme next, introducing additional characters and actions:

It's about two wolf with the piggies. It's a bad, bad wolf. He eat the piggy – now he eat the duck.

These examples suggest that not only should children's stories be treated as cultural productions, but also, as the stories about oranges and bins demonstrate, 'one child's production could not be understood without situating it in other children's productions' (Dyson, 2010: 16). In her studies of children's written narratives, Dyson found that even when they are supposed to be working alone, the collegial interest children demonstrate in each other's meaning making leads them to deliberately 'copy', remix and re-contextualise each other's compositions. Dyson (2010: 17) calls this 'deliberate coordination of composing'. There were many examples of coordination of composing during Helicopter Stories sessions, suggesting this is another function of intent participation.

While traditional fairy-tale and superhero themes were popular with both girls and boys in nursery classrooms, gender-related themes were more common amongst the older children in the London study, replicating the findings of Nicolopoulou et al. (2014). For example, in St Aidan's reception class, a distinctive 'military' subculture developed with ten of the eleven boys producing twenty-two stories where armies and army vehicles combined forces to defeat bad guys. By contrast, a series of horses galloped their way through the nine girls' stories, usually accompanied by princesses, princes, knights, fairies and butterflies (fifteen stories in all).

In addition, interesting literary tropes emerged. As Dyson (2010) has established, when composing their own narratives children borrow and revoice words and phrases used by their peers. For example, by the third week of the study, Bournehill reception children began to use their own version of the canonical opening 'Once upon a time'. This became, 'Once upon a time/one day there was a princess', or simply 'There was a princess'. Originally introduced by Sahana in week 2, this opening was adopted by both boys and girls, as in Daniel's story told in week 4:

Once upon a time there was a princess and the princess went to the castle. The princess saw a prince and the prince ran away. There was another castle next to the first castle. So the princess went to the second castle, and the princess saw the prince and the princess was in love with the prince. And they all lived happily ever after. The end.

In some cases, this opening was used even when the following tale did not strictly conform to the traditional 'princess' theme, as in Summer's story from week 5:

> Once upon a time there was a princess and there was a horse. And there was a pig, then they lived in a castle. And there was a knight and the knight went to the sweetie shop. And then they had a party at the castle.

Ruth's story, told in week 3, offered an even more radical departure from the 'princess' theme. In this example, although she uses the opening 'There was a princess', this is followed by more everyday events and the later introduction of a helpful Power Ranger:

> There was a princess. And there was a grandad. And he went to a shop and then he had a dog. And there was some little chicks. And he bought the little chicks. And there was a little boy and his ice cream fell on the floor. He bought some food and some water. And there was a Pink Power Ranger. The Pink Power Ranger took the little boy home.

Being abducted and/or rescued by a Power Ranger or superhero was a popular theme in this class, giving rise to stories with considerable dramatic potential and roles for several characters. As discussed earlier, identifying the acting parts and lead character was of immense importance to the intent participants gathered round the storyteller. In all settings it was noticeable that as children became familiar with storytelling and story acting, they began to compose stories with acting parts for as many of their peers as possible, as in Monesha's story told in week 7, which contained multiple acting parts (underlined).

> First there was <u>Goldilocks</u> and the <u>three bears</u>. The <u>mummy bear</u> cooked some porridge for dinner and <u>Hello Kitty</u> was making some cornflakes for dinner. And <u>Barbie</u> had a big, big friend called <u>Teddy</u>. And the second name of Teddy was Ravi. And <u>Power Rangers</u> had a fire in their house and the <u>ambulance</u> came to put it out. The end, and then they bowed.

The final words of this story 'and then they bowed' clearly anticipate its later performance. This suggests that the practice of storytelling/story acting can give rise to a community mindset where the anticipated performance and number of actors takes precedence over plot structure and narrative coherence. This is borne out by observations that third-party participants appeared more interested in the number of acting parts than in listening to the story.

Conclusion

This chapter has investigated the relationship between the nature and quality of children's intent participation in Helicopter Stories sessions and the sociocultural transmission of distinctive narrative themes and literary tropes identified in each setting. As not all storytelling sessions were filmed, it was only possible to explore this relationship in detail for 25 per cent of the training sessions and it was not always possible to determine exactly how many children were present at any one time. Similarly, although there were 90 recordings of children telling their stories, it was only possible to demonstrate sociocultural transmission with any degree of reliability when the order of the sessions captured on video coincided exactly with the order of stories in the class storybook.

Nevertheless, the analysis of this data has established that at the personal level, Rogoff's construct of learning through guided participation offers a convincing account of how storytellers and practitioners co-construct meaning. At the interpersonal level, the construct of intent participation was found to require further elaboration. Although physically present, not all of the storyteller's peers could be said to be listening and watching with keen attention all of the time. Differing degrees of participation were evident depending on children's proximity to the storytelling duo and on the nature of their more peripheral activities. In the main, first-party participants were clearly fascinated by the relationship between speech and writing. Second-party participants were more obviously listening to the story as it unfolded and judging its potential entertainment value. Finally, possibly in anticipation of their later participation in story-acting sessions, the third-party peripheral participants monitoring the session from afar only returned for the final reading of the story. These children appeared to be more interested in its dramatic potential and in ascertaining how many acting parts it offered.

At the cultural level there was considerable evidence of sociocultural transmission. Distinctive themes and local narrative and cultural conventions specific to each setting were identified, suggesting that the children had acquired the level of narrative consciousness necessary to appreciate, understand and emulate each other's cultural productions. This was most compelling in cases where one child introduced novel and original characters, actions, themes or literary tropes that were subsequently appropriated by his/her peers over a sustained time period. It could be argued, therefore, that intent participation facilitates collective meaning making and the social construction of local community narratives that, regardless of their level of narrative competence, all children can draw on for inspiration.

Notes

1   It was not always possible to gauge the exact number of children present at any one time as the focus of the videos was on the child storyteller and adult taking the story. In my observations, therefore, I was only able to count the number of children who were actually in the video frame. Other children may have been present, but out of shot.

2   See for example, the National Bookstart list celebrating fairy tales, compiled in 2013 by BookTrust, (the largest reading charity in the UK): http://www.bookstart.org.uk/events/national-bookstart-week/duckling/#/static/bookstart/duckling/

References

Bell, N., Skalicky, S. and Salsbury, T. (2014) Multicompetence in L2 language play: A longitudinal case study. *Language Learning, 64*: 72–102.

Braun, V. and Clarke, V. (2006) Using thematic analysis in psychology. *Qualitative Research in Psychology, 3*(2): 77–101.

Cremin, T., Swann, J., Flewitt, R. S., Faulkner, D. and Kucirkova, N. (2013) *Evaluation Report of MakeBelieve Arts Helicopter Technique of Storytelling and Story Acting.* The Open University. Available at: http://www.makebelievearts.co.uk/docs/Helicopter-Technique-Evaluation.pdf

Crystal, D. (2001) *Language Play.* Chicago, IL: University of Chicago Press.

de Haan, M. (1999) *Learning as Cultural Practice: How children learn in a Mexican Mazahua community.* Amsterdam: Thela Thesis.

Dyson, A. H. (2010) Writing childhoods under construction: Re-visioning 'copying' in early childhood. *Journal of Early Childhood Literacy, 10*(1): 7–31.

Faulkner, D. (2011) Angels, tooth fairies and ghosts: Thinking creatively in an early years classroom. In D. Faulkner and E. Coates (eds), *Exploring Children's Creative Narratives* (pp. 39–62). London: Routledge.

Faulkner, D. and Miell, D. (2005) Collaborative story telling in friendship and acquaintanceship dyads. In K. Littleton, D. Faulkner and D. Miell (eds), *Learning to Collaborate: Collaborating to learn* (pp. 7–30). New York, NY: Nova Science Publishers.

Hudson, J. and Nelson, K. (1986) Repeated encounters of a similar kind: Effects of familiarity on children's autobiographical memory. *Cognitive Development, 1*: 253–271.

Marsh, J. and Millard, E. (2000) *Literacy and Popular Culture: Using children's culture in the classroom.* London: Sage.

Nelson, K. (2007) *Young Minds in Social Worlds: Experience meaning and memory.* Cambridge, MA: Harvard University Press.

Nelson, K. (2010) Developmental narratives of the experiencing child. *Child Development Perspectives, 4*(1): 42–47.

Nelson, K. and Fivush, R. (2004) The emergence of autobiographical memory: A social cultural developmental theory. *Psychological Review, 111*: 486–511.

Nicolopoulou, A., Cates, N. B., de Sá, A. and Ilgaz, H. (2014) Narrative performance, peer group culture, and narrative development in a preschool classroom. In A. Cekaite, S. Blum-Kulka, V. Grover, and E. Teubal (eds), *Children's Peer Talk: Learning from each other* (pp. 42–62). New York, NY: Cambridge University Press.

Paley, V. G. (1990) *The Boy Who Would Be a Helicopter: The uses of storytelling in the classroom.* Cambridge, MA: Harvard University Press.

Robbins, J. (2007) Young children thinking and talking: Using sociocultural theory for multi-layered analysis. *Learning and Socio-Cultural Theory: Exploring modern Vygotskian perspectives, 1*: 46–65.

Rogoff, B. (1990) *Apprenticeship in Thinking.* New York: Oxford University Press.

Rogoff, B. (2003) *The Cultural Nature of Human Development.* New York, NY: Oxford University Press.

Rogoff, B., Paradise, R., Arauiz, R. M., Correa-Chavez, M. and Angelillo, C. (2003) Firsthand learning through intent participation. *Annual Review of Psychology, 54*: 175–203.

Stein, N. L. (1988) The development of story telling skill. In M. B. Franklin and S. Barton (eds), *Child Language: A book of readings* (pp. 282–297). New York, NY: Cambridge University Press.

6

STORIES IN INTERACTION

Creative collaborations in storytelling and story acting

Joan Swann

Introduction

> They make [storytelling] their own and they bring themselves to it … and they are
> listened to by their peers and by the teacher and I know I have seen them develop
> so much self-confidence.
>
> *(Early years teacher, cited in Cremin et al., 2013: 45)*

A major theme that emerged in the UK evaluation of MakeBelieve Arts'
Helicopter Stories discussed in Chapter 2 was the way children were supported in
their storytelling and story acting. Support came both from the adult acting as
sympathetic scribe, and the attentive audience when stories were acted out on
stage. In the present chapter I see such supportive activity not simply as giving
voice to the child narrator, but as an extended process of collaborative creativity.
The initial transcription of a child's story involves an adult scribe collaborating with
the child and, in various ways, co-creating the narration. Other children may also
contribute to this process (see Faulkner, Chapter 5). In acting out the story, the
adult managing the activity, children acting out roles, and children and adults who
make up the audience, all contribute to an enhanced performance of the narrative.
Through these collaborative and facilitative processes all participants contribute to
the production of a child's story. The value to the child is not simply that people
listen to them, but that they work on the story: the story is worth the effort that
others bring to its development.

To examine this issue further, I look closely at how stories emerge from the
interactions between those involved in storytelling and story acting. I draw on
insights from the applied linguistic study of conversational narrative as well as the
anthropological study of stories in performance. A particular benefit of this
combined 'interactional' approach is that it allows detailed scrutiny of the processes

of storytelling and story acting, revealing the subtle, step-by-step interactional activity that produces children's stories.

An interactional approach to storytelling and story acting

Vivian Gussin Paley's work documents the power of story through close observation of young children interacting with each other, and her own interactions with children. *The Boy Who Would Be a Helicopter*, for instance, shows Jason, initially an outsider, begin to play with others, engage in classroom stories and 'come home' to the classroom (Paley, 1990: 146). Paley provides sympathetic and highly reflexive accounts of classroom life. It is through observation and reflection that she seeks to understand the daily preoccupations of the children in her care, and her own role in relation to the children and their learning. The principle is not unlike the 'insightful observation' associated with several language researchers, classically Barnes (1976), whose observation and recording of classroom interaction sought to relate children's talk, with each other and with teachers, to processes of learning:

> Classroom learning can best be seen as an interaction between the teacher's meanings, and those of his pupils, so that what they take away is partly shared and partly unique to each of them.
>
> *(Barnes, 1976: 22)*

More recently, and more systematically, educational researchers such as Mercer and Littleton have focused on the role of collaborative, exploratory talk in the development of children's thinking (e.g. Mercer, 2000; Mercer and Littleton, 2007; Littleton and Mercer, 2013). In my own earlier work I have also looked, at a greater level of interactional detail, at how such exploratory talk is embedded in, and partly conditioned by, the collaborative construction of children's relationships and identities (e.g. Swann, 2007, 2009a). These ideas on the educational importance of collaborative interactional activity underpin the present chapter. My focus here, however, is on collaboration in storytelling and story acting. To understand these processes, I step outside education and draw on insights from research on story and performance.

Studies of the way narratives are produced in interaction between people have often focused on conversational narratives, across a wide range of settings. While researchers give slightly different labels to their work this falls broadly within the tradition of applied linguistics, meaning here the study of 'real-world' language use and language issues. Norrick (2000), for instance, studied conversational narratives within a large corpus of stories, including stories told between friends and in families; Tannen (2007) compared a corpus of American and Greek conversational stories collected across diverse settings; Coates (1996) looked at stories that emerged in conversations between women friends chatting together, often in each other's houses; and Maybin (2006) included conversational narratives in her study of eleven- to twelve-year-old children's talk, mainly in playgrounds and classrooms.

In all these contexts the talk is relatively informal and storytelling is a collaborative process. Stories may be narrated by two or more speakers – a practice Norrick refers to as 'co-narration' – but even where a single speaker is the main teller of a story this is developed with contributions from others. Other speakers may prompt the telling of the story and comment on or add to this as it is being told; successive stories, or story fragments, may also build progressively on previous stories. Studies have looked both at the formal properties of conversational narratives, and also their social and interpersonal functions: how they convey certain values in their representation of experience, for instance, and their role in promoting shared values and rapport between speakers.

Storytelling in conversations is a performance, attended to by others taking part in the conversation and standing out from the surrounding talk. It is perhaps best characterised as an emergent and fleeting performance, however, surfacing briefly in the flux of talk. In this sense it differs from the telling of 'Helicopter Stories' – a more clearly demarcated interactional activity in which time is set aside for storytelling and where stories, through their transcription, become durable and lead to a fully fledged, staged performance. The study of conversational storytelling may nevertheless usefully inform the study of Helicopter Stories, providing insights into collaborative narrative activity and an approach to documenting this.

Another field of enquiry relevant to the study of storytelling and story acting is linguistic anthropology and the associated field of folklore studies, particularly with respect to the study of narrative in performance. Anthropologists and folklorists traditionally engaged in a process not unlike Helicopter storytelling, transcribing oral narratives that were recounted to them, in this case by informants in communities they were studying. This produced collections of, particularly, folk narratives in which certain cultural themes could be explored. The study of performance was a major breakthrough in these fields (Hymes, 1975; Bauman, 1986). Bauman argued that the story text, as transcribed by a researcher, was abstracted from the context in which it would normally occur when it was performed to an audience. The text was a 'thin and partial record of a deeply situated human behaviour' (Bauman, 1986: 2). Focusing on performance could reveal the artistry and skill of the narrator as well as the significance of the audience, both as people for whom the performance was enacted and as contributors to the performance itself. In a study of Limba storytelling in Sierra Leone, for instance, Finnegan (1967, 2006) contrasts the 'thin' story text with a performance created by the narrator and his audience that was 'profound, allusive, and full of both sharply observed individuality and universal drama' (2006: 184). What produced the thin record of the story was partly that this was restricted to the verbal text, as recounted by the narrator. Studies such as Finnegan's take account of a range of other modes that make up the performance: perhaps music, song and the storyteller's use of his/her voice and body (see further Finnegan, 2007). While the intellectual roots are different, the study of different communicative modes in performance, including but not limited to verbal language, is consistent with the multimodal approach to children's meaning making outlined by Flewitt (Chapter 9, this volume).

Limba story performances may seem a long way from young children's stories in US and British classrooms. In this chapter, however, I draw on insights from the study of stories in performance in the analysis of children's story acting. I try to illustrate the way story acting adds to the original story text dictated by children to their teachers, and the important role played by other participants, including audience members, in the construction of the performed story.

The interactional approach I draw on comes from my own earlier work analysing informal talk in educational and other settings (e.g. Swann, 2007; 2009a) and the analysis of performances by professional storytellers (e.g. Swann, 2009b). The analytical process involves playing and replaying recordings, here video-recordings, of storytelling and story-acting episodes; making a close transcription of these episodes; and qualitative scrutiny of recordings and transcripts with a focus on the content of the interaction, e.g. particular themes that emerge in the narratives; and a complementary focus on interactional strategies – how storytelling and story acting are conducted, in this case with an interest in collaborative strategies that amount to the co-creation of a child's narrative. Transcription plays a significant part, perhaps the most important part of the analytical process. The interaction is transcribed verbatim, including any hesitations, repetitions, overlaps, pauses, false starts and other characteristics of informal talk. Aspects of voice are noted – e.g. a phrase spoken more loudly or quickly than the surrounding talk, 'smile voice', laughter accompanying the talk. Communicative modes such as gesture, body orientation and gaze are also included, not just in the transcription of story-acting performances but also in storytelling. Scrutiny of the videos shows that the collaboration between teacher and child in storytelling is a multimodal, not simply linguistic, achievement. How all these features are captured, selected and noted by the researcher is a subjective process, and it is in this sense that transcription has been seen as necessarily theoretically motivated (Ochs, 1979), not simply as a neutral process of representing interactions. Certainly transcription is not pre-analytical. It is in the act of transcribing (making certain representational choices, playing with particular formats, layouts etc.) that particular interpretations are revealed to, or more accurately, constructed by the analyst.

An analysis of storytelling and story acting

I shall illustrate this complex, multimodal process of co-creation with the stories of a single child, George, who was four years old at the time of the research. George attended one of the settings studied as part of the UK MakeBelieve Arts project (see Chapter 2): an early years unit that included three mixed-age nursery/reception classes, forming part of an inner-London primary school referred to as Charrington School. The children spent some of their time in class groups, but the unit was largely open plan and also operated a free-flow system that allowed children access to different areas and activities supported by adults, including outdoor play. MakeBelieve Arts trainers worked with class teachers in the introduction and embedding of storytelling and story acting within the early years curriculum, and the examples I discuss below come from sessions facilitated by George's class teacher, a MakeBelieve Arts trainer, or both.

Notes from George's class teacher record that he had excellent language skills and was 'very good at writing stories', but for the first four weeks of the programme he was unwilling to tell a story. Our observations show that he hung around watching storytelling sessions but did not take part himself. Furthermore he often seemed to be on the fringes of activity during free-flow periods (e.g. he stood at the back of a group of boys playing on a computer and watched, but did not interact with the other children). Supported by the class teacher and the MakeBelieve Arts trainer, George began to tell stories from the fifth week, and the class teacher's logbook notes that his confidence increased: after his initial unwillingness he 'can't wait to tell his story'. He also began 'to interact much more with others and seems to be having fun!' The extracts below, taken from observations and transcribed video recordings, illustrate this process in action. They show how George began to participate in storytelling, the very subtle support he received from the trainer and class teacher, and responses from other children during story acting.

George begins to tell stories

George had an unusual beginning in storytelling. During the fifth session of the programme he remained unwilling to tell a story, though he watched when others did so. There was a lull in the session while the trainer, Liz, waited for the class teacher to bring a child who was due to tell the next story. George and two other children were sitting next to the trainer, and she said to George: 'The day when I get a story from you it will be my happiest day.' George replied that he couldn't think of a story, then rephrased this in the third person: 'when George couldn't think of a story...'. The extract in Figure 6.1 shows what happened next. Transcription conventions for this and other extracts are included at the end of the chapter.

George's initial musing ('when George couldn't think of a story') is uttered as if speaking to himself. It is not clear if it is intended as a story title, but that is how the trainer interprets it in her questions in sequences 1 and 2/4 in Figure 6.1. George's 'yes', accompanied by a nod, shows he accepts this, and so his first story begins. It is a story about a story – of how he wanted to do a story but couldn't think of one, till his class teacher told him that his story didn't need to be fantastic, so he thought of a story that, as he says later in his narrative, was 'just a little bit good'. The trainer is clearly delighted by this. She shares the story with the teacher at the end of the session, and George comes up to listen.

Figure 6.1 illustrates the starting point of an extended process of co-creation – how a turn in a conversation (George saying he can't think of a story) becomes an ambiguous reflection ('When George couldn't think of a story'), framed by the trainer as a story title. While this is clearly George's story, the trainer's framing is part of the creative process that produces the narrative. As the trainer asks if she

Seq	Time	Dialogue		Action	
		S	Talk	George	Trainer
1	0	Tr	Let me write that down should I write that as a title	Sitting on the floor to the side of Tr, looking down at a wooden toy car he is holding; as Tr speaks he looks towards her and the story book	Leans over her book; at the end of her question, looks towards G
2	0.4	Tr	"When George couldn't think of a story" [(.)	On *George* he looks up more directly at Tr	Leans further forward, turns to look more clearly at G's face
3		G	[yes	Nods	
4		Tr	should we write that down ((laughing voice))	Maintains gaze on Tr	Maintains gaze on G
5	0.7	Tr	<"when George couldn't think of a story"> and what happens in this story	Looks down at toy car, handling this. On *think*, he turns back to Tr. Shuffles round so he is angled more towards her	Gazes at the book; reads back G's words slowly as she scribes these; when finished she looks up at G to ask her question, smiling.
6	0.18	G	erm (.) one day when Liz was doing Helicopter Stories George really wanted to do one …	Oriented towards Tr. Looks down towards car, handles this as he speaks.	Maintains gaze on G, still smiling. On *Liz* leans slightly closer, then on *Helicopter* looks down towards book, holding pen as if preparing to write.

(Seq = sequence; Time = elapsed time in minutes/seconds; S = Speaker: G = George, Tr = Trainer, Liz)

FIGURE 6.1   When George couldn't think of a story

should write down George's words, she looks towards George, and she and George maintain mutual gaze as she repeats her question and George responds. As the trainer writes the title, George shuffles round towards her, a non-verbal confirmation that he is continuing his narration. The trainer looks towards George and smiles as she asks him what happens in the story, and maintains her gaze and smile as he begins to narrate. The trainer's support for George and George's acquiescence in the storytelling process are, then, coordinated by gaze, facial expression, body orientation and body movement as much as verbally.

This collaborative process continues through into story acting. When the story is acted out, George plays himself and other children play the trainer and the class teacher. There is limited action in the story, but the trainer, as stage manager, gets the audience to join George in miming 'thinking' when he is trying to think of a story, and this works well. When the audience applauds at the end of the story one of the boys claps towards George, smiling. The trainer/stage manager, George and other actors, and audience members work together to co-create the performance of George's narrative.

Later stories: Talking castles and secret agents

The serendipitous elicitation of George's first story is a catalyst – he tells a story every week after this. He is a reflective narrator, thinking carefully about his words – a process that requires sympathetic scribing. Figure 6.2 shows an instance of this, from a story George tells a week after his first story, about two talking castles. The castles' chatter is interrupted by a witch who walks between them. The teacher transcribes this ('And then the witch went in between them to stop them talking') and George accepts her transcription. The extract in Figure 6.2 begins with a pause that follows this acceptance.

Seq	Time		Dialogue	Action	
		S	Talk	George	Teacher
32	2.54		(10)	G looks to left, turns slightly away, glances towards the book, to right and then turns back to book	T's gaze initially on G; as he glances towards the book, she looks down at the page and holds her pen ready
33	3.04	G	<erm> (2) and then the witch thought (1) that (1) and then the witch thought (1) that (2)	G leans slightly forward towards book; he moves around to squat in front of T, maintaining gaze on the book	T gazes at the book; on G's first *thought* she glances quickly at him, then back to the book; as G repeats his utterance, she begins to write
34	3.14	T	"and then the witch"	G looks at the book, watching T writing	T glances at G then looks back to the book, reading out as she continues writing
35	3.16	G	thought that they had learnt their lesson	G maintains gaze on the book	T looks at the book and writes

(G = George; T = Teacher)

FIGURE 6.2   The witch and the talking castles

George pauses in his storytelling for twelve seconds before he continues (sequence 33 'and then the witch thought that …'). The pause is noticeably long but the teacher remains silent and does not intervene. She holds her pen ready, however, showing she is prepared to write. When George begins to speak in sequence 33 his delivery is somewhat hesitant, with brief pauses between words and a repeated utterance. The teacher gazes alternately at George and the book. She begins to write on his repetition and as he shuffles round towards her. This seems to 'fix' the utterance, and George then quickly continues his narrative clause (sequence 35).

In this and other instances the adult scribe needs to decide when to intervene to support a child, e.g. with a prompt, and when to remain silent. The latter strategy clearly works with George, although in Figure 6.2 the teacher offers support with her gaze (towards George then following his own gaze down towards the book) and actions (holding her pen ready). A further striking example comes from the beginning of a story about secret agents told two weeks later in the programme. This time the trainer is scribing George's story, and she waits for him to complete his story opening. George and the trainer are both seated on the floor, with George to the left of the trainer. The teacher is also present: she watches and listens to the storytelling but does not intervene – see Figure 6.3.

This is an extraordinary piece of elicitation. George takes almost a minute to complete his first narrative clause, with prolonged gaps between utterances. It is almost painful to the observer, but the trainer listens completely silently. She remains attentive to George, shown in her gaze patterns, and she holds the book so that George can see the page that will be used for his story. She inclines her head and looks more closely at George as he begins to speak, very quietly, then transcribes the clause as usual. The process continues for the remainder of the story, though without further very long pauses. At the time, the incident is not responded to as unusual by the trainer, or the teacher who is observing, although in a later reflection it is clear it stood out for them and that it required confidence on the part of the trainer to leave the initial lengthy pause unbroken.

Figure 6.1, showing George's first story, seems to be a clear instance of co-creation, where the trainer's action in framing George's utterance as a story title helped to produce the narrative. The trainer also prompted George to continue (sequence 5, 'And what happens in this story'). In Figure 6.2, on the witch and the talking castles, the teacher did not explicitly prompt George, although she offered non-verbal support; her scribing and reading back George's utterance also ratified this as a finished part of the narrative and may have encouraged him to continue the narrative clause. In Figure 6.3, from the secret agents story, the trainer starts George off ('do you want to tell me your story'), then sits silently and with relatively little movement in the gap between his two utterances. But this absence of activity itself seems to be a form of co-creativity, leaving George space to reflect and formulate his first narrative clause.

Seq	Time	S	Talk	George	Trainer
			Dialogue	*Action*	
		S	*Talk*	*George*	*Trainer*
1	0	Tr	all right George so this is your page do you want to tell me your story	G is oriented towards Tr, looking up; his gaze takes in Tr and book. On *story* he looks away from Tr, gazing straight ahead	Tr has her pen poised over the book, looking slightly down and towards G
2	0.3	G	erm (1) once upon a time (3) there \<were\>	Looks up, ahead then slightly to right towards Tr; in the pause after *time* he glances up at Tr, then slightly away and ahead into the room	Slightly inclined towards G. Maintains gaze towards G, holds pen and book ready
3	0.8			Shuffles slightly, gazes to left; then forward and slightly up; and ahead again	Gazes towards G, holding book and pen so that book page is visible. Adjusts posture – more erect. Looks up then down again towards the book; glances briefly at G then away, slightly down
4	0.38		((vocalization))	On vocalization looks to left, then back towards the book then ahead	On vocalization, looks down towards G; holds book at an angle so page is clearly visible. Maintains this position
5	0.45	G	once upon a time there was four ((very quiet)) (16)	Maintains gaze straight ahead and rocks slightly on hands as he speaks; remains still with gaze still ahead, then turns head and gazes left	Inclines head, gazes more directly at G as he speaks; then sits back up, gaze slightly down, not directly at G
6	1.02	G	secret agents	Still facing/gazing left	Inclines head, looks directly at G as he speaks
7	1.03	Tr	"once upon a time there was four secret agents" yeah (.) shall I write that down	Turns towards Tr as she speaks; on *shall I write that down*, nods. As Tr prepares to write, shifts his position to face her, gaze directed towards book	As she repeats G's words, bends slightly towards G, nodding. When G nods in answer to her question, she puts pen to paper

(G = George; Tr = Trainer)

FIGURE 6.3 Secret agents

Acting out the talking castles story

Although initially reticent in telling stories, George was willing to take part in story acting. The acting out of his own stories, however, encouraged him to take the initiative in performance. His performances were not marked but they were inventive, as in the extract in Figure 6.4, from George's story about two talking castles (see also Figure 6.2). The full text of the story, as transcribed by George's teacher, is:

> Once upon a time there were two talking castles, and they never stopped chatting to each other. But one day when the talking castles were still chatting along came a witch. And then the witch went in between them to stop them talking. And then the witch thought that they had learnt their lesson so she went away. And they hadn't learnt their lesson.

Our video analysis shows the part played by different participants in the performance of this story. Figure 6.4 illustrates the performance of the third sentence: 'And then the witch went in between them to stop them talking'. The interaction between multiple participants is highly complex, and I have used a different transcript format from the storytelling extracts above in an attempt to capture this. The transcript separates out the narrator, here the class teacher; three characters, two castles and a witch; and the audience – in this case the direct intervention of a girl is significant. For more on transcription conventions, see the note at the end of the chapter. The transcript is complicated to read, but it is explained and interpreted below.

It is 46 seconds into the acting out of George's story. George and another boy, Harry, are on stage as the two castles. They are chatting, repeating 'bla bla bla'. The teacher has called Sam, a child who speaks English as an additional language, on to the stage as the witch. Sam is standing next to the castles, occasionally glancing at the teacher. The teacher continues her story reading in sequence 17: 'and then the witch went in between them' (i.e. the castles). Sam is uncertain what to do and looks towards the teacher. She directs Sam's performance vocally, in her emphasis on the second syllable of *between*; by gaze, looking towards Sam; and by gesture as she indicates the castles. George is in role as the first castle but also looks towards Sam. Harry is oriented towards George, but his gaze also takes in Sam. Sam looks towards the teacher, then George, but does not move or change his stance. The teacher continues reading: 'to stop them talking' (sequence 18). She looks up at Sam as she reads, and leans towards him. Sam still hasn't moved. A girl sitting next to the teacher taps him gently on the leg, and in sequence 19 the teacher asks Sam: 'just show me how you'd go in between them', pointing with her finger at the castles. It may be that Sam doesn't understand the instruction, or that he is unsure more generally about the requirements of performance. It is clear, however, that he is the focus of attention, and that he needs to do something. He makes two downward movements with his right arm and exclaims a couple of words – these are unclear. The teacher leans forward and gazes directly at Sam (sequence 20). He

Seq	Time	Narrator (T)		Characters			Audience
		Speech	Action	Castle 1 (G)	Castle 2 (H)	Witch (S)	Action/speech
					Action/speech		
17	0.46	"and then the witch went in betw<een> them"	On *the witch*, looks up towards S; on *between*, maintains gaze on S, slight smile, quick gesture towards castles	G is in role as castle, arms raised and moving up and down, vocalizing 'bla bla bla ...'. Shifts gaze from H towards S, gaze moves around and down to his left, then back towards S	H is in role as castle, arms raised vocalizing 'bla bla bla ...' He faces G, but gaze is also able to take in S, to his right	S is oriented towards castles; on *between*, gazes slightly to right towards T	Audience members fairly attentive throughout episode
18	0.50	"to stop them talking"	Glances down to book then up to S; on *to stop* leans slightly forward	In role, gazes forward to H, then towards S	In role, arms moving but slightly lowered, bent at elbow; gaze forwards to G and then slightly towards S	S maintains stance, brief glance to G then gaze back towards T	Girl next to T reaches arm out, taps S gently on leg
19	0.52	just show me how you'd (go in between them)	Gaze maintained on S; reaches arm towards S, points finger towards castles then lowers arm	In role, gaze towards S, slight smile as S raises arm	In role, gaze more clearly on S as S raises his arm	Raises right arm, bent at elbow; two strong downward movements towards Castle 1; on second stroke, exclaims (unclear); glances back to T	Girl still tapping

FIGURE 6.4 Two castles and a witch in performance (continues overleaf)

Seq	Time	Narrator (T)		Characters				Audience
		Speech	Action	Castle 1 (G)	Castle 2 (H)	Witch (S)		Action/speech
					Action/speech			
20	0.56	would you like to go in between them to stop them talking	Sitting forward, looking directly at S	In role, gaze on S then shifts forward to H, smiling	In role, gaze forwards towards G	Body slightly oriented towards castles, gaze towards T (perhaps out of role)		
21	0.58		Gaze towards S, smiling	In role, shifts gaze to S as S moves towards him	In role, gaze towards S, slight smile	Nods towards T, turns away and moves closer to castles, facing G as Castle 1		
22	0.59		Gaze still on S	In role, keeps arms up, but on *stop talk* he falls silent and stops moving; gaze directly towards S	In role, keeps arms slightly raised; gaze shifts between S and G; on *stop talk* he stops moving, seems to take cue from G	Still facing G, exclaims 'stop talk'		

(T = teacher; G = George; H = Harry; S = Sam)

FIGURE 6.4 continued

returns her gaze as she asks him: 'would you like to go in between them to stop them talking'. This time Sam nods towards the teacher (sequence 21) and moves closer to the castles. In sequence 22 he exclaims 'stop talk' and the castles stop moving and chatting. Sam here adds to the narrative – there is no direct speech in the teacher's script. But his intervention is managed and supported by others – the teacher/narrator, a girl audience member, and the two actors/castles who acknowledge him in their gaze and a smile. Figure 6.5 is drawn from a video still, illustrating a tiny element of this process.

The performance of the castles by George and Harry is also of interest. They are used to children taking on the role of inanimate entities – the sun, a tree, buildings – and here an erect stance and outstretched arms represent a castle. There are two castles and they are performed in a similar way. The castles are not actually inanimate, however – they chat together and move their bodies. George and Harry's performance of the castles requires close coordination – they face each other, adopt a similar posture, raise and lower their arms, repeat the nonsense

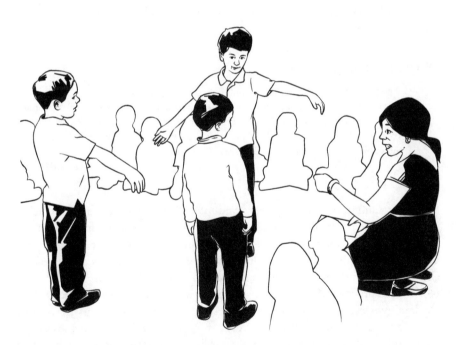

FIGURE 6.5   '… and then the witch went in between them'

The teacher is uttering the second syllable of 'between', drawing this out to give increased emphasis. Her gaze and a slight smile are directed towards Sam. Her left arm is moving towards the castles. Sam has turned his head slightly right to see the teacher. George (behind Sam in the illustration) and Harry (facing George) are in role as the castles, their arms moving and vocalizing 'bla …'. George had been looking down to his left but he has moved his head up and right and his gaze is now towards Sam. Harry is facing forwards towards George, but his gaze also takes in Sam.

syllable 'bla bla bla ...'. Their movements are coordinated by reciprocal gaze and joint gaze elsewhere – here towards Sam as the witch. While not obvious from a single viewing of the performance, transcription and analysis suggest this is led by George. He is the first person to come on stage and initiates the castle stance and vocalization, mirrored by Harry. In Figure 6.4, his castle stance is more marked and more consistent than Harry's (e.g. in his arm movements), and he is slightly ahead of Harry in gaze shifts.

This brief extract is illustrative of how this and other performances are organized. Performances extend the written narrative, here for instance showing how the castles interact – their synchronized movement as they chat. Sometimes new elements are introduced: the witch's command to the castles. The performance itself requires close coordination: the teacher as narrator, and the characters, monitor each other. Characters' gaze may be in role, but also allows them to coordinate their actions, most evident in George and Harry's interaction as castles. George is slightly in the lead here – an interpretation inferred from the observation that his actions begin just ahead of Harry's and tend to be more marked. These are all subtle and fleeting processes, evident from playing and replaying the video, and close transcription.

Discussion and conclusion

> The way that theatre ignites its audience can happen whether in a classroom 20 minutes before the end of the morning or in a darkened auditorium at an evening's performance by professional actors. The theatre of the children portrays a microcosm of the world as they see it. Their questions, explorations, fears or sense of adventure are explored through the world of play.
>
> *(Lee, 2016: 58)*

Storytelling and story acting together constitute a theatrical experience in which a story is scripted and then staged. The theatrical element is emphasized by MakeBelieve Arts, as a theatre and education company. For instance, the company often adopts the metaphor of the adult managing the activity as a 'stage manager', eliciting a child's story and orchestrating its enactment (Cremin et al., 2013: 64–66). In this process, MakeBelieve Arts shares with Paley a focus on respecting children's voices (e.g. transcribing a child's story verbatim, remaining 'true' to this in performance). Theatre itself, however, is a highly collaborative activity, in which any production of a scripted play relies on contributions from a range of participants: author, actors, director, stage manager, set designer ... etc. It is recognized that there are differing interpretations of 'the same' dramatic text and it's possible in principle to distinguish between the text, its production as drama, and its performances, these last also involving interactions with particular audiences. While the production and enactment of young children's stories is not quite such a multifaceted activity, I have suggested that it is also highly collaborative: the adult scribe supports the child in dictating their story; scribing itself requires a degree of interpretation; in reading out the story the teacher/narrator performs this; actors, in their performance of characters, create meanings that add to the original text; audience members at least attend to and interpret the performance and may intervene in this in various ways.

The interactional approach adopted above, drawing on insights from the applied linguistic study of conversational narratives and the anthropological study of stories in performance, shows how this collaboration is achieved by all participants moment-by-moment and at an intricate level of detail: the trainer in Figure 6.1 framing George's utterance as a story title; the trainer or teacher, here and in later extracts, closely attending to George's words and sometimes waiting still and silently for him to speak; George himself carefully planning his narrative clauses and monitoring the teacher or trainer as they write; the teacher narrator in the story acting sequence in Figure 6.4 emphasizing a syllable and supporting the performance of an initially hesitant child; actors taking on roles that amplify the verbal text and sometimes introduce new elements (Sam's 'stop talk'); audience members attending to the performance and in one case following the narrator in seeking to encourage an actor. All these are multimodal activities, and transcription illustrates the integration of verbal language with aspects of voice, gesture, facial expression, body movement and orientation, and subtle patterns of gaze in managing collaboration between participants. This occurs throughout storytelling and story acting as participants routinely co-create stories and their performance.

The collaborative creativity evident in storytelling and story acting is consistent with ideas that are prevalent in the contemporary study of creativity across a range of activities: both high-status activities such as art, literature and scientific discovery, and more everyday activities such as play and problem solving, are increasingly recognized as multi-party and collaborative (e.g. Craft, 2002; Carter, 2004; John-Steiner, 2006; Maybin and Swann, 2007; Pope, 2005; Swann et al., 2011). Creativity is collaborative partly in the sense that creative ideas, practices or artefacts are never entirely novel but tend to link to or build on the work of others. This occurs in storytelling and story acting as children recycle and adapt themes and motifs from earlier narratives (see examples in Faulkner, Chapter 5, this volume). My focus in this chapter, however, is on collaboration in the sense of people (writers, artists, scientists, conversationalists) working creatively together. John-Steiner (2006), for instance, documents creative partnerships between well-known artists and scientists, amongst others. And in a study of everyday linguistic creativity, Maybin and Swann (2007) consider the collaborative production of conversational joking, a conversational story and playful online chat. This second sense of collaborative creativity is consistent with the analysis above, in which different participants are seen as co-creators of a child's narrative. I have tried to show that the close transcription and analysis of interactions between participants in storytelling and story acting reveal the subtle, moment-by-moment collaborations through which narratives are co-created: the way children's stories are thereby valued, but also the value added through this process.

Transcription conventions

Transcriptions of storytelling and story acting represent verbal language alongside other communicative modes, with slightly different conventions adopted in each case.

Storytelling

Transcriptions of spoken interaction usually follow a 'dialogue' format, transcribing the interaction turn by turn. The term 'turn' however, doesn't apply well to other communicative modes, so I have preferred to chunk the interaction into numbered 'sequences'. Sequences have no theoretical significance – they are a way of segmenting the interaction and making the transcript easier to read.

I have distinguished a 'dialogue' section, in which talk is transcribed verbatim. Transcription conventions here include:

"when George …"	Elements of the story text that are read out or repeated by the teacher are in quotation marks.
[(.) should we [yes	Square brackets indicate the beginning of overlapping speech.
(.), (2)	Pauses are indicated in curved brackets; (.) = a brief pause, below 1 second; (2) = a pause of 1 second or above, duration given in seconds.
(go in between them)	Text in curved brackets = uncertain transcription.
((laughing voice))	Text in double curved brackets indicates a noticeable shift in voice quality in the previous utterance (the extent of this is underlined).
<"when George …">	Text within angle brackets is uttered more slowly than surrounding text.

Sometimes researchers indicate other communicative modes (posture, gesture, gaze etc.) in separate lines above the verbal transcript (see Fine, 1994 for an example from folklore). This can make transcripts hard to read, and here I have preferred to give these forms of communication as a running commentary in a separate 'Action' section, with one column for each interactant.

Story acting

The layout for story-acting transcripts is slightly different, with separate sections for interactants with different roles – the narrator who reads out the story, characters on stage, and audience members.

The narrator transcript separates 'speech' and 'action'. Because actors and audience members speak very little, speech and action are combined within their columns.

When actors speak in role, their words are in single quotation marks. Other conventions are as above.

References

Barnes, D. (1976) *From Communication to Curriculum*. Harmondsworth: Penguin Books.

Bauman, R. (1986) *Story, Performance, and Event: Contextual studies of oral narrative*. Cambridge: Cambridge University Press.

Carter, R. (2004) *Language and Creativity: The art of common talk*. Abingdon, Oxon: Routledge.

Coates, J. (1996) *Women Talk: Conversation between women friends*. Oxford: Blackwell Publishers.

Craft, A. (2002) *Creativity and Early Years Education: A life wide foundation*. London: Continuum.

Cremin, T., Swann, J., Flewitt, R., Faulkner, D. and Kucirkova, N. (2013) *Evaluation Report of MakeBelieve Arts Helicopter Technique of Storytelling and Story Acting*. MakeBelieve Arts and The Open University. http://www.makebelievearts.co.uk/docs/Helicopter-Technique-Evaluation.pdf.

Fine, E. C. (1994) *The Folklore Text: From performance to print* (2nd edn). Bloomington, IN: Indiana University Press.

Finnegan, R. (1967) *Limba Stories and Storytelling*. Oxford: Clarendon Press.

Finnegan, R. (2006) 'It's not just the words…': The arts and action of performance. In S. Goodman and K. O'Halloran (eds) (2006) *The Art of English: Literary creativity*. Basingstoke: Palgrave Macmillan.

Finnegan, R. (2007) *The Oral and Beyond: Doing things with words in Africa*. Oxford/Chicago: James Curry/University of Chicago Press.

Hymes, D. H. (1975) Breakthrough into performance. In D. Ben-Amos and K. S. Goldstein (eds), *Folklore: Performance and communication*. Approaches to Semiotics 40. The Hague/Paris: Mouton & Co.

John-Steiner, V. (2006) *Creative Collaboration*. New York: Oxford University Press.

Lee, T. (2016) *Princesses, Dragons and Helicopter Stories: Storytelling and story acting in the early years*. Abingdon, Oxon: Routledge.

Littleton, K. and Mercer, N. (2013) *Interthinking: Putting talk to work*. Abingdon, Oxon: Routledge.

Maybin, J. (2006) *Children's Voices: Talk, knowledge and identity*. Basingstoke: Palgrave Macmillan.

Maybin, J. and Swann, J. (2007) Everyday creativity in language: Textuality, contextuality and critique. *Applied Linguistics, 28*(4): 497–517.

Mercer, N. (2000) *Words and Minds: How we use language to think together*. Abingdon, Oxon: Routledge.

Mercer, N. and Littleton, K. (2007) *Dialogue and the Development of Children's Thinking*. Abingdon, Oxon: Routledge.

Norrick, N. R. (2000) *Conversational Narrative: Storytelling in everyday talk*. Amsterdam: John Benjamins.

Ochs, E. (1979) Transcription as theory. In E. Ochs and B. Schieffelin (eds), *Developmental Pragmatics*. New York: Academic Press.

Paley, V. G. (1990) *The Boy Who Would Be A Helicopter: The uses of storytelling in the classroom*. Cambridge, MA: Harvard University Press.

Pope, R. (2005) *Creativity: Theory, history, practice*. Abingdon, Oxon: Routledge.

Swann, J. (2007) Designing 'educationally effective' discussion. *Language and Education,* *21*(4): 342–359.

Swann, J. (2009a) Doing gender against the odds: A sociolinguistic analysis of educational discourse. In E. Eppler and P. Pichler (eds), *Gender and Spoken Interaction* (pp. 18–41). Basingstoke: Palgrave Macmillan.

Swann, J. (2009b) Stories in performance. In J. Maybin and N. J. Watson (eds), *Children's Literature: Mapping the field* (pp. 249–266). Basingstoke: Palgrave Macmillan.

Swann, J., Pope, R. and Carter, R. (eds) (2011) *Creativity in Language and Literature: The state of the art.* Basingstoke: Palgrave Macmillan.

Tannen, D. (2007) *Talking Voices: Repetition, dialogue, and imagery in conversational discourse.* New York: Cambridge University Press.

7

DRAMATIC CHANGES

Learning in storytelling and story acting

Gillian Dowley McNamee

Introduction

One morning in preschool, four-year-old Keisha is baking a birthday cake for her baby doll along with her best friend, Zoe. They have been absorbed in conversation for about 15 minutes. When their teacher, Veronica Adams, checks in with them, Keisha announces that she has a story to tell. Mrs Adams has her notebook in hand and writes down Keisha's words as she offers them in phrases. 'The wolf says, – "I will huff – and I will puff – and I will blow your house down".' Mrs Adams reads this back to her and asks, 'Anything else?' Keisha says no and goes right back to stirring a pot of beads and blocks, her cake ingredients.

Later, Mrs Adams guides the eighteen three- and four-year-olds in acting out the stories dictated by children during the morning activity time. The children sit around the edge of a large blue rug that becomes their stage. After a song and nursery rhyme, Mrs Adams announces, 'Time for stories. Keisha, your story is about the wolf. Do you want to be the wolf?' 'Yes.' Keisha is on her feet with a big smile and stands on the stage in the middle of the group. Mrs Adams reads, 'The wolf said, "I'll huff and I'll puff ..." Go ahead Keisha, you say it!' Keisha breathes like a wolf and says in a deep voice, 'I'll huff and I'll puff and I'll blow your house down!' Mrs Adams says, 'Good job, Keisha. That's a good wolf scene you have given us. Next story is Jessica's ...'

Keisha is distressed, 'You didn't write the part about the little girl!' Mrs Adams pauses, 'You didn't tell me about a little girl. What's that part?' Keisha steps right into her dictation voice, 'Little Red Riding Hood said, "I'll go to my house."' Without missing a beat, Mrs Adams calls the girl sitting next to her and says, 'You be Little Red Riding Hood. Let's do this again.' Mrs Adams reads the entire story – the two sentences, and the girls enact the completed narrative. Keisha is now ready to sit down as Mrs Adams moves along to Jessica's story.

Mrs Adams teaches in an urban neighbourhood school where families face economic challenges. Many of the children are learning English as a second language. She is participating in a professional development seminar studying the story dictation and dramatization teaching practices of Vivian Gussin Paley and their contribution to the foundations for learning to read and write. This chapter describes one morning of story dictation and dramatization in Mrs Adams' classroom as a case study of children's development in this configuration of activities. To examine the teaching and learning taking place, I bring the thinking of Russian psychologist L.S. Vygotsky to the discussion.

Vygotsky approaches an individual's development as it relates to the communities of people where he or she grows up and lives. His theory is ideal for thinking about learning and teaching in school. He explains a child's change over time not only in relation to one key person in a setting such as a parent or teacher, but accounts for the influence of others in the group, be it family or classmates. Vygotsky's signature concept describing the development of thinking is the zone of proximal development (1978: 84). He describes learning as happening twice. Development begins among people where the individual benefits from participation and guidance in a task from more experienced others (peers and adults), and later sustains thinking and problem solving from more internally regulated guidance derived from one's own initiative, focus and purpose. Learning in a zone of proximal development is a dynamic give and take between the individual and the group, with an individual gradually becoming aware of mastering and managing skills in activities important in the group.

For young children, Vygotsky describes pretend play as the quintessential activity that opens the way to change over time. As Vygotsky says,

> Play creates a zone of proximal development of the child. In play a child always behaves beyond his average age, above his daily behavior; in play it is as though he were a head taller than himself. As in the focus of a magnifying glass, play contains all the developmental tendencies in a condensed form and is itself a major source of development.
>
> *(Vygotsky, 1978: 102)*

Vygotsky's insights in concert with Vivian Paley's discoveries about storytelling and story-acting activities can help illuminate the potential power in work such as Mrs Adams' with her children in influencing each child's development.

The important characteristic of the storytelling and story-acting activities is their fundamental social purpose; the activities are propelled by children's desire to have their thoughts recorded daily in order that they can be read to the group and acted out. Vivian Paley noted early on in her writings how she discovered the significance of acting out stories with one boy, Wally, who was having a particularly bad day in school.

> We acted out [his] story immediately for one reason – I felt sorry for Wally. He had been on the time out chair twice that day, and his sadness stayed with

me. I wanted to do something nice for him, and I was sure it would please him if we acted out his story.

It made Wally very happy and a flurry of story writing began and continued all year. The boys dictated as many stories as the girls and we acted out each story the day it was written if we could.

Before we had never acted out these stories. We had dramatized every other kind of printed word – fairytales, storybooks, poems, songs, but it had always seemed enough to write the children's words. Obviously it was not; the words did not sufficiently represent the action, which needed to be shared. For this alone, the children would give up playtime, as it was a true extension of play.

(Paley, 1981: 12)

Vivian Paley's discovery that children will gladly give over play time to storytelling when dramatization is included as it is 'a true extension of play' is the insight that led me to connect her writings with Vygotsky's. Paley points out how young children telling stories that the teacher guides them in acting out makes it possible for the written word to influence learning – intellectual, social, and emotional – in an integrated, dynamic, transformative way. Her writings demonstrate the accumulated effect such learning can have on children's literacy learning in particular from ages three to seven (McNamee, 2005, 2015; Cooper, 2009).

There is one additional idea from Vygotsky about learning in pretend play that can further our understanding of the significance of storytelling and story acting. Keisha's pretend play in baking a birthday cake for her baby doll with Zoe, and her story about the wolf, are new psychological achievements for her. Using her imagination to create such hypothetical possibilities is in its very beginning stages of development, and she is currently deep into the practice of imagining with others. Vygotsky notes that,

Imagination is a new psychological process for the child; it is not present in the consciousness of the very young child, is totally absent in animals, and represents a specifically human form of conscious activity.

(Vygotsky, 1978: 93)

When children begin to pretend, their thinking is no longer constrained by the physical properties of an object or action in the present. They cross a threshold into the mental space where they can use actions, objects and words to represent something in the past, future or in a hypothetical world.

With the development and rapid expansion of skills in pretend play, children are able to have ideas and explore them in endless permutations. As Paley's writings demonstrate, storytelling and dramatization provide a stage (literally and figuratively) for children to engage in the practice of using their imagination in words alone – the bedrock of schooling. The hypothesis explored in this chapter is: When classrooms for young children are organized around pretend play, and have teachers who are skilled in leading storytelling and story acting, young children are positioned for an education that cultivates their greatest human potential.

The analysis of children's storytelling and acting offered here focuses on six stories dictated by Keisha and five classmates during a morning in November. The conversations around dictating and acting out stories provide insights into children's thinking and the influence of friendships as it unfolds in the context of the school day. In the dramatization of stories, we find the space where teachers and children close gaps in understanding, as Keisha and Mrs Adams did about the wolf and Little Red Riding Hood. What can we uncover about children's learning as they dictate and act out stories together, and what can this tell us about their potential change over time during the school year?

Mrs Adams is in her fourth year of teaching young children, and works with an assistant teacher, Mrs Johns. I participate in their classroom every week or two as a 'visiting teacher' to observe and assist them. I do so in order to experience and think further about the dynamics and challenges they describe in our professional development seminars and coaching conversations. I am an experienced teacher educator who carried out my own teacher preparation in Vivian Paley's classroom as her assistant teacher many years ago. I offer Mrs Adams and Mrs Johns a model of another teacher interacting with their children and interpreting classroom events. In discussing the classroom events, I provide support to their developing professional skills in one-on-one conversations as well as in seminars with other teachers with whom we work (McNamee, 2015).

Starting the school day: Creating space for stories in school

The children's school day begins with a hot breakfast sitting at tables together. When children finish, they clear their dishes and move to a large open space on a rug. They pick a book to read and talk with friends until the teachers are ready to guide the group in their activities for the day.

Today Keisha devours her breakfast and eagerly pulls me to the library area, takes the first two books within reach from the shelf, and says, 'I'll read this to you. Listen to me read.' I am ready. More children come crowding onto the rug with a book. Four-year-old Fernando arrives dragging his feet, face a bit downcast; he is slow to move into the daily routines. Marco has his favourite book so he chooses another listlessly while pushing to get as close to me as he can. His goal seems to be physical proximity to a trusted teacher.

Keisha becomes forceful. 'Listen to me! You all got to listen to the story. Look. You're not looking.' She notices me scanning the group, helping children find a space with a hand signal. When I do not give her my undivided attention, she becomes aggressive about getting it. Keisha reads the two books, and then grabs another. She announces, 'I'll read this to you!' She starts to read and then she calls out, 'You all not listening. I got to start over.' And she goes back to the first page. She does this three times, declaring more emphatically each time, 'You are not listening! I gotta start over.' I begin to feel exasperated, but I watch and listen. This has become my way to gauge a problem – watch the reactions of the children. The children are glued to the book she holds up. All is well.

Mrs Adams calls for group time with the hand gesture for one of their favourite games, 'Sparkle'. The children count off one by one around the circle up to ten. The eleventh child is the sparkle who waves their arms and fingers in the air like fireworks while everyone cheers. The children love this routine. They quickly move to the edge of the rug for the counting.

Mrs Adams and Mrs Johns sit on small chairs at different ends of the rug. The children often argue over who is going to sit next to a teacher. Today Zoe, Keisha's best friend, asks Mrs Adams if she can sit beside her. Mrs Adams agrees. Keisha is sitting across the circle where there is an open space. She starts to get up. Mrs Adams tells her to sit right where she is. Zoe follows up in a loud clear voice, 'Keisha, I need some alone time.' This is startling; everyone pauses for a moment and wonders. What is going on? Zoe is Keisha's friend but Zoe is asking for space. Keisha settles down. She listens to Zoe. A few minutes later, Keisha starts to get antsy again, but Zoe calls out forcefully, 'Keisha, I need my space!' I am in awe of the way Zoe sets boundaries for Keisha, and equally in awe that Keisha listens. How is it that these four-year-old girls are finding ways to regulate their feelings in words? What has Mrs Adams been saying to create such respect and safety in this classroom community to make it possible for children to work out their needs? I will ask her these questions when we meet at the end of the day.

Mrs Adams moves the group into singing today's nursery rhyme, 'Twinkle twinkle little star'. Keisha grows restless. She crawls toward me whispering, 'Tie my shoe.' I tell her, 'Not now.' I keep my eyes on Mrs Adams. In her squirming around, Keisha slips over to sit between Luis and Zoe. Luis is the youngest and smallest child in the class and Zoe's other best friend. Zoe plays a role like that of a big sister to him. Zoe and Luis accept Keisha's arrival at her new place on the rug. A few minutes later, Mrs Adams says to her, 'Keisha, control your body.' She is twirling around and pulling her shoelaces.

From the moment the children enter the classroom, they are steeped in literacy practices – conversation, book reading, and singing songs. The first word they write each day coming into the classroom is their name, or their closest approximation of it. Keisha exhibits the confident command of a good reader and writer who knows the daily routines, and knows how to select books that will draw readers to her. She can lead the group with her authoritative teacher persona, and yet she needs the help of her teacher and friends to control her distractibility and fidgetiness.

Keisha shows that she is listening carefully. She provides structure for others and yet needs the reminders and directives from peers and teacher to manage herself. The space for learning in these relationships is reciprocal. The control for learning and source of the wisdom in the lesson shifts among members of the classroom community, and moves around the group in rhythms. Sometimes the teacher carries the insight that the group can benefit from, and sometimes 'the lesson' is coming from a child. This give and take in relationships is the holding ground for learning, the space inside of which literacy learning advances. This is Vygtosky's space for learning, the zone of proximal development where the child is in a prime position to benefit from adult guidance and collaboration with more capable peers.

Children's learning here, and later during storytelling and acting, is not happening inside of discrete bounded instructional lessons. While teacher-initiated and guided activities are the building block of the school day, children's learning is far more fluid in terms of who is teaching and when. Learning ebbs and flows in relationships among many people. Children's learning becomes evident from their attentiveness to what is happening in the moment, in their imagination, and in their preoccupations (worries, anticipations, sadness) from home and school events. How teachers navigate learning around the contours of what their children imagine, and what is real, is the excitement of classroom teaching and learning.

Focusing the group – one class/one story

Mrs Adams reads *The Three Billy Goats Gruff* with great expression and with the children's full attention. When she gets to the Billy Goats on the bridge, she asks a child to come to the centre of the circle to act out the littlest Billy Goat. The children love doing this. When the third Billy Goat is about to confront the troll, Mrs Adams has an idea. She says, 'Zoe, go get the baby doll in the house corner.' Zoe hesitates. She does not move. Mrs Adams says, 'Come on, go get the baby doll.' Zoe said with some exasperation, 'OK'. It is clear that she does not like the thought of whatever Mrs Adams has in mind for bringing a baby doll into the scene with the Billy Goats and the troll.

Mrs Adams calls Eduardo into the circle to be the biggest Billy Goat. She says, 'Pretend this baby doll is the troll.' This turns out to be a terrible move, Mrs Adams gradually realizes, using the baby doll in her green tutu and pink shirt, to act the part of the troll. Mrs Adams asks Eduardo to act out the Billy Goat knocking the troll into the river. She lays the baby doll on the floor where Eduardo can pretend to kick it, acting out the troll's fate as the Billy Goats went up the hillside to make themselves fat. Zoe is horrified. The other children become confused along with her. Mrs Adams gets the message; she says at the end of the story, 'Uh-oh, I can tell Zoe's mad about me using the baby doll in this story.' She moves the group along good-naturedly, calling children to line up for the bathroom.

Mrs Adam's miscalculation with the baby doll as a prop for the troll illustrates how pretend play and dramatization of stories work for young children. The children are aware that there is nothing mean, threatening and scary about the baby doll. The vulnerability of a baby is the opposite of what they imagine in trying to understand the villain in this story. They are better off having nothing but their imagination for the menacing troll. The children's reaction to this misstep in teaching provides evidence of the strength in their thinking. How does a teacher repair such a mistake? We can wonder and watch. The children have a lot more to tell us.

Wolf, pigs and princesses

The children head off to activities in different play areas of the classroom with clarity of purpose. I was sure that Zoe was going to insist that one of the teachers get right to work with her on a dictated story because she has already asked several times for someone to write 'her script'. Zoe's grandmother reports that Zoe will be in their church fashion show, and that during rehearsals, one of the Women's Club leaders has a script for the event on a clipboard that children and parents will follow. Thus Zoe asks her teacher to write 'her script' when the invitation is offered for children to dictate a story.

Today, however, Zoe goes right to a table with Keisha, declaring she has to bake a cake for her baby. She takes the baby doll with pink shirt and green tutu along with her. The playtime becomes a therapy session for the baby doll. Zoe keeps her baby at her side for the next hour, pampering her.

Mrs Adams follows Fernando to the easel where he picks up a paintbrush alongside Ana. Fernando has not said a word yet in school today. Mrs Adams tells me later that she decides to approach Ana first about a dictated story to create an opening for connecting with Fernando. She asks Ana if she has a story to tell. Ana, who speaks in a barely audible whisper, is ready.

> Once upon a time there was a girl. The wolf come and get her. And the pig came and got the big bad wolf and saved grandma. There was a princess with Snow White and the big bad wolf was their friend.

Mrs Adams asks, 'Who do you want to play when we act this out?' Ana answers, 'Princess'. Mrs Adams, said, 'Good story. I like the way the wolf becomes friends with the princess and Snow White in this story.'

While Ana dictates her story, Fernando talks ever so quietly to himself as he makes big swirls of green. It is hard to understand him but he is absorbed in painting. Mrs Adams follows up with him, 'Fernando, would you like to tell a story?' He replies right away: 'The big bad wolf eat the three little pigs. They fix the house.' Mrs Adams echoes each word as she writes it down, and then adds, 'You are thinking about the three little pigs and the wolf. Ana has one of the pigs in her story too, and the wolf.' Fernando is on the wavelength of Ana and other classmates who are thinking about imagery from the stories their teacher reads to them. In the children's imagination, there is no problem with characters that get eaten; they can still move on with their day, and even make friends with the wolf.

For Fernando and Ana, the invitation to tell a story hoists them into the position of engaging in literacy practices – using their imagination to construct scenes to be recorded, like those in books read to them, that others can listen to and appreciate. The children do this even though they are not doing the reading and writing yet themselves. They watch each and every word they use to conjure up the outlines of a scene with its unfolding actions scribed onto a page that the teacher can read back to them as well as read to the group later. The children, without knowing it, are apprentices to the crafts of writing and reading. They are participating in the physical training and mental discipline of how authors transform imagery into words on paper. The children are on their way to becoming writers and readers who can give voice to meaning in their daily lives in writing with school friends (McNamee, 2015; Cooper, 2009; Lee, 2015).

A birthday: Squares, bears, the alphabet and pegs

Mrs Adams circles by Keisha and Zoe who are absorbed in making birthday cakes. They each have a metal cookie tray with magnetic alphabet letters placed in every direction filling it. They use little counting cubes to fill in the spaces and then place small counting bears on top of the squares. Zoe announces: 'We baking cakes. My baby havin' a birthday. Teacher, will you help us bake a cake? We gotta bake her a real nice cake.' The two girls are side by side decorating cakes in like fashion with bears and squares falling all over the place. Jessica is at the table playing quietly alongside them bringing out the pegboards and pegs to add to the table's resources. All three girls mix these ingredients, and put pegboards on top of the cookie trays to now be filled with letters, bears, and squares. The cakes are colourful structures. The baby doll in her pink tutu is happily laying in Zoe's lap.

Right next to these girls in the doll corner are Fernando, Ana, Isabella, Lena and Luis playing pizza restaurant. The cooking intensifies at both the game table and in the doll corner. I notice Mrs Adams' look of concern about the mounting mess. I whisper to her that I will sort the materials later, that the play is so good it is worth letting it go into what could be considered a real mess. She looks at me with a grimace of appreciation; she will not have to clean up alone. She nods in agreement. I have given us permission to wonder about what will happen next.

Mrs Adams asks Zoe if she is ready for her script, her story. She says, 'No, I have to bake for my baby' whom she holds tightly in her arm. Mrs Adams next asks Keisha who says, 'Yes, I want my story.' She dictates, 'The wolf says, "I will huff and I will puff and I will blow your house down."' She then goes back to her cake baking.

Mrs Adams approaches Jessica about a story. She says yes and starts right in. 'My mommy and my daddy and my sister, and my mommy and daddy keep fighting and my mommy go to the hospital and she bleeding.' Mrs Adams stops writing and puts her pen down. Mrs Adams and I have thought about what to do in such circumstances when a child begins to retell painful family events. Mrs Adams pauses, and then says to Jessica, 'I am sorry that your mommy and daddy were fighting.' Jessica says, 'Yeah, they fighting and my mommy bleeding and they be shouting …'

Mrs Adams lets her talk, and then waits. Jessica says nothing further. She is a quiet child who is attentive to the tasks asked of her in school. Mrs Adams tells her, 'I am glad that you told me the sad story about your mommy and daddy.' She pauses; she and I are both holding our breath to see what will happen next. Mrs Adams has been aware that there has been tension in Jessica's home. She will check in with Jessica's mother when she comes later, and touch base with the school social worker.

Mrs Adams continues by saying, 'I wonder if you want to tell a story that we can act out, one about bears or pigs or wolves.' Mrs Adams references some of the favourite characters in children's stories of late. Jessica nods and without hesitating starts in:

> I love my school. I love my teacher. I love my friends. I love Ana. I love Zoe. I love Keisha. I love Lena because they's my friends. I like to be in school. I like the movies. We watch the movies. The princess died because she didn't know. She got killed by Prince Droid.

Jessica's story calls forth sources of strength – friends in school who offer a safe spot in the face of danger along with brave efforts by literary heroes. In this moment, she finds a way to benefit from the presence of friends playing with her inside an imaginary story before she goes home. This is social and emotional learning tied directly into cognitive learning, inseparable partners in literacy learning that will carry a child for a lifetime.

Finally Zoe is ready for her 'script' to be written down. Mrs Adams comes over to sit by her and her baby doll. With the table piled high with birthday cake ingredients, Zoe dictates:

> My baby's going to turn six years old. She going to eat nachos, potato chips, cupcakes, ice cream, Doritos, tacos. She know how to say, 'I love mommy' (said in a baby voice). She know how to say, 'Run, baby, run!' She know how to say, 'Jump, baby, jump!' She even know how to say her own name. She can jump.

As Zoe dictates, she bounces the baby doll on her knees while gently smiling at her. Zoe has revived the baby after the appearance on stage as the troll. Zoe now has the baby fully immersed in a baby's world. Zoe is the one who is growing up to become six, as the baby doll in her story will, but she must not be rushed. She, and her baby doll, need the reassurance of mothering and taking small steps in play as well as in reality. Zoe is able to create a way to mend and comfort herself in play along with offering creative possibilities in her friendship with Keisha and Jessica who are her steadfast partners in cooking. The birthday party helps each of the girls manage in the daily steps and missteps of growing up in school. This happens also for each of the children playing alongside one another in the doll corner where there are clothes and food all over the floor.

Vivian Paley summarizes her unspoken message to children about their play, storytelling and story acting as follows:

> Let me study your play and figure out how play helps you solve your problems. Play contains your questions, and I must know what questions you are asking before mine will be useful.

Even this is not accurate enough. Today I would add: Put your play into formal narratives, and I will help you and your classmates listen to one another. In this way you will build a literature of images and themes, of beginnings and endings, of references and allusions. You must invent your own literature if you are to connect your ideas to the ideas of others.

(Paley, 1990: 18)

Paley articulates here the role of her listening and guidance connecting the children to one another, and ideas that have been invented and written about that the children can inherit over time. She is describing how she creates a zone of proximal development for children, the protected place for learning and teaching in her classroom.

As we listen to children's dictated stories in Mrs Adams' classroom, we watch how the children are drawn to weaving elements of literature into their attempts to formulate their own images of possible worlds. The children's thinking is connected to that of the authors Mrs Adams reads to them, and to their peers as authors. Mrs Adams is finely attuned to the narratives emerging, and the connections children are making. She gathers up the children's narratives in her conversations with each for the larger goal to come: acting them out.

Last-minute rescue

The children have been playing at various activities for a good 45 minutes when Mrs Adams calls for clean-up time. I pick up trays, buckets, and saucepans full of the birthday cake ingredients and put them on a shelf to sort later. In the middle of putting away blocks and table puzzles, Isabella tugs at my shirtsleeve saying, 'I have a story.' This is her first request ever to tell a story. She speaks Spanish predominantly but is learning some English. Mrs Adams and I both have had the goal to seek more storytelling with Spanish-dominant children. Isabella is offering me a chance to do so. How could I resist such a request with the possible insights it might afford?

I quickly pull her aside and ask, 'What happens in your story?' I scribble as fast as I can. Her voice is strong and clear, making sure I understand her words.

One princess and one baby and one castle and one prince. The monster tear down the castle. He drag out the princess and the prince rescue the princess.

Isabella constructs a scene complete with key characters, setting, plot and resolution, all in three tight sentences of 28 words. She marks her narrative debut in English with a lively imagination, and a full set of literary resources at her fingertips. She is digging deep into her new language for words to portray her story yearning to be told.

It is a huge effort for any child, and particularly those acquiring a new language, to identify one scene from the many different ones crowding their mind at any one moment in order to tell a story. Isabella focuses on one image that she anticipates her peers and teacher will listen to. She realizes she has to describe it well, and particularly under the time constraints of clean-up time. The scene cannot be too messy or complicated. Story dictation requires discipline, focus and clarity. The child is efficient in her word choices, offering the listener a scene she imagines – characters, dilemma, and a happening of some sort. Isabella has the courage of prince and princess in authoring her story in this moment, a few short minutes before it will be enacted.

Dramatizations

I join Mrs Adams on the rug to gather up the excited energy in the room. The children are nearing the end of their school day and anticipate going home. Mrs Adams calls for twinkling stars: the wiggling of fingers to accompany the singing of 'Twinkle twinkle little star'. Mrs Adams moves right to acting out each story that has been dictated. From my own experience plus coaching advice from Vivian Paley (McNamee, 2015), I advise Mrs Adams in such moments to push ahead with determination and goodwill to act out each story, letting the momentum of the narratives carry the group. The noisy energy can be a testament to engagement rather than disruption. It emulates the spirit of Elizabethan theatre, as Vivian Paley describes, where the audience is a lively partner in the staging of stories. Several times Mrs Adams quiets the group to regain focus. The noise level returns when the stage fills with characters for the next story, but we come to see that as part of a good day in school. When the teacher accepts the children's liveliness as part of what theatre enactments engender, and knows that the children appreciate every second of the story acting, goodwill carries everyone to the close of the school day.

Mrs Adams reminds the children that she will point to one child after another around the circle, offering each a chance to be an actor as needed in the stories. They will all get a turn to act, and perhaps several. She also adds, 'Remember, no touching. Just like in your playing, actors *pretend*.' Ana's story is first: 'Once upon a time there was a girl.' Mrs Adams narrates as Ana comes into the circle happily as a princess. Mrs Adams asks each child sitting next to her, 'Do you want to be the wolf?' Luis scrambles onto the stage. To Eduardo she asks, 'Do you want to be the pig?' He is ready to go. To Maria, 'Do you want to be the grandma?' They enact their part as Mrs Adams narrates each phrase.

Fernando's story follows with the wolf and three pigs having their run-in. It takes less than 60 seconds to enact: three pigs, a wolf eating them, and the three pigs fixing their house. Both story scripts are sparse and yet concise. The stepping in and out of scenes increases every child's mental flexibility within hypothetical worlds, and all of it happens in words alone.

Keisha's story provides insight into how the impromptu nature of story acting can help an author see when there is an essential missing piece in portraying an idea. In the acting out of her story, author, actors, audience and stage director handle such adjustments with ease. Everyone benefits from the more polished narrative that Keisha completes with the addition of Little Red Riding Hood in a second sentence, and from acting out the story twice.

Jessica's second dictated story about being in school with friends is acted out with Jessica choosing the role of narrator. Mrs Adams feeds her the lines: 'I love my school.' She then coaches Jessica, 'Show us what it is like when you walk into our classroom loving school.' Without saying a word, Jessica walks around the stage happily. As Mrs Adams reads, 'I love my friends,' Jessica continues to walk. Mrs Adams reads the names of her friends who each smile from their seat on the edge of the rug. For the princess and Prince Droid, Mrs Adams invites the next two children to the rug to enact the final moment. Mrs Adams is nimble in taking the children's literary wishes and turning them into moments where children become 'a head taller' as Vygotsky says, as actors trying on new personae, and as contributing members to an appreciative audience. The classroom storytelling culture will help children like Jessica benefit from the narrative lifelines around them.

In Zoe's story, Zoe plays the part of the mother and Lena is the baby growing up. The two girls stand in the centre of the stage with Zoe gazing at her baby. Mrs Adams reads the script slowly through the long list of her baby's favourite foods. It offers a fantasy every child savours: enjoying tacos, potato chips, cupcakes, and ice cream. Mother and baby are in their element; the baby eats, talks, and jumps while her proud mother watches. Mrs Adams notes, 'Zoe's baby likes to eat like the very hungry caterpillar in yesterday's story [*The Very Hungry Caterpillar* by Eric Carle, 1969].' The weaving of influences from a variety of authors is evident in this literary community.

Isabella's story provides the grand finale to the day's acting. A teacher could not ask for more: a heroic scene of a prince rescuing a princess, and this story from a child learning English as her second language. Six children, one-third of the class, have been authors on this day, and twenty-one individual roles have been enacted. One story involved the whole class as actors. All of this was orchestrated through the teacher and children's imagination guided by the printed word awaiting their full expression in acting.

The children go to tables for fruit and crackers before they leave for home. There are no stragglers today; the classroom empties quickly. Mrs Adams and I finish the clean-up while we compare notes on each of the children in the day's activities.

Assessing change

Story acting is the time of day when we see children benefit from as well as demonstrate their acute awareness of ideas that are in the air during their school day. Three aspects of the psychological space for learning are evident in the storytelling and story-acting activities that Mrs Adams leads. First is the space for relationships among children and teacher that intricately link the details of the school day. As any teacher knows, academic learning is not a process of managing the personal and interpersonal needs of children separate from the more intellectual and academic. Social and emotional learning is intertwined in all that they do together throughout the day.

Second, the space for learning is in the moment, 'in the air' as J. Bruner says, in the space among people (Bruner, 1978: 44). Story acting becomes the lesson everyone is studying – whether the content derives from a teacher or the children. The influence of story acting is most effective in the school day when there is a rhythm of teacher and child content being offered to the group for consideration, explication, and seeding the ground for new possibilities to wonder about.

The third aspect of the space for learning in Mrs Adams' classroom is the opportunity for imagination, the children's and the teachers'. Sometimes an attempt at imagining misfires, as it did when Mrs Adams thought of using a baby doll in dramatizing a story. However, within the framework of dramatization, there is the expectation for change and new ideas. There is room for the dynamic shifting ground for potential, what is possible in a hypothetical situation. Story dictation and dramatization place the child's learning and growth in the province of abstract logical thinking, the place schooling hopes high-achieving students will inhabit. Children come through the school door as characters in costume in their imagination, ready to don them in a moments' notice in the next story to be told and acted out. When there are opportunities for dramatizing stories, all eyes are on learning.

The presence of dramatic play mediated by words provides evidence of children achieving academic goals. The children gravitate toward the space where they can wonder, have conversations, and pretend. When given the invitation to have a story written down, the children demonstrate their willingness to take a piece of their imaginary thinking and commit it to written words to be offered to the group in the growing give-and-take of story imagery. Dictating is exciting, but teacher and children alike are on the edge of their seat wondering what someone will portray next, and what new ideas will emerge as they are acted out. The stage for story acting is the 'seeing space' as Trisha Lee calls it, 'the place where people come to see the truth about life and the social situation' (Lee, 2015: 67).

The work of Paley and Vygotsky helps us appreciate how story acting offers one of the most powerful learning opportunities in a school day because it joins the power of speech with the imagination to revisit and reorganize our perceptions of the world as well as create new possibilities to think about. Dramatizing stories creates new connections between the child's imagination and spoken word, and then between the spoken with written word. The activities provide ties between child and teacher, and child with their peer group as sources of influence and motivation to continue speaking and thinking together.

Dramatization of stories is unique in that it requires the basic teaching skills of listening, observing closely, and harnessing the imagination of everyone in exploring new ideas. Dramatization holds children's interest, motivation and focus. It is a step forward from pretend play toward a new achievement in human development as children become thinkers in written language as well as spoken. The teacher holds the ingredients of higher-order thinking at everyone's fingertips:

imagination, spoken word, and written, held in a tightly orchestrated structure of authors and actors on a stage.

The movement of children from spoken language into a written language culture is complex and exhilarating. By age three, children arrive at preschool ready to cultivate their human potential using words to create imaginary worlds with one another. What Vivian Paley discovered with storytelling and story acting is that teachers can build on children's pretend play skills to expand and transform them into written possibilities through an apprenticeship in storytelling and acting. Dramatic change is under way when a teacher listens closely with pen in hand as children explain who the wolf is, and how characters make friends with the villains as well as the heroes in their stories.

References

Bruner, J. (1978) Learning the mother tongue. *Human Nature*, September: 43–49.

Cooper, P. (2009) *The Classrooms All Young Children Need: Lessons in teaching from Vivian Gussin Paley*. Chicago, IL: University of Chicago Press.

Lee, T. (2015) *Princesses, Dragons and Helicopter Stories: Storytelling and story acting in the early years*. London, UK: Routledge.

McNamee, G. D. (2005) The one who gathers children: The work of Vivian Gussin Paley and current debates about how we educate young children. *Journal of Early Childhood Teacher Education, 25*: 275–296.

McNamee, G. D. (2015) *The High Performing Preschool: Story acting in Head Start classrooms*. Chicago, IL: University of Chicago Press.

Paley, V. G. (1981) *Wally's Stories*. Cambridge, MA: Harvard University Press.

Paley, V. G. (1990) *The Boy Who Would Be a Helicopter*. Cambridge, MA: Harvard University Press.

Vygotsky, L. (1978) *Mind in Society: The development of higher psychological processes*, eds M. Cole, V. John-Steiner, S. Scribner and E. Souberman. Cambridge, MA: Harvard University Press.

8

VIVIAN PALEY'S 'PEDAGOGY OF MEANING'

Helping Wild Things grow up to be garbage men

Patricia M. Cooper

Introduction

Laura, a former teacher education student of mine, writes, 'And did you know Max grew up to be a garbage man? Can I count this as a story?'

Laura was referring to a picture she attached in her e-mail, which shows a little guy named Oscar, a three-year-old English language learner, sitting next to a toy garbage truck on a classroom table. Laura had asked him if he wanted to tell a story, and, pointing to the driver's seat, he said, 'Max'.

The answer as to whether Oscar's one-word reference counted as a 'story' is simple: of course. I base my response on what I know about story and, just as important, what I know about Oscar. He is an English language learner in Laura's preschool class. Polish is his first language. I also know that Laura regularly engages him and the other children in the paired activities of storytelling and story acting first described by early childhood teacher and author Vivian Gussin Paley (1981). They comprise what I call her 'storytelling curriculum' (Cooper, 2009; Cooper et al., 2007). Laura says the children, almost all of whom are English language learners, often tell and act out their stories in a mixture of Polish, English and gestures.

Another thing I know is that Laura, who doesn't speak Polish, makes a practice of reading the children's favourite books over and over again for both their pleasure and their English language development. Maurice Sendak's (1963) *Where the Wild Things Are*, with its anti-conformist, wild thing, hero Max, is one Oscar likes best. Laura tells me (in a separate e-mail) that after re-reading the book once again, Oscar jumped up and told her, 'I love you', and then – bit her hand.

Obviously, we can't know for sure what story Oscar would tell if he had all the English words he needed. That his father drives a garbage truck? (He does). That Max (Oscar) is the sort of boy who eventually settles down and grows up to be a responsible citizen? (In other words, no need to worry.) Again, we can't be certain. What we do know from developmental theory, however, is that when you're three years old, the things you imagine are often the things you are trying to understand or control. From this perspective, it is easy to see Oscar's story – one word or a head full of words and thoughts he cannot yet express in English – as an imaginative embrace of Max's wise decision to leave the wild rumpus and get on with the business of growing up.

My confidence in this assessment comes from my experience as a classroom teacher, teacher educator, and researcher of Paley's storytelling curriculum, which, I argue, lies at the heart of her 'pedagogy of meaning' (Cooper, 2009). First, according to Paley, the stories young children tell and act out are an 'extension' of their natural interest in pretend play and all its benefits (Paley, 1981: 12). Viewed from Vygotsky's (1978) work on the role of imaginative play between three and six years old, storytelling and story acting can be seen as foundational activities to such developmental accomplishments as separation, self-concept, and self-regulation.[1] Over the years, Paley came to view the storytelling curriculum as her best pedagogical effort to satisfy young children's developmental thirst for imaginative release in school. 'If readiness for school has meaning', she writes, 'it is to be found first in the children's flow of ideas, their own and those of their peers, families, teachers, books, and television, from play into story and back into more play' (Paley, 2004: 11).

This chapter explores storytelling and story acting from the inside out to showcase the constructivist and moral character of Paley's pedagogy of meaning. I also show that prevailing educational trends in kindergarten writing instruction that exclude imagination-based writing compromise these essential pedagogical goals, while simultaneously deflating children's development as storytellers, sense makers, and, ultimately, readers and writers.

The power of pretend play

Imaginative thinking and play in preschool and kindergarten

A thorough review of the research on imaginative play in or out of school is beyond the scope of this analysis. Nevertheless, it is important to place the imagination-based stories that comprise storytelling and story acting in a historical and theoretical context if we are to appreciate the complexity of Paley's achievement, as well as resist efforts to replace imaginative play, including imaginative narrative compositions, in preschool and kindergarten.

Briefly, play in early childhood has long been constructed in terms of categories unfolding in a linear, developmentally progressive sequence: social, physical, object, constructive, dramatic, or games with rules. Parten's (1932) classic study on the six levels of growth in children's social play (observer, solitary, onlooker, parallel, associative, and cooperative) suggests the recursive nature of play, wherein the individual categories grow more complex as children mature. In addition, the borders between categories are naturally somewhat porous, leading to a good deal of overlap. For example, even children below three can learn to deliberately blend different types of play, as is what typically happens in block play.

More recent scholarship, including Xu (2010), suggests play sequences or sub-categories may not be universal, but are dependent on experiential and cultural factors, such as community expectations and parenting values. Further, other research suggests dramatic play in particular is a function of culture and opportunity (Goncu and Gaskins, 2007; Lancy et al., 2010). Although the present discussion recognizes this tension in the literature, it is governed by Vygotsky's theory of imagination-based play as a foundational problem-solving activity for children between three and six (Vygotksy, 1978).

The common showcase for dramatic play in early childhood is role-playing imaginative-based subjects not directly related to functioning in real time. Indeed, this is hard to miss when watching young children at play. (Henceforth, the term dramatic play is used interchangeably with imaginative, creative, pretend, and fantasy play, and refers to those instances involving imagination-based thinking, including that exhibited in storytelling and story acting.) American philosopher and educator John Dewey, however, warns against making observable data the proving ground of young children's imaginative thinking. Dewey, an acknowledged influence on Paley's teaching philosophy, theorizes that if story form is the natural intellectual activity of young children, the defining criterion of true imaginative play, he argues, is the child's underlying mental attitude or psychological engagement. The test of imaginative play's success depends on whether it guides the child to a 'higher plane of perception and judgment' of some idea or event (Dewey, 1900/1990: 127). In this sense, Dewey aligns with Vygotsky to see the significance of what children do and say in imaginative play, not from how it seems to us, but what it *means* to them.

Modern interest in the role of young children's imaginative play in development is broad reaching and ongoing (for example, see Hirsh-Pasek et al., 2009; Johnson et al., 2005; Pellegrini and Boyd, 1993; Singer et al., 2006). In general, research highlights its cross-developmental benefits, which advance young children's social, emotional, and identity development, as well as cognitive and linguistic skills (Ashiabi, 2007; Bodrova, 2008; Lillard et al., 2013). Much of the research also reports a steady erosion of time for imaginative play in American preschools and kindergartens in favour of an academic curriculum, despite the fact that the National Association for the Education of Young Children (NAEYC) has long promulgated imaginative play as a key feature of 'developmentally appropriate practice' (Copple and Bredekamp, 2009). Ironically, critics have noted that NAEYC has steadily increased its emphasis on the need for literacy sub-skills instruction in preschool and kindergarten (Cooper, 2009; Dickinson, 2002), adding to conflict and confusion in the field over the necessity of play in preschool and kindergarten. It must also be acknowledged that Lillard et al.'s (2013) descriptive review of the literature on the value of imaginary play concludes that the findings are on average more correlational than causal.

Vygotsky's theory of imagination-based play

Paley's work is also influenced by Vygotsky (1978), who argues that imaginary play is the highest level of preschool development (Vygotsky, 1978: 72). Its primary characteristic, he writes, is the reflexive way it scaffolds children's learning, creating, as it were, its own 'zone of proximal development' (Vygotsky, 1978: 102). We can infer from Vygotksy's oft-quoted belief (including by Paley) that a child in pretend play 'behaves beyond his average age, above his daily behaviour; in play it is as though he were a head taller than himself' (Vygotsky, 1978: 102). He is practicing skills he does not currently possess, while building the psychic and cognitive muscle needed for the ultimate possession of those he will need in the future. Berk (1994), Berk et al. (2006), and Bodrova and Leong (2007), among other Vygotskyan researchers, make the case for imaginative play's contribution to children's self-regulation in these terms.

Vygotsky sees imaginary play as the young child's natural option for the acquisition and practice of symbolic thinking, as well as the best preparation for later acquisition of scientific concepts and abstract reasoning. He writes that it emerges sometime in the third year 'at the point when unrealizable tendencies appear in development'. He suggests that rather than becoming overwhelmed by these tendencies, young children employ imaginative play to solve problems unsolvable in their real lives (Vygotsky, 1978: 93). Such problems can be as simple as a wished-for toy that doesn't arrive, or unease over a displeased mother, or, on a more intuitive level, a feeling of powerlessness in an unsafe world.

Paley's pedagogy of meaning

As I argue elsewhere, analysis of Paley's oeuvre reveals a two-pronged teaching philosophy (Cooper, 2009). First, she aims to be a moral teacher, the functional equivalent of which she describes as being a *fair* teacher. Her focus is equity across the relational or interpersonal spectrum. 'Is this classroom in which I live', she asks in *White Teacher* 'a fair place for every child who enters' (Paley, 1970/2000: xv). I categorize Paley's efforts in this direction as her 'pedagogy of fairness' (Cooper, 2009).

The second prong of Paley's teaching philosophy is her 'pedagogy of meaning', mentioned above. By this, I mean Paley's implementation of curricula that scaffold young children's investigations into or engagement with things, first, compatible with their *present* identity and knowledge base, and, second, the pull of new identities and knowledge. In this, we again see Dewey's influence.

I view Paley's pedagogy of meaning as threefold: 'From the perspective of praxis, a pedagogy of meaning requires the preschool and kindergarten teacher to create classroom life in and across three contexts; the probable, the personal, and the instructive' (Cooper, 2009: 48). As I write, preparation for the probable – the now – in the classroom includes classroom activities and schedules that fit usual expectations of competency and interest. Opportunities for choice of topic or content make way for the personal, and opportunities for problem solving make up the instructive – the future.

All of the above brings us to imagination-based play and stories. Like any good early childhood educator, Paley runs a well-rounded classroom that supports learning across the content areas. Nonetheless, she maintains that dramatic play, 'the serious and necessary occupation of children' (Dyson, 2009: 122), is the ideal classroom activity. We can see that the storytelling curriculum, which Paley believes is the natural extension of dramatic play (Paley, 1981: 12), adjusts automatically to individual children's competency levels and immediate interests. It also easily accommodates children's interests in the moment, as it simultaneously signals the future child through boosts to psychosocial development, as well as cognitive and language skills.

Paley's storytelling curriculum

Various efforts beyond Paley's own offer explicit descriptions of the storytelling curriculum and how to implement it (Cooper, 1993, 2009; McNamee, 2015; McNamee and Chen, 2007; Lee, 2015). Suffice to say for this analysis what Paley means by storytelling is the young child's response, usually oral, to some variation on the question 'Would you like to tell me a story?' Stories may be short (one word) or long (one page) depending on age, language, and purpose. Children whose language differs from their teachers may rely on gestures or small objects, and even classmates, to convey their stories. Still others with communicative disorders may rely on sign language or assistive technologies. An interesting fact is that with only a little exposure to what happens in storytelling, almost all children, even the very youngest, understand the teacher will act as scribe and write their story down to act out later on. I should underscore this does not assume that all three- and four-year-olds (and in some classrooms two-year-olds) have the cognitive awareness to *intentionally* create an oral narrative, let alone a coherent one. That is, the path to becoming a storyteller often begins in a pre-story, reporting-like stage, usually associated with toddlers.

Content, at first, is most often driven by something that actually happened to the storytellers, or some fact of their real lives. This type of story can be very meaningful to a child. For example, two-year-old Janie's first story – 'Mommy goes to work. Janie goes to school. We have snack. It's raining' – might be an attempt to simply record the day, or it might be Janie's reminder to herself that if Mommy is elsewhere, she is safe at school. What I mean to submit is that children in this stage have yet to harness the power of stories to solve problems by *removing* them from the confines of only real solutions.

This same limitation may apply to the uninitiated older storyteller, who hasn't grasped the freedom in storytelling yet. Becoming a storyteller and story actor assumes it's developmentally possible for children to eventually understand that to tell a story is not an invitation to report on the here and now (though it may use realistic elements), but an opportunity to share ideas not anchored in the moment.

Naturally, as children's language and understanding of what constitutes a story mature, their use of 'extended discourse', that is, language not based on the immediate situation, expands (Dickinson and Tabors, 2001).

Story acting is the dramatization of children's stories through the semi-formal process of enacting the words the teacher reads aloud. Props are rarely used. Typically, the author plays the main character, and classmates are invited to play additional characters as needed. Dialogue read by the teacher is repeated by the actors, who often will add more spontaneously. Again, it doesn't take children long to realize that if they tell a story, it will be acted out (usually on the same day), unless they request otherwise (which almost never happens).

The marriage of storytelling and story acting

Telling stories to the teacher, as well as acting out those found in books, holds long-standing and respected roles in preschool and kindergarten. Paley, however, is to be singularly credited with bundling the children's dictated and personal stories with acting them out as a regular choice in the classroom day. She reported her discovery of this powerful pairing when she followed one little boy's story dictation with its dramatization simply because she wanted to do something she thought a sad little boy in trouble might like (1981).

> The first time I asked Wally if he wanted to write a story, he looked surprised.
> "You didn't teach me how to write yet," he said.
> "You just tell me the story, Wally. I'll write the words."
> "What should I tell about?"
> "You like dinosaurs. You could tell about dinosaurs."
> He dictated this story.
> The dinosaur smashed down the city and the people got mad and put him in jail.
> "Is that the end?" I asked. "Did he get out?"
> He promised he would be good so they let him go home and his mother was waiting.
> We acted the story immediately for one reason—I felt sorry for Wally. He had been on the time-out chair twice that day, and his sadness stayed with me.
>
> *(Paley, 1981: 12)*

Bringing to mind Oscar's story in the introduction, Paley introduces us here to the idea that the content of children's stories is always deeply personal, however disguised. Wally (dinosaur) was feeling out of control, then over controlled (teacher who got mad), and finally rescued by his mother (mother dinosaur). She also introduces us, if not herself, to the teacher's role in fostering the child's ability to release himself from dinosaur jail or whatever restrictions inhibit his attempts to be whole or good.

Story themes

True stories. One question that hovers over Paley's interest in story content is what makes a 'true' story. In her Foreword to Paley's *Wally's Stories* (1981), Courtney Cazden reflects on the meaning of the imaginary content in the stories children tell with appreciation: 'When you are five, there is much in the world that needs to be accounted for, and these accounts are "stories" to us adults when children prefer magical explanations to those we call "true".' Paley might argue that the stories children tell – whatever the content – are not actual magical explanations of how the world works, but rather true explanations involving magic, *if by true we mean the most meaningful and by magic the most reasonable.* This is evident in Paley's defining interest in the child's pursuit of identity. Reeny, the child at the centre of her 1997 *The Girl with the Brown Crayon*, is a case in point. Paley characterizes Reeny's exploration of race and royalty in her princess stories as sending a personalized message to the world: 'This is who I am, and, so far, this is what I know to be true' (Paley, 1997: 4). Clearly, for Paley, true content is what makes sense to the child at a given time and place, as they seek to understand themselves and the circumstances of their lives. This doesn't mean, however, that story content reflects reality. As Dyson (2013) argues, 'a major aspect of children's *real* life is *pretend play*' (Dyson, 2013: 70; italics in original). Echoing both Dewey and Vygotsky, Paley says story content need only have felt meaning to the child, powerful enough to stimulate the problem solving and intellectual engagement so critical to long-term healthy development, from the psychosocial to the cognitive. The importance of all three thinkers around this point takes on even greater significance in light of the new Common Core Standards and a very popular writing curriculum in favour of non-fiction or 'true' stories, defined as reality-based, which I discuss below.

Prevalent themes. Paley was attracted to exploring thematic content in children's stories from the start. In *Bad Guys Don't Have Birthdays: Fantasy Play at Four* (1988), she finds bad guys, birthdays, and babies occupy the preschool-aged child. Stories involving fairness, magic, and power focus the kindergarten storyteller's mind, she writes in *Wally's Stories* (1981). Two more themes we might add for both age groups are royalty of all ranks and the animal kingdom. On first blush, we might also think to add superheroes as a distinct theme, only to realize that any discussion of good guys and bad guys in the play of four- and five-year-old boys is but a short hop to superheroes. I return to superheroes in a moment, but for now I'll simply note that, like most aspects of development, few themes stand alone in children's stories. This is how princess stories give way to babies and bad guys to a fear of the dark, depending on necessary detours of circumstance and growth. In fact, we might say 'it all depends' guides most young storytellers' plot developments.

Grand themes. In line with the consummate teacher she is, Paley's views on thematic content evolved as her classroom investigations into storytelling and story acting continued. At first, she locates particular themes, like lost bunnies and sleeping giants, inside of three major ones, friendship, fantasy, and fairness (Paley, 1988: 107). With regard to friendship, for example, Paley writes that each story told and acted out functions as an invitation to the storyteller's classmates to 'come play with me in my story' (Paley, 1981: 167). But, unlike story-based free play, which often can get beyond an individual child's control as she adjusts to other children's participation demands, children's dictated stories offer pre-ordained 'dependability' and the 'powerful certainty of outcome' (Paley, 1981: 122). For example, a more popular or domineering child may consistently grab the role of a mother rabbit looking for her lost bunnies in a free play event. But the child assigned the bunny role can reinvent herself as the mother rabbit without any opposition storytelling. Also, while free play can often break before a hoped for conclusion, almost all dictated stories come to a satisfying ending. That is, bunnies are found, bad guys are killed or jailed, and the pizza gets delivered in time for bed.

Eventually, Paley adds a fourth theme she finds in children's stories: fear. She writes that fear is the 'other side of friendship and fantasy' (Paley, 1988: 107), and explores the worry of isolation, the need to be rescued. Perhaps Paley's most stunning example of how fear makes its appearance in stories is that of Jason, a child who exhibits autistic-like behaviours in *The Boy Who Would Be a Helicopter: The uses of storytelling in the classroom* (1990). Paley refuses to label him, but Jason's daily fantasy play and storytelling involve an almost panicked concern with fixing his helicopter's broken blades. Paley tries hard to identify what aggravates his anxiety, but fails. Near the end of the school year, however, Jason creates a three-seater vehicle to rescue children he sees as being left at school. He invites Sara to take part in their rescue, to 'hold hands', as he flies off. It takes little imagination to see that he has, in effect, rescued himself and the others, Paley concludes:

> Jason may be revealing the biggest piece of the story. In his fantasy play no one has arrived to take the schoolchild home; *the child is lost at school.* Jason's helicopter will be the agent of rescue from school to home. The ultimate fear and loss, Jason tells us, is separation.
>
> *(Paley, 1990: 147)*

It is a seminal moment in Paley's teaching philosophy, but her work on the significance of story theme schemata is still not done. She lastly believes that she has been mixed up. Fear, friendship, and fairness are but only penultimate sub-themes of fantasy, which she comes to see as the uber motif, serving up a universal methodology for the successful exploration of all other themes. This is easy to see in the following stories, told and acted out in a Houston pre-kindergarten classroom. On the surface, they may appear bland or derivative to the adult reader, but upon closer inspection all clearly reveal the children's use of fantasy to integrate and explore fear, friendship, and fairness in the effort to grow up.

The Three Ninjas
By Paul
Once upon a time there was three Ninjas. They had two enemies. They were secret agents. They had a battle in a forest. The enemies jumped out of

a helicopter when they got to the forest and the good guys were going across trees jumping on the branches. They were fighting for a golden crystal. When the battle got over the good guys won. And then the good guys got the golden crystal. The End.

The Losting Animals
By Raina
Once upon a time there was a tiger and snake and a zebra that were lost in the forest. And they couldn't find their homes. So they spread up and find their homes. And when they were walking they saw some eagles and giraffes and monkeys. And they find their homes. The End.

The Friends That Fought and Never Again
By Mina
Once upon a time there was a cat and a dog and a rabbit and a turtle. Their owners were giving them food. But one day they escaped and they went under the fence. So, they saw each other. And they said, 'Hi, I am rabbit.' And the turtle said, 'Hi, I'm turtle.' And the cat said, 'Hi, I'm cat.' And they all wanted to be friends. But one day they started to fight. And the cat said, 'Hey turtle, you go so slow.' And the dog said to the rabbit, 'You jump so high.' And they started to fight a lot. So they went back home and they never fighted again. The End.

Paley's open attitude towards story content results from her deep understanding of why children are so drawn to storytelling and story acting. She tells us, 'The children's stories, lacking great plots and memorable prose, answered one of the children's most important questions: what do other children think about?' (Paley, 1981: 66). The sub-text captures the essence of Paley's pedagogy of meaning: children's interests, not teacher judgments, lead pedagogical decisions.

Embracing the unrestricted and the unoriginal content in stories

Both Paley and those who write on the stories young children tell (e.g. Cooper, 2009; Lee, 2015; McNamee, 2015) attest that the children's fantasy-based story content falls on a continuum between fantastical realism to downright out-of-this-world make-believe. An example of the first could be Drew's story of her birthday party with a hundred balloons. Hypothetically possible, but not plausible. Yet, the story does not stray far from a realistic frame of reference. Many birthday parties come with lots of balloons. In contrast, what surely leaves realism behind is Mariette's story of Princess Mariette, whose birthday cake is baked by fairies, and has *one thousand* candles.

As a teacher educator of Paley's storytelling curriculum for more than three decades, I am confident in saying that teachers agree with her on the contribution fantasy-based stories make to young children's thinking and healthy development.

But this doesn't mean they all agree with her on what constitutes acceptable story content, at least not at first. Many teachers new to storytelling struggle with the twin issues of unrestricted and unoriginal story content.

Unrestricted and unoriginal content. By age four, most children (though of course not all and not all the time) revel in telling fantasy-based stories. The specific content varies, but a significant proportion represent the sub-themes mentioned above. Teacher trainees, however, often react with horror when I advise them not to restrict the children's content matter in stories. 'You mean, they get to write about *anything*?' The teachers' response betrays their instantaneous concern that children will want to write about something from popular culture. A television show. YouTube. Worse, it might be a superhero movie or, heaven forbid, *Frozen*. In other words, children might want to write about things the teachers hear them talk about.

Experience proves the teachers right. Left to decide on their own, young children will just as often create plots based on television, movies, and other media, as they will the seemingly more innocent fare of babies and small animals. Anne Haas Dyson (2003) links permission to tell stories based on popular culture phenomena at the centre of children's investment in writing stories and other language and literacy-driven activities in a low-income African American community. Exhibiting her debt to Dewey and Vygotsky once again, the pedagogical question for Paley here is not how to discourage children's interests in particular story content, but why they are interested in the first place.

Borrowed content. Teachers often question why children persist in telling unoriginal stories. It's not just a story theme that may repeat among the storytellers. Sometimes it's the very plot, borrowed from popular culture or a shared class experience. Many beginning storytelling curriculum teachers fail to see the value in this approach, and urge children to tell their 'own' story, not to do what other children do.

Borrowed content is not a problem for Paley, for originality is not the point of the storytelling curriculum, nor is creative writing. Paley does not only expect repeated variations on a theme, she values them as the individual child's attempts to request or prove membership in the classroom community. To return to Jason and his helicopter, the point of borrowed content in storytelling and story acting at its extreme is to avoid isolation. In a more everyday sense, it is simply to make friends through common interests.

Boys and girls and superhero stories. The superhero story is one of the best examples of borrowed content at work. Contrary to expectations, however, it is as telling for girls as it is for boys. Focusing on the expected first, as a young kindergarten teacher I never doubted the appeal of superhero stories to the boys in my class, though I for sure underestimated the strength of their attraction. My reckoning came when after weeks and weeks of taking down *Star Wars*-themed stories; I decided I had had enough. I just couldn't scribe one more Hans Solo or Darth Vader adventure. I told the children I was taking a break. No *Star Wars* stories for the month of January. Secretly, of course, I was hoping to absent them long enough for the children to move on to another topic of interest. The children cooperated, and *Star Wars* disappeared from their stories. I was sure better minds had prevailed. Then, on a frosty winter morning, Peter came to the storytelling table. He began: 'One day, Hans Solo …' I picked my pen up from the paper, and said, 'Remember, no *Star Wars*.' Peter smiled mischievously, and pointed to our classroom calendar, as if he had been anticipating this delicious moment for a long time. 'February 1st', he said. I sighed and continued scribing.

Paley notes that with its basic plot structure and predictable language, the superhero story makes the fewest narrative demands on the storyteller. As a result, most sound alike. Authorship is barely conceivable. She has a breakthrough: 'This must be the point then, I decided. Such stories are used to mask, not reveal, individuality' (Paley, 1981: 129). One reason might be that boys, concerned over the power of the bad guy, give up their individuality in exchange for protection.

I wrote earlier that I find Paley's insight into the boys' retreat from individual identity in the name of safety simply extraordinary (Cooper, 1993, 2009), as it gives lie to the idea that little boys are out of control or more cognitively immature than girls. Nor does the stereotyping bother her. Paley associates most things superhero with boys and things princess-y with girls throughout her work. *Boys and Girls: Superheroes in the doll corner* (1984) opens: 'Kindergarten is a triumph of sexual stereotyping' (Paley, 1986: xiii). The children at play (and story), she says, are seeking a 'new social definition for "boy" and "girl"' (Paley, 1986: xv), even as she acknowledges that adults may disapprove or inquire about the chicken or egg nature of these stereotypes. But this is not the mystery she seeks to solve. Instead she puzzles over what purpose superhero and princess stories serve for boys and girls.

What then do we make of princess stories? What safety lies in their attraction to little girls? First, I need to acknowledge that the princess stories that emerge from the storytelling curriculum are no less mundane and ordinary than the average Ninja Turtle story. Stories without the authors' names on the top are as equally interchangeable as the boys'. Thus, we must ask if princess stories, too, are attempts at times to blend in, to cover up their personal essence, and steer clear of the group's power by assuming their own.

This brings us to Disney's *Frozen*. Although it's always reasonable to question why Disney animators insist on such overly shapely female characters (see Elsa's transformation in the 'Letting Go' segment), in all my years in early childhood education I can't think of another event in popular culture that has exerted such a grip on young children's imaginations, particularly girls'. Perhaps it's because the central characters, Princesses Elsa and Anna, finally make clear what little girls have known all along. Princesses *are* superheroes. Just those of the royal stripe. Yes, princesses no doubt rely more on magic than strength (a distinction between superheroes and princesses Paley's Deana treasures in *Wally's Stories* (1981)), but their effect on the world is no less diminished for it.

Paley suggests *Frozen*'s eminent appeal may be attributable to something we've not asked of the boys' superheroes to date. This is the unbreakable sibling bond hiding beneath the story of Elsa's runaway powers. 'There is magic enough to suit all tastes', Paley says, 'but essentially the story is about two sisters. The younger one represents all of us, rejected by an older sibling, but filled with love, loyalty, and optimism, nonetheless' (2015, personal correspondence).

Contrary to some expectations in the field, however, the child's urge to fit in, to gain control through donning a cape in a make-believe story, is not bad news. Despite the early childhood classroom's characteristic homage to individuality, young children should not be spared a basic opportunity in life. This is to create, or borrow, an avatar who will help them practice control over what they intuitively know they are too young and alone to control in real life, including power, sex, and death. Arguably, they depend on this practice in early childhood to counter these actual dilemmas in middle childhood and adolescence.

The careful reader may point out that whatever virtues can be found in boys' and girls' superheroes, more palpable fare in this vein is available from fairy and folk tales or other rich literature. Why can't children borrow from them for story ideas? Surely, this would make their stories more productive, and more rigorous. Assuming we've made such literature available to them, the fact is they can and very often do. Creating a false choice between fairy tales and modern-day superhero and princess stories is not the answer, though.

Exceptions to unrestricted content. Are there exceptions to this endorsement of unrestricted story content? I would argue yes. A prime example for me is 'bathroom stories', which reliably arrive in the early childhood classroom sometime in the fourth year. These stories are to be distinguished from the bathroom stories of two-year-olds, who sometimes tell about new potties or pull-up diapers. They are also different from bathroom jokes that have filtered down from the pervasive scatological humour found in modern movies. I'm referring to stories involving exposed bottoms, defecation, and urination told by young children after toileting is mastered and physical autonomy is well under way (see Erikson, 1950/1985). These are generally immature attempts by the storyteller in a bid for attention denied him by more popular children. Assuming no deeper problem than this, the wise teacher will simply encourage the child to think of something to tell about that the other children like to listen to.

A second example of story content that I do not allow is that which hurts another child's feelings. In this case, I simply suggest teachers talk with the storyteller about her refusal to allow stories that are unkind in spirit or word. Occasionally young children tell stories that clearly expose trouble at home. Teachers find it very upsetting, and often refuse to write the story down so as to protect both the child and the family. I suggest to teachers that they take the story down so the children will feel listened to, but they should explain that acting it out with the whole class might upset the parents if they don't ask permission before doing so. Children as young as four intuitively understand the dilemma the story has raised, and rarely press the point.

Acting in other children's stories. One delightful offshoot of the storytelling curriculum is when audience members and actors are able to utilize the content in other children's stories for their own personal growth. Three-year-old Sam, for example, agreed to act in Maura's story about going to Disneyland with her family. In acting out the story, Sam, who plays her brother, must pretend to go up and down a big slide at the water park. The teacher, on the sideline, wonders if Sam wants to act this out by holding his mother's hand up the stairs (I learned later that Sam is something of a cautious child). Sam immediately rejects her directorial suggestion, as well as the extended hand of the child playing the mother. 'By myself', he says in a low voice. The teacher, wisely, honours his request. 'Oh, you're big enough to go down by yourself?' Sam nods as he starts to pretend climbing stairs. Then he adds in a much smaller voice, as if almost to himself, '*Just in pretend.*' The larger story for Sam is risk taking. He has borrowed his classmate's story to overcome his own fears.

When stories *can't* come to school

This last section considers a growing phenomenon in early childhood writing education related to storytelling. As noted earlier, the daily schedule not only includes less time for fantasy play and fantasy-based stories. Exacerbating this problem is the fact that fantasy content in young children's oral and written narratives is frequently discouraged or outright banned in today's early childhood classrooms. I describe this trend as 'when stories *can't* come to school' (a riff on the title of an early book of mine on Paley's storytelling curriculum). Two distinct forces currently at work in early childhood education make my case. The first is the Common Core State Standards for ELA (www.corestandards.org), and the second is Lucy Calkins' influential writing workshop curriculum (1983/1994, 2015).

The Common Core Standards for writing in grades kindergarten through second grade with regard to 'types and purposes' are: 1) opinion pieces on topics and texts; 2) informative and explanatory texts; and 3) narratives. Expectations of competency increase by grade. Central to this discussion are the standards for narrative writing, the third type and purpose of writing instruction. In kindergarten, children are expected to write about a 'single event'. In first grade, they are to write on 'two or more appropriately sequenced events', in second on a 'well-elaborated or short sequence of events'. It is not until third grade that children are expected to write on 'real or *imagined* experiences' (italics mine). The upshot of standards that leave imaginative writing until third grade is that it instantly becomes devalued in the K-2 curriculum. We can expect, then, that it will fail to be emphasized, if included at all.

Lucy Calkins is founder and director of the Teachers College Reading and Writing Workshop, a well-known and widely disseminated reading and writing workshop curriculum. A signature requirement of writing instruction in the kindergarten year is that all content be 'true', but not true in a Vygotskyan or Paley-like sense, where what is true is what children think about. Rather, from the beginning, Calkins has meant true *as in real life*. 'When we ask [children] to choose their own topics for writing, they often write about superheroes or retell television dramas. In word and deed, our children ask: Does my life really matter?' (Calkins, 1983/1994: 6).

I find Calkins' characterization of young children's imagination-based stories troubling and out of sync with the lives of real children. I have never met a child who is questioning whether his life matters by indulging in superhero or television play. Instead, taking a page from Paley's notebook, I see young Batmen and Princess Leias as very much alive, attuned to the world, and eager to figure out their place in it.

Of course, if we need a technical reason to invite children's preferences for superhero, princess, and otherwise unoriginal content into the storytelling curriculum, we can always turn to language and literacy development. To ban popular culture, to ban children's imaginative writing, in the classroom is to automatically reduce the opportunity for free-flowing discourse between the children and us. Not only does this impede the aforementioned social bonding and group membership, foundational achievements of early childhood, we reduce opportunities to scaffold their language, literacy, and content knowledge, and, in the long term, their mental engagement with text. Thus, Calkins' goal to improve non-fiction writing by excluding imagination-based writing when the young clearly crave its indulgence is as wrongheaded as is the omission of it from the Common Core Standards for K-2.

Conclusion

On the face of it, Paley's storytelling curriculum is a straightforward affair. Young children dictate stories to the classroom teacher, and then act them out with their classmates, who serve as actors or audience members. To see storytelling and story acting in action is not necessarily to be awed. The children, as always, are charming, yet their stories can be as opaque to the observer as they can be unoriginal. Their acting abilities are equally limited. Research, however, allows us to dig deeper to support Paley's contention that the storytelling curriculum exemplifies what children need most from early childhood education: a platform of pretend on which to 'practice problems' (Paley, 1990: 80). Research shows, for example, that participation in storytelling and story acting can support such critical cognitive problems in early childhood as learning to take perspective, control the elements of narrative, and understand the concepts of print. Paley, though, clearly prizes the storytelling curriculum most for the way in which it allows children to practice solving the three F problems of early childhood: fear, friendship, and fairness, under the umbrella of the uber F, fantasy play. In this, the imagination-tolerant storytelling curriculum manifestly exemplifies Paley's pedagogy of meaning: to teach the children we have in the manner that is the most sense-making to them.

Yet, contrary to recommendations in the research, imaginative play is less and less valued in early childhood praxis today because children's psychosocial development, and even alternative routes to sub-skill mastery, are seen as unconnected to academic achievement. The modern teacher's loss here is no different from the children's. When we fail to find meaningful ways, like the storytelling curriculum, for Max to grow up and become a garbage man, and Sam to risk climbing higher, and Peter to save the universe from Darth Vader, we fail to become the problem solvers we, too, must be if we are to embody teaching as a 'moral act' (Paley, 1990: xii), a goal we deserve to *enact* every day.

Note

1   Although not the focus of the current analysis, it is also worth noting that researchers and educators have found demonstrable links between storytelling and story acting and children's language, narrative, and overall literacy development (including, but not limited to, Cooper 2005; Cooper et al., 2007; Dyson, 2003, 2009; Dyson and Genishi, 1994a, 1994b; Genishi and Dyson, 2009; McNamee, 2015; McNamee and Chen, 2007; Nicolopoulou, 1997; Nicolopoulou et al., 2015; Nicolopoulou et al., in press).

References

Ashiabi, G. S. (2007) Play in the preschool classroom: Its socioemotional significance and the teacher's role in play. *Early Childhood Education Journal, 35*: 199–207.

Berk, L. E. (1994) Vygotksy's theory: The importance of make-believe play. *Young Children, 50*(1): 30–39.

Berk, L. E., Mann, T. D. and Ogan, A. T. (2006) Make-believe play: Wellspring for development of self-regulation. In D. Singer, R. M. Golinkoff and H. Hirsh-Pasek (eds), *Play = Learning: How play motivates and enhances children's cognitive and social-emotional growth*. New York, NY: Oxford University Press.

Bodrova, E. (2008) Make-believe play versus academic skills: A Vygotskian approach to today's dilemma of early childhood education. *European Early Childhood Education Research Journal, 16*: 357–369.

Bodrova, E. and Leong, D. J. (2007) *Tools of the Mind: The Vygotskian approach to early childhood education*. Upper Saddle River, NJ: Pearson.

Calkins, L. M. (1983/1994) *The Art of Teaching Writing* (2nd edn). Portsmouth, NH: Heinemann.

Calkins, L. (2015) *Units of Study in Opinion, Information, and Narrative Writing: Grade K: A common core workshop curriculum*. Portsmouth, NH: Heinemann.

Cooper, P. M. (1993) *When Stories Come To School: Telling, writing, and performing stories in the early childhood classroom*. New York, NY: Teachers and Writers Collaborative.

Cooper, P. M. (2005) Literacy learning and pedagogical purpose in Vivian Paley's storytelling curriculum. *Journal of Early Childhood Literacy, 5*(3): 229–251.

Cooper, P. M. (2009) *The Classrooms All Young Children Need: Lessons in teaching from Vivian Paley*. Chicago, IL: University of Chicago Press.

Cooper, P. M., Capo, K., Mathes, B. and Grey, L. (2007) One authentic early literacy practice and three standardized tests: Can a storytelling curriculum measure up? *Journal of Early Childhood Teacher Education, 28*(3): 251–275.

Copple, C. and Bredekamp, S. (eds) (2009) *Developmentally Appropriate Practice in Early Childhood Programs: Serving children from birth through age 8* (3rd edn). Washington, DC: NAEYC.

Dewey, J. (1900/1990) *The School and Society: The child and the curriculum*. Chicago, IL: University of Chicago Press.

Dickinson, D. K. (2002) Shifting images of developmentally appropriate practice as seen through different lenses. *Educational Researcher, 31*(1): 26–32.

Dickinson, D. K. and Tabors, P. O. (eds) (2001) *Beginning Literacy with Language: Young children learning at home and at school*. Baltimore, MD: Paul H. Brookes.

Dyson, A. H. (2003) *The Brothers and Sisters Learn to Write: Popular literacies in childhood and school cultures*. New York, NY: Teachers College Press.

Dyson, A. H. (2013) *ReWriting the Basics: Literacy learning in children's cultures*. New York, NY: Teachers College Press.

Dyson, A. H. and Genishi, C. (1994a) *The Need for Story: Cultural diversity in classroom and community*. Urbana, IL: National Council of Teachers of English.

Dyson, A. H. and Genishi, C. (1994b) Visions of children as language users: Language and language education in early childhood. In *Handbook of Research in the Education of Young Children*, ed. B. Spodek (pp. 122–136). New York, NY: Macmillan.

Dyson, J. P. (ed.) (2009) Interview with Vivian Gussin Paley. *American Journal of Play, 2*(2): 122–138.

Erikson, E. (1950/1985) *Childhood and Society*. New York: Norton.

Genishi, C. and Dyson, A. H. (2009) *Children, Language, and Literacy: Diverse learners in diverse times*. New York: Teachers College Press.

Goncu, A. and Gaskins, S. (eds) (2007) *Play and Development: Evolutionary, sociocultural, and functional perspectives*. Mahwah, NJ: Lawrence Erlbaum.

Hirsh-Pasek, K., Golinkoff, R. M., Berk, L. E. and Singer. D. G. (2009) *A Mandate for Playful Learning in Preschool: Presenting the evidence*. New York, NY: Oxford University Press.

Johnson, J. E., Christie, J. and Wardle, F. (2005) *Play Development and Early Education*. New York, NY: Pearson.

Lancy, D. L., Bock, J. and Gaskins, S. (eds) (2010) *The Anthropology of Learning in Childhood*. Lanham, MD: AltaMira Press.

Lee, T. (2015) *Princesses, Dragons, and Helicopter Stories: Storytelling and story acting in the early years*. New York, NY: Routledge.

Lillard, A. S., Lerner, M. D., Hopkins, E. J., Dore, R. A, Smith, E. D. and Palmquist, M. (2013) The impact of pretend play on children's development: A review of the evidence. *Psychological Bulletin, 139*(1): 1–34.

McNamee, G. D. (2015) *The High-Performing Preschool: Story acting in Head Start classrooms*. Chicago, IL: University of Chicago Press.

McNamee, G. D. and Chen, J. (2007) *Bridging: Assessment for teaching and learning in early childhood classrooms, preK-3*. Thousand Oaks, CA: Corwin.

Nicolopoulou, A. (1997) Children and narratives: Toward an interpretive and sociocultural approach. In *Narrative Development: Six approaches*, ed. M. Bamberg (pp. 179–215). Mahwah, NJ: Lawrence Erlbaum.

Nicolopoulou, A. K, Cortina, K. S., Ilgaz, H., Cates, C. B. and de Sa, A. B. (2015) Using a narrative- and play-based activity to promote low-income pre-schoolers' oral language, emergent literacy, and social competence. *Early Childhood Research Quarterly, 2*(31): 147–162.

Paley, V. G. (1979/2000) *White Teacher*. Cambridge, MA: Harvard University Press.

Paley, V. G. (1981) *Wally's Stories: Conversations in the kindergarten*. Cambridge, MA: Harvard University Press.

Paley, V. G. (1984) *Boys and Girls: Superheroes in the doll corner*. Chicago, IL: University of Chicago Press.

Paley, V. G. (1988) *Bad Guys Don't Have Birthdays: Fantasy play at four*. Chicago, IL: University of Chicago Press.

Paley, V. G. (1990) *The Boy Who Would Be a Helicopter: The uses of storytelling in the classroom.* Cambridge, MA: Harvard University Press.

Paley, V. G. (1997) *The Girl with the Brown Crayon.* Cambridge, MA: Harvard University Press.

Paley, V. G. (2004) *A Child's Work: The importance of fantasy play.* Chicago, IL: University of Chicago Press.

Parten, M. B. (1932) Social participation among preschool children. *Journal of Abnormal and Social Psychology, 27*(3): 243–269.

Pellegrini, A. D. and Boyd, B. (1993) The role of play in early childhood development and education: Issues in definition and function. In B. Spodek (ed.), *Handbook of Research on the Education of Young Children* (pp. 105–121). New York, NY: Macmillan.

Sendak, M. (1963) *Where the Wild Things Are.* New York, NY: Harper and Row.

Singer, D. G., Golinkoff, R. M. and Hirsh-Pasek, K. (eds) (2006) *Play = Learning: How play motivates and enhances children's cognitive and social-emotional growth.* Oxford: Oxford University Press.

Vygotksy, L. S. (1978) *Mind in Society: The development of higher psychological process.* Cambridge, MA: Harvard University Press.

Xu, Y. (2010) Children's social play sequence: Parten's classic theory revisited. *Early Child Development and Care, 180*(4): 489–498.

9

EQUITY AND DIVERSITY THROUGH STORY

A multimodal perspective

Rosie Flewitt

Introduction

With the politically and economically motivated migration of peoples around the globe, many preschool and primary schools in England are enrolling an increasing number of young children who speak languages other than English. Whilst this phenomenon adds rich diversity to the classroom, it also presents challenges for teachers about how to create inclusive communicative and social spaces for individual children from ethnic and linguistic minority backgrounds, particularly when working within the constraints of national curricula that assume 'homogeneity and stability represent the norm' (Creese and Blackledge, 2015: 20). Through the lens of two young boys in the early stages of learning English, this chapter explores how Vivian Gussin Paley's storytelling and story-acting pedagogy (Paley, 1990, 1992, 2004) has creative and enabling potential for children to express themselves through multiple modes, such as actions and gaze as well as words, and how valuing multimodal narrating and acting can promote equity and celebrate diversity in the early years classroom.

The chapter draws on data from an evaluation of 'Helicopter Stories' training offered by a London-based theatre and education group, as described in Chapter 2, focusing on the stories told by three-year-old Jaime and five-year-old Wang Tai, in the preschool and Reception classes of one inner-city primary school in England. Both boys were described by their teachers as emerging speakers of English, and not fully integrated in classroom life. When the Reception class teacher began the 'Helicopter Stories' training programme, she expressed the hope that the storytelling and acting approach might create opportunities for non-native and less confident speakers of English 'to be able to show themselves in a different light to the other children because they might be very good at making up stories or acting out stories which other children will enjoy'.

The chapter begins by discussing multimodality, its relevance for stories and early literacy, its compatibility with sociocultural theories of learning and its potential for celebrating diversity and difference in the classroom. Through detailed analysis of a selection of stories told by the two boys, the chapter argues that valuing the communicative potential of all modes in storytelling and acting, rather than always prioritising oral and written language, enables young children from diverse backgrounds to share their personal interests, perspectives and expertise holistically, creatively and practically in ways that link with their imagination and promote their intellectual and social inclusion in the classroom.

Valuing children's multimodal storytelling and story acting

Storytelling is primarily associated with the spoken or written word, but multimodality offers a very different perspective on communication and learning by taking into account the wide range of modes we all use to make and express meaning. The term *mode* derives from social semiotics (Halliday, 1978), and refers to the ways that meaning can be represented through different 'signs' (semiosis) such as gesture, gaze, facial expression, movement, vocalisations *and* language. It also refers to the range of modes that we encounter in diverse texts, such as words, images and layout in printed texts, and wider modal combinations in digital media, such as spoken and written words, still and moving images, screen design, sounds, music and so forth. When communicating, children and adults choose 'the forms for the expression of their meaning which best suggest or carry the meaning, and they do so in any medium in which they make signs' (Kress, 1997: 12). One simple example that may resonate with early years practitioners is that young children rarely use the word 'big' without accompanying it with widening eyes, arm gestures or whole body movements to indicate a large size. From a multimodal perspective, this reflects a process of intentional choice making: the word 'big' is the usual 'sign' in the English-speaking world to signify the concept of 'bigness'. Yet it is a very small word, and gestures convey far more effectively the magnitude of its meaning. Sometimes, or oftentimes for young children with emerging language skills, words are simply not enough to get the feel of an idea across: 'Feelings show us the limits of our language. They bring home to us that language is not omni-competent; for we know far more than we can say' (Gibson, 1989: 58).

Although scholars have studied individual modes of expression such as gesture (Kendon, 2004; McNeill, 1985) and gaze (Kendon and Cook, 1969; Goodwin, 1980), including how gestures are used by storytellers, the communicative function of silent modes has tended to be seen as an *accompaniment* to speech rather than as communicating meaning *in their own right*. A multimodal perspective on communication recognises and values how different modes are selected purposefully during interaction, and how modes work together to create rich layers of meaning in a 'multimodal ensemble' (Kress et al., 2001). The term 'ensemble' draws an analogy with how each instrument in an orchestra contributes to a musical performance. Similarly in interaction, each mode makes a unique contribution to communicative performance. This significant shift in perspective 'is not simply a rephrasing of the field of study often called "nonverbal communication"' (Scollon and Scollon, 2014: 206), but offers radically new insights into how meanings are constructed through the intentional interplay of multiple modes.

One further tenet of multimodality is that all modes are shaped by social and historical norms, their use evolves in socioculturally situated practice but is also influenced by the particular motivations and interests of the sign-maker in a particular social context. To illustrate this with an example: a young child at home might habitually pull gently on their parent's clothes to indicate they would like the adult's attention, but will quickly learn that this way of communicating is not appreciated in school. In time, the child will 'redesign' their method using the orchestration of multiple modes to achieve their goal – most likely by learning to wait, using alert body posture and position to indicate waiting, gaze direction to indicate they are expecting a response, and ultimately using talk to express meaning once invited to do so. Waiting your turn in class has fairly fixed rules, yet at other times children have to work out unspoken rules for themselves. In busy classrooms young children tend to use whatever mode(s) of communication they feel most comfortable with, and often opt for the silence of gesture and/or gaze rather than language, particularly if they are unsure what is expected of them (Flewitt, 2005).

Multimodality is highly compatible with sociocultural theories of learning (Vygotsky, 1978, 1986), and with Vygotsky's proposal that learning is most effective in the so-called 'zones of proximal development' (ZPD), or areas of potential learning (Vygotsky, 1978), defined as 'the distance between the actual developmental level as determined by independent problem solving and the level of potential development as determined under adult guidance or in collaboration' (Vygotsky, 1978: 86). This draws attention to the social nature of learning, which is not shaped merely by an individual's 'competence', but by 'a complex web of social, historical and cultural beliefs that the individual encounters through everyday practice' (Nind et al., 2014: 345). From a sociocultural perspective, mental processes are social in origin, and are mediated through interaction using diverse symbolic tools, including language and material artefacts (Wertsch, 1991).

Researchers working with multimodality have extended sociocultural theorising to show how gaze, gesture, body orientation, movement, images, sounds and talk are interdependent and integral to meaning making, and how children often express the subtlety and sophistication of their understanding through silent modes. For example, Binder and Kotsopoulos (2011) illustrate how a literacy curriculum that embraces visual arts pedagogy creates opportunities for young children who have not yet mastered written language to develop personal narratives in non-traditional forms of literacy – in this case through the creative endeavour of planning and making quilt squares, and then composing poems. In this nine-week study, twelve children in a culturally and linguistically diverse Canadian kindergarten classroom were encouraged to bring in artefacts that were important to them, and to use these to design and make a quilt square which reflected why they were important. Having made the quilt squares, they were then invited to compose 'I

Am' oral poems, where the visual narratives of the quilt squares laid the foundations for and enhanced the language-based poetry. Through this creative and multimodal approach to literacy, the children were able to represent their own importance in the social world and document their personal narratives in non-traditional forms of literacy, empowering them to make their thoughts public and to change how they viewed and situated themselves in the classroom.

Working with six- to seven-year-old children in a primary school in the north of England, Pahl (2009) showed how multimodal meaning making can reveal deep insights into children's conceptual understanding. In this study, the children used shoe boxes to make 'panorama boxes' of an environment of their choosing, such as the ocean, the jungle, the desert or the Arctic. They then researched, made and placed animals and artefacts in their boxes, of the kind that would be found in their chosen environment. By observing the material choices the children made, Pahl was able to see how they drew on their individual knowledge and experience, and how their personal histories shaped their understandings of the concepts they were being asked to recreate. These insights would not have been evident through their talk alone.

Both these studies highlight how learning processes are complex: learning is not just a mental process, but is highly dependent on individuals' personal histories and on how educational practices are mediated. Learning is also highly social: studying the early writing practices of four-year-olds in an ethnically diverse pre-kindergarten class in the USA, Kissel (2009) identified that using images, movement and talk, and creating a peer audience for the children's stories, introduced new possibilities for their engagement with writing and narrative, especially when working with their peers, who supported each other and shared ideas as writers.

These studies exemplify how creative activities that encourage expression through multiple modes that have purpose, an audience, and encourage interaction between peers offer a fertile environment for early literacy. By valuing all modes of signification, practitioners can begin to conceptualise literacy differently, and to rethink the concept of 'text' as multimodal, with an increased focus on visual, embodied and new media texts (Unsworth 2001). Regardless of their language fluency, from a multimodal perspective all young children are offered an equal chance to present themselves to the world, and to be viewed as competent and creative explorers of multiple semiotic resources who make intentional choices in their meaning making.

Methodology

The data presented in this chapter relate to the multimodal narratives of young children in the early years unit of an inner-city primary school. This school was one of four locations that formed part of the evaluation of an eight-week training programme for practitioners in Paley's story-based pedagogy, as described in Chapter 2. The school featured in this chapter had a regular intake of children from migrant families who were housed temporarily in the local area, a high percentage of children who were eligible for Free School Meals (a measure used as an indicator of poverty), and also a significant number of children who either had been or were in the process of being identified as having special educational needs (SEN). The children in the early years unit were ethnically diverse, with approximately half registered with English as an Additional Language (EAL). Teacher–parent contact was limited principally because many children were bussed into school from a distance (due to a lack of available school places nearer their sometimes temporary homes). It can be argued that this diverse unit is fairly typical of schools in today's 'global cities' around the world (Butler and Hamnett, 2011), which are increasingly characterised by a high concentration of children from different ethnic minority populations, where some families may be experiencing displacement, and where teachers face the potentially rich but challenging environment of working with children who have diverse learning needs and may not share fluency in a common language.

This particular school had also undergone rapid and extensive change: shortly after receiving an unfavourable inspection report by Ofsted[1] two years prior to the study, it had been put into 'Special Measures',[2] a new school leadership team had been brought in by the local education authority, all the class teachers had been replaced, the old school had been demolished and a brand new school had been built on the same site. The children and new staff had moved into the well-resourced new school just one month before our study began, but the teachers reported that they had all settled extremely well into their light, spacious and airy new learning environment. Despite the sudden injection of funds to improve the school with purpose-built facilities and the recruitment of a highly skilled and motivated teaching team, the Executive Head described the school as still 'dealing with a chessboard of problems', including the need to improve home–school relationships and to meet the varied learning needs of all its diverse pupils.

The data selected for consideration in this chapter therefore focuses purposively on the stories of two children in the early years unit who reflect these challenges, and whose teachers felt were not fully engaging in classroom life. Brief details of the children are presented in Table 9.1.

TABLE 9.1 Child details*

Pseudonym (gender)	School class	Age at start of study (yrs.mnths)	Ethnicity	Language status	No. of Helicopter stories told during study
Jaime (male)	Preschool	3.7	W. European	Portuguese/ EAL	5
Wang Tai (male)	Reception	5.6	Asian	Mandarin/ EAL	2

* Details taken from official school records data. EAL denotes the child is listed with English as an Additional Language.

As described in Chapter 2, the methodological approach in this study was naturalistic, and used the ethnographic tools (Green and Bloome, 1997) of:

- observations of the children's storytelling and story acting;
- the collation of children's stories as scribed by the teachers and trainers;
- 'logbooks' made by teachers of any progress they noted in individual children throughout the training programme;
- three rounds of interviews with lead teachers in each classroom;
- scrutiny of school records, student data and profiles.

Although the data presented for close analysis here focus on two boys' storytelling and story acting, the analysis is also informed by scrutiny of the 67 total number of stories told and acted out in the preschool class and 42 stories in the Reception class of this setting. Through the lens of multimodal ethnography (Flewitt, 2011), I discuss how conceptualising stories as multimodal narratives creates empowering spaces for young children to share their thoughts, feelings and understanding through spoken and silent modes in an inclusive classroom culture.

Multimodal storytelling and acting in the early years classroom

During the storytelling and story-acting training programme, trainers worked with practitioners to establish the 'Helicopter Stories' principles, as described in Chapter 2. Across all the study settings, we observed that whilst some children were eager from the outset to volunteer their own stories, many others held back. Gradually, as the storytelling became more firmly embedded in classroom practice, even the most reticent children gravitated towards other children's stories in the telling, and participated peripherally in the storytelling and scribing process. Eventually, encouraged gently by their teachers, they began to tell their own stories, and took great pleasure in watching their classmates act them out. Like many other children in their respective classes, three-year-old Jaime and five-year-old Wang Tai observed other children for a few weeks before volunteering their own stories. Over the eight-week programme, Jaime told five stories about dinosaurs (during Weeks 3, 4, 5, 7 and 8) and Wang Tai told two stories about Transformers[3] (during Weeks 6 and 7), both deriving their principle narrative force from popular culture.

Jaime's stories

Jaime was in his second term in preschool, having joined the class part-way through the school year. From a Portuguese-speaking home, he was described by his teacher as quiet, not knowing other children in the class, and with very little spoken English. He 'didn't settle initially', and 'cried a lot' during his first half-term, but had become more content since moving to the new school and acquiring a new school uniform, which he was proud of: 'he's bright and strong-willed and stubborn and he decided he was going to do it, so that was good'. During the first two weeks of the training programme, Jaime often attended closely to other children's stories and took part in story acting. He volunteered his first 'Helicopter story' during Week 3 of the training programme, by which time he was familiar with its format and procedures. Jaime's first story was one word in length, embellished at the time of telling with arm gestures to indicate a large size, and scribed as: '*(uses gesture) monster*'.[4] His second story was considerably longer and brought action, a dinosaur theme and references to popular and fictional media characters: '*Dinosaur. Pig. Dinosaur do "Rah Rah Sheepy". 2 dinosaur. Tin Tin*'. His third story had a more focused plot: '*Dinosaur. It does this (shows action)*'. His fourth and fifth stories were scribed respectively as '*Dinosaur, Raa*', and '*Dinosaurs. T-Rex*'.

A performative lens on the language used in these five stories might deduce that no significant progress had been made in Jaime's literacy or narrative competence during the eight-week programme – he began with a one-word story and ended with a two-word story, with some elaboration in-between. However, there was far more learning going on than was expressed through language – for the teacher, for Jaime, and for his peers. Although short, Jaime's stories were treated with full respect by his teachers and classmates. When he told his stories, Jaime experienced the undivided attention of the teacher scribe, as well as one or more peers and sometimes also a Helicopter trainer, as shown in Figure 9.1a. This level of closely focused and expectant teacher attention can be somewhat unusual in an early years classroom, and for some children might be intimidating, yet by the time Jaime told his first story in Week 3, it had become normalised practice by its frequent occurrence during Helicopter storytelling. Furthermore, the core 'Helicopter' pedagogic principle that children's language use is never corrected offered the 'freedom' for Jaime to take risks and grow in confidence as the following analysis illustrates. The fixed 'Helicopter Stories' rules contributed significantly to the inclusive and equitable nature of the story-based pedagogy, as one teacher involved in the training observed:

> It is a good tool in that no matter when you have come into the setting, where you have come from, what your background is, it goes back to that equality again. The rules are the same for everybody, the opportunities are the same for everybody, the choice is there, the freedom is there.
>
> *(Teacher interview)*

During all the observed storytelling episodes, the classroom storybook that teachers used to scribe the children's stories acted as a central pivot around which the adult and child participants arranged their bodies in an encircling space which affirmed the centrality of the child's story, with a mutual interest in the telling and scribing of that story. Figure 9.1a illustrates the nature of the interactive spaces offered by this story-based pedagogy for children's learning. The teacher is scribing, and her body posture, direction and length of gaze, hand position, tilt and proximity of her head all indicate respect for and inclusion of Jaime's contributions. Similarly, Jaime's classmate's posture (Figure 9.1a) reinforces the unity of purpose and interest.

This fine-tuned combination of modes of affirmation gives a sense of congruence, sincerity and distinctiveness to the storytelling interactions.

Jaime's second story creatively wove together themes and characters from different sources, with powerful (dinosaur) and less powerful protagonists (pig, sheepy), a script (Rah Rah Sheepy) embellished with intertextual reference to a well-known social hero making a surprise entrance at the end of the story (Tintin).[5] This story evidenced his developing English vocabulary and, for the first time since he had joined the class, the teacher could see his thoughtful and creative interest in storytelling, and the rich funds of interest and literary knowledge that he brought to school from home (Gonzalez et al., 2005). Jaime's third story, although shorter than his second, depicted a scene that lent itself well to performance, with stage directions conveyed through action, and a plot that was presented in a simple but nonetheless perfectly formed sentence in English: '*It does this (shows action)*'. Both the second and third stories indicate Jaime's creative planning for the acting out of his story, reinforcing his sense of ownership and control, which Jeffrey and Woods (2003) suggest can unleash innovation. As one practitioner commented, the children did not look to adults as if to query 'Am I doing it right?', rather, their storytelling and story-acting manner asserted a mutually agreed 'We're doing it'.

Jaime's fourth story ('Dinosaur, Raa') may have drawn on Henrietta and Paul Stickland's popular book for young children 'Dinosaur Roar!', reflecting his interest in his reading experiences in English, and also echoing the noises in his second story ('Rah Rah Sheepy'). This time, Jaime's 'Raa' was theatrical, guttural and delivered with gusto, as the acting out field notes show:

> Jaime's enactment began quietly. He hunched his shoulders and raised his arms slightly, making claw-like hands to indicate the form of a dinosaur. He then paused and gazed slowly around the audience, before roaring such an unexpected and impressive 'Raa' that everyone was taken aback, laughing delightedly at his uncharacteristically animated portrayal. Seeing his peers' and teachers' approbation made him smile broadly, almost in disbelief, and spoke volumes about the value of his active involvement for his growing sense of identity as an included and 'licensed' member of the classroom.
>
> *(Field notes written immediately after the story acting)*

A multimodal lens on the telling of Jaime's short yet precise fifth story, scribed as '*Dinosaurs. T-Rex*', illustrates how the timing and physicality of the teacher's responses affirmed its importance as part of the now established classroom practice of storytelling and story acting. From the multimodal transcription presented in Figure 9.1 we can see that during the fifteen-second pause between Jaime's first and second utterances, he receives encouraging and positive feedback from the teacher in multiple modes: her body is angled towards him, her gaze is fully focused either on him or on his story, the act of repeating his words and scribing them simultaneously affirms their importance in the classroom context and creates time for Jaime to plan further additions to his storytelling. There is a physical unity in this shared storytelling endeavour, expressed through the similar postures of the storyteller and story scribe, both sitting straight-backed and angled slightly towards each other, in their mutual gaze towards the storybook, and in the fine-tuning of their interpersonal gaze exchange (see Figure 9.1a–d). As their joint attention moved from a focus on Jaime's storytelling to the teacher's story scribing, Jaime watched intently as his spoken story appeared in the form of words on a page. For each story, the teacher's scribing presented an opportunity for children to experience the relationship between the spoken and written word, and the arrangement of their words on paper. The teacher's echoing of Jaime's utterances as she scribed (at times 0.04 and 0.21) further validated his contribution, and encouraged him to embellish his story whilst respecting his authorial right to end it at the moment of his choosing.

Further affirmation of the importance of his story was offered by the presence and intense focus of Jaime's classmate, in Figure 9.1a and b. The trainer recognised how important his teacher's and peers' attention was for Jaime:

> When (the teacher) was taking that story with Jaime … it was the most interesting thing to him because they all just sat round on the sofa just watching, and they didn't need anything else it was just listening and just watching (the teacher) write that story, and there wasn't any interruptions. It almost felt like … suspense to be honest like 'let's just listen and watch and see what happens'… you just get that curiosity, and that children wanting to know surprise, and wanting to experience that surprise by just being there, I think they're really powerful, powerful moments.
>
> *(Trainer interview)*

Jaime's teacher felt the Helicopter Stories had enabled his growing confidence and inclusion in classroom learning. At the outset of the study she explained that he had sometimes spoken in 'babble': 'it wasn't Portuguese and it wasn't English and he had this made-up language that he thought that he could communicate in'. With increasing confidence, which the storytelling experiences had contributed to, she reported 'his language has improved but he is still telling stories about dinosaurs, it is quite interesting, makes me laugh, single words really again, but generally in the classroom he is talking and he is understanding so much better' (end of training interview). Indeed, all the teachers in this study cited examples of the storytelling and story acting having boosted children's confidence both socially and in terms of their use of spoken and written language, particularly in the case of quiet children and those with EAL. As one reported:

> I think it is about giving the children confidence to experiment with language and to use language – and to actually speak. For some children, you know, to say anything at all in some cases, or to tell us a story and then to get up and act it … that's a huge thing.

Video still	Elapsed time	Participant	Action	Gaze	Speech
a)	0.00	Teacher	The teacher writes Jaime's name in the book	To book	
	0.02	Jaime	Twists her head and body towards Jaime, pencil poised over the storybook, ready to scribe	Fixed on Jaime	Do you want to tell me a story?
	0.03	Jaime	Sitting on sofa, body turned towards teacher	To storybook, glances up to teacher when speaks	Dinosaurs
	0.04	Teacher	Right arm begins to move towards storybook page as soon as Jaime begins to speak, scribes 'dinosaurs'	Gaze turns to storybook page	Dinosaurs
b)		Jaime	Body towards teacher, tilts his head forward so he can see the teacher's scribing	Watches closely as the teacher scribes	
	0.07	Teacher	Twists head back towards Jaime, with pen poised	Gaze to Jaime	Anything else?
	0.07–0.11	Jaime	Leans slightly towards storybook	Gaze fixed on storybook	
	0.12	Teacher	Pen poised	Gaze to Jaime	D'you want me to write anything else in your story?
	0.13	Jaime	Nods his head (barely perceptibly)	Gaze to storybook	
	0.15	Teacher	Moves hand slightly as though ready to write	Gaze to Jaime	Right go on then tell me the rest of your story

FIGURE 9.1 Multimodal transcript of Jaime telling his fifth story (continues overleaf)

Video still	Elapsed time	Participant	Action	Gaze	Speech
c)	0.18	Jaime	Tilts head upwards	Gaze up to teacher	T Rex
	0.19	Teacher	Leans closely in to Jaime, so her ear is next to his face	Gaze to storybook	Say it again (quietly)
	0.20	Jaime	Head tilted upwards	Gaze to teacher	T Rex
	0.21	Teacher	Sits up straight and scribes	Gaze to storybook	T Rex (uses same intonation as Jaime)
	0.21	Jaime		Fixed gaze on storybook as teacher scribes	
	0.25	Teacher	Lifts arm with a flourish when has finished scribing	Gaze from storybook to Jaime	Ok?
	0.26	Jaime	Nods almost imperceptibly	Gaze fixed on storybook, looking up and down the page	
	0.27	Teacher	Reads Jaime's story out loud, pointing to words as she speaks	Gaze to storybook	We've got dinosaur (.) T Rex
	0.27	Jaime	Nods approvingly as teacher speaks	Gaze from book to teacher	

Video still	Elapsed time	Participant	Action	Gaze	Speech
	0.28	Teacher	Turns body slightly towards Jaime	Gaze to Jaime	Any more?
	0.29	Jaime	Shakes head several times	Gaze fixed on teacher as he shakes his head	
	0.30–0.35	Teacher	Sits up straight, twists torso towards Jaime	Gaze from book to Jaime to book	No? Ok (.) brilliant so d'you wanna be the dinosaurs or d'you wanna be the T Rex dinosaur?
	0.36–0.40	Jaime	Scratches nose, points towards storybook with index finger	From book to teacher to unfixed gaze straight ahead	T Rex dinosaur
	0.41	Teacher	Circles 'T Rex' in the storybook	Gaze to book	
	0.42	Jaime	Twiddles his hands together	Gaze fixed on teacher	
	0.43	Teacher	Nods	Gaze to book, then to Jaime	T Rex ok T Rex dinosaur Ok? Alright (.) brilliant Thank you very much.
	0.44	Jaime	Gaze remains fixed on teacher until she has finished speaking, then he stands and leaves the sofa area		...you can go now

FIGURE 9.1   continued

Wang Tai's stories

Wang Tai was five and a half years old at the beginning of this study, and in his second term at the school. His home and local community language was Mandarin, and he was described by the Reception teacher as a 'keen learner' with 'developing English' who had not yet formed close friendships in school. During the first weeks of the 'Helicopter' training, Wang Tai observed other children's stories and enthusiastically joined in their acting out. He did not tell his own story until training weeks 6 and 7, by which time the story-based pedagogy was firmly established in classroom routines. The teacher's scribed version of both his stories are presented in Figure 9.2.

A striking aspect of Wang Tai's storytelling was his lively enactment of each story in the telling, with animated and expansive whole-body movements depicting action in his unfolding narratives. The multimodal transcript presented in Figure 9.3 features a brief extract of Wang Tai's second story and illustrates how narrative detail and his enthusiasm for storytelling were expressed eloquently through elaborate actions accompanied simultaneously or split seconds later by short

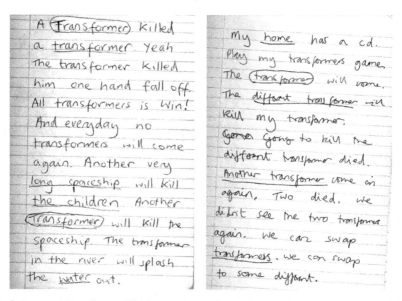

Week 6 story: A Transformer killed a transformer Yeah. The transformer killed him one hand fall off. All transformers is win! And every day no transformers will come again. Another very long spaceship will kill the children. Another transformer will kill the spaceship. The transformer in the river will splash the water out.

Week 7 story: My home has a cd. Play my transformers game. The transformer will come. The different transformer will kill my transformer. Going to kill the different transformer died. Another transformer came in again. Two died. We didn't see the two transformers again. We can swop transformers. We can swop to some different.

FIGURE 9.2 Wang Tai's stories

Video still	Elapsed time	Participant	Action	Gaze	Speech
	1.40	Teacher	Finishes scribing previous utterance. Raises head with a look of surprise and exaggerated anticipation, then tilts head towards Wang Tai	Fixed on writing as she scribes. Gaze to Wang Tai	...one hand fall off
	1.45	Wang Tai	Body turned towards teacher, half standing, half sitting on sofa, raises his left hand with clenched fist and extends it behind him, then swings left arm down in a sharp, swift movement	Towards his own arm as it moves, then towards teacher	and then um
	1.47		Extends right arm horizontally across his body, and glides it back slowly, keeping it horizontal, across his own body	Straight ahead	all the transformers
	1.49		Extends right arm straight up vertically with a flourish, almost standing as the thrust of his arm movement pulls him upwards	Towards teacher as he utters 'win'	is win

a)

FIGURE 9.3 Wang Tai tells a story

utterances. When telling this story, Wang Tai often bounced from sitting to standing as though barely able to contain his enthusiasm for the unfolding narrative, as shown at the end of Figure 9.3. Looking down the 'Action' column in the transcript, we can see a wealth of descriptive detail that his mastery of English could not yet capture: the aggression and determination of the raised, clenched fist and decisive downward arm movement in 1.45, accompanied by a thoughtful 'and then um', which the teacher does not transcribe; the slow steady gliding of his right arm across his body which seems to suggest transformers in steady flight at 1.47, represented in words by 'all the transformers'; and finally thrusting his right arm skywards with a clenched fist which for transformers, as elsewhere, is used to show solidarity and support – a highly symbolic action that is consolidated in the flourish 'is win!'. From this brief extract we can see rich layers of meaning in a 'multimodal ensemble', with a disconnect between Wang Tai's lively yet limited English vocabulary and the rich creative detail of his narrative imagination, as enacted during his storytelling, and which came to life again during his story acting.

Here then was rich potential for Wang Tai to connect with many of his classmates' interest in action heroes. Although none of Wang Tai's peers shared his knowledge of 'Transformers', perhaps not surprising given their film classification PG-13, other action superheroes from popular culture featured no less than sixteen times in the forty-two stories told in this class. Altogether, Power Rangers fought, kicked or killed in six boys' and five girls' stories, along with Superman and Batman swooping into action twice, and Goldman and Supergirl once. Although Wang Tai's stories are abrupt in their violence, with 'kill' and 'died' each mentioned twice, the events featured in his literary narratives are similar to other children's story plots. For example, three girls' stories featured death:

'The dragon eat a rat and the dragon died.'
'Trish was dead because the dragon deaded Trish by putting the fire on her.'
'The dragon made the princess dead.'

Further references to violence in the children's stories in this class included fighting opponents (four mentions), eating them (four mentions), kicking (three mentions), smashing (one mention), and cutting them. Readers may be wary of the aggression in these stories, yet as Katch (2001) notes, it is important to distinguish between experimenting with ideas about pretend violence, which does not hurt others, and real violence, which causes physical or emotional pain, and may be connected with exclusion. Furthermore, children often use incongruity to produce humorous stories, such as the unexpected violation of rules and acts of violence, particularly when their story characters act to empower themselves (Loizou et al., 2011). Through Wang Tai's oral and enacted stories, the teachers became aware of the influences of popular culture resources from home on his emerging sense of narrative, and his playful manipulation of themes that reflected his interests and those of other children in the class, and ultimately facilitated his inclusion in other children's play.

Discussion: The multimodal nature of storytelling and story acting

From very early childhood, oral, written and enacted stories weave through children's lives and form part of how they come to understand the social and cultural worlds they inhabit (Flewitt and Maybin, 2016). They are a major 'organising device' (Langer, 1953: 261) that enable children to make sense of and order real or imagined experience, providing them with opportunities to explore their own interests, and to address affective and cognitive issues they have experienced in real life. Put simply, stories are 'the coin and currency of culture' (Bruner, 2002: 15), where 'culture' refers to the Vygotskyan sense of how societies organise the tasks and tools that facilitate communication within and between social groups, such as oral and enacted stories.

Paley (1990) suggests that children use stories to work their way into the adult world, and to imagine others' worlds. We have seen how the stories told by Jaime and Wang Tai were dynamic, requiring the performer/actor to fill in detail in the storyline by interpreting words through action. Like many children across the study sites, these two boys created stories around topics of particular interest to them, sometimes mixing their sources of inspiration from personal experience, their home lives and popular culture (as in Wang Tai's stories), and sometimes mixing topics of interest from diverse literary sources (such as Tintin, sheep and dinosaurs in Jaime's stories). Over time, the children's references to each other's stories helped to build a sense of solidarity, as they appropriated others' embryonic story plots and real, 'popular', 'traditional' or imagined characters. In this way, the Helicopter Stories created spaces for children to learn about each other's interests, backgrounds and ways of being, to perceive differences as desirable and to feel they were all valued members of a trusting community where they could take risks – as Jaime did when enacting his dinosaur's roar.

For all children, talk is just one mode amongst many used for self-expression, and young children often tell more through their actions than they do through their words (Corsaro, 2003; Flewitt, 2012). In this chapter, I have argued that gaze, gesture, actions and talk are all interdependent and integral to communication and meaning making. For many young children, speaking in class is challenging, particularly if the dominant classroom language is different to their home language(s), and oftentimes the subtlety and sophistication of their understanding is made visible through silent modes (Flewitt, 2005; Whitebread et al., 2009). Over time, the repeated practice of Paley's story-based pedagogy affirmed the value of all children's stories. However short or partially formed they may have been in words, rich layers of meaning could be attributed to them in their telling and acting. As the analysis in this chapter has illustrated, the valuing of multiple modes of expression in storytelling and scribing contributed to children's growing confidence, sense of themselves as capable storytellers and story actors, as valued members of the classroom community, and to their willingness to participate. These learning experiences formed powerful moulds for the development of positive learner dispositions, identities and friendships.

Paley's story-based pedagogy offers ways to support learning in a principled manner that is dynamic and responsive to children's interests and enthusiasm. Furthermore, it provides a framework to extend the literacy curriculum in creative and inclusive ways that enable teachers to break away from the 'disabling discourses' (Hamilton, 2015: 203) around literacy that young children and their teachers all too often experience, especially when working in the context of reductive curricula (Wohlwend, 2008). Starting from the central tenet that every child has strengths, this story-based curriculum creates spaces for children's strengths to be recognised, valued and built on sensitively, and for 'the surprising and unexpected, not just the predefined and the normative' (Moss, 2012: vii). The multimodal storytelling and acting pathways offered by Paley's approach permit all children – regardless of their linguistic and ethnic background – to share ideas in the classroom, building each child's sense of identity and worth in an inclusive community of peers and teachers. Celebrating children's stories in this manner offers the kinds of playful, multisensory and multimodal experiences that teachers instinctively know are essential for inclusive classroom cultures. As Paley attests:

> The children I teach are just emerging from life's deep wells of private perspective: babyhood and family … Then, along comes school. It is the first real exposure to the public arena. Children are required to share materials and teachers in a space that belongs to everyone. Within this public space a new concept of open access can develop if we choose to make this a goal. Here will be found not only the strong ties of intimate friendship but, in addition, the habit of full and equal participation, upon request.
>
> *(Paley, 1992: 21)*

Notes

1   The inspection of publicly funded schools in England is carried out by the Office for Standards in Education, Children's Services and Skills (Ofsted), a non-ministerial department of the UK government.
2   At the time of this study, the term 'special measures' was a status applied by Ofsted when inspectors considered a school was failing to supply an acceptable level of education and appeared to lack the leadership capacity necessary to secure improvements.
3   A popular media franchise about transforming alien robots, with comic books, videos and toys, which younger children encounter principally through product placement deals with fast-food outlets.
4   All nouns were underlined by the teacher scribe to indicate a part that could later be acted out.
5   *The Adventures of Tintin* is a series of comic albums created by the Belgian cartoonist Georges Remi (1907–1983), who wrote under the pen name Hergé, which recount thrilling adventures and mysteries solved by the heroic young reporter Tintin, assisted by his faithful dog Snowy.

References

Binder, M. and Kotsopoulos, S. (2011) Multimodal literacy narratives: Weaving the threads of young children's identity through the arts. *Journal of Research in Childhood Education, 25*(4): 339–363.

Bruner, J. (2002) *Making Stories: Law, Literature, Life.* Cambridge, MA: Harvard University Press.

Butler, T. and Hamnett, C. (2011) *Ethnicity, Class and Aspiration. Understanding London's new East End.* Bristol: The Policy Press.

Corsaro, W. A. (2003) *'We're Friends, Right?': Inside kids' cultures.* Washington, DC: Joseph Henry Press.

Creese, A. and Blackledge, A. (2015) Translanguaging and identity in educational settings. *Annual Review of Applied Linguistics, 35*: 20–35.

Flewitt, R. S. (2005) Is every child's voice heard? Researching the different ways three-year-old children make meaning at home and in a preschool playgroup. *Early Years: International Journal of Research and Development, 25*(3): 207–222.

Flewitt, R. S. (2011) Bringing ethnography to a multimodal investigation of early literacy in a digital age. *Qualitative Research, 11*(3): 293–310.

Flewitt, R. S. (2012) Multimodal perspectives on early childhood literacies. In J. Larson and J. Marsh (eds), *The Sage Handbook of Early Childhood Literacy* (2nd edn) (pp. 295–309). London: Sage.

Flewitt, R. S. and Maybin, J. (2016) From crib talk to YouTube. In J. Maybin (ed.) *Narrative, Language and Creativity: Contemporary approaches.* Milton Keynes: The Open University.

Gibson, R. (1989) The education of feeling. In P. Abbs (ed.) *The Symbolic Order: A contemporary reader on the arts debate* (pp. 53–61). Philadelphia: The Falmer Press.

Gonzalez, N., Moll, L. C. and Amanti, C. (eds) (2005) *Funds of Knowledge: Theorizing practices in households, communities and classrooms.* New Jersey: Lawrence Erlbaum Associates.

Goodwin, C. (1980) Restarts, pauses and mutual gaze in turn taking. *Sociological Inquiry, 50*(3–4): 272–302.

Green, J. and Bloome, D. (1997) Ethnography and ethnographers of and in education: A situated perspective. In J. Flood, S. B. Heath and D. Lapp (eds), *A Handbook for Literacy Educators: Research on teaching the communicative and visual arts* (pp. 1–12). New York, NY: Macmillan.

Halliday, M. A. K. (1978) *Language as Social Semiotic.* London: Arnold.

Hamilton, M. (2015) The Peckett Way: Negotiating multimodal learning spaces in a user-run community education project. In M. Hamilton, R. Heydon, K. Hibbert and R. Stooke (eds), *Multimodality and Governmentality: Negotiating spaces in literacy education* (pp. 201–219). London: Bloomsbury/Continuum Books.

Jeffrey, B. and Woods, P. (2003) *The Creative School: A framework for success, quality and effectiveness.* London: RoutledgeFalmer.

Katch, J. (2001) *Under Deadman's Skin: Discovering the meaning of children's violent play.* Boston, MA: Beacon Press.

Kendon, A. (2004) *Gesture: Visible action as utterance.* Cambridge: Cambridge University Press.

Kendon, A. and Cook, M. (1969) The consistency of gaze patterns in social interaction. *British Journal of Psychology, 60*(4): 481–494.

Kissel, B. T. (2009) Beyond the page: Peers influence pre-kindergarten writing through image, movement, and talk. *Childhood Education, 85*(3): 160–166.

Kress, G. (1997) *Before Writing: Rethinking the paths to literacy.* London: Routledge.

Kress, G., Jewitt, C., Ogborn, J. and Tsatsarelis, C. (2001) *Multimodal Teaching and Learning: The rhetorics of the science classroom*. London: Continuum Books.

Langer, S. K. (1953) *Feeling and Form*. London: Routledge and Kegan Paul.

Loizou, E., Kyriakides, E. and Hadjicharalambous, M. (2011) Constructing stories in kindergarten: Children's knowledge of genre. *European Early Childhood Education Research Journal, 19*(1): 63–77.

McNeill, D. (1985) So you think gestures are non-verbal? *Psychological Review, 92*(3): 350–371.

Moss, P. (2012) Foreword. In L. Miller, C. Dalli and M. Urban (eds), *Early Childhood Grows Up: Towards a critical ecology of the profession* (pp. v–viii). Dordrecht: Springer.

Nind, M., Flewitt, R. S. and Theodorou, F. (2014) Play and inclusion. In K. Cologon (ed.), *Inclusive Education in the Early Years: Right from the start* (pp. 341–357). Australia and New Zealand: Oxford University Press.

Pahl, K. (2009) Interactions, intersections and improvisations: Studying the multimodal texts and classroom talk of six- to seven-year olds. *Journal of Early Childhood Literacy, 9*(2): 188–210.

Paley, V. G. (1990) *The Boy Who Would Be a Helicopter: The uses of storytelling in the classroom*. Cambridge, MA: Harvard University Press.

Paley, V. G. (1992) *You Can't Say You Can't Play*. Cambridge, MA: Harvard University Press.

Paley, V. G. (2004) *Child's Play: The importance of fantasy play*. Chicago, IL: Chicago University Press.

Scollon, R. and Scollon, S. W. (2014) Multimodality and language: A retrospective and prospective view. In C. Jewitt (ed.), *The Routledge Handbook of Multimodal Analysis* (2nd edn) (pp. 205–216). London: Routledge.

Unsworth, L. (2001) *Teaching Multiliteracies Aross the Curriculum: Changing contexts of text and image in classroom practice*. Buckingham: Open University Press.

Vygotsky, L. S. (1978) *Mind in Society*. Cambridge, MA: Harvard University Press.

Vygotsky, L. S. (1986) *Thought and Language*. Cambridge, MA: MIT Press.

Wertsch, J. V. (1991). *Voices of the Mind: A sociocultural approach to mediated action*. Cambridge, MA: Harvard University Press.

Whitebread, D., Coltman, P., Pino Pasternak, D., Snagster, C., Grau, V., Bingham, S., Almeqdad, Q. and Demetriou, D. (2009) The development of two observational tools for assessing metacognition and self-regulated learning in young children. *Metacognition Learning, 4*: 63–85.

Wohlwend, K. (2008) Kindergarten as nexus of practice: A mediated discourse analysis of reading, writing, play, and design in an early literacy apprenticeship. *Reading Research Quarterly, 43*(4): 332–334.

10

PROMOTING DEMOCRATIC CLASSROOM COMMUNITIES THROUGH STORYTELLING AND STORY ACTING

Ben Mardell and Natalia Kucirkova

Introduction

We live at a time of unprecedented migration – between rural areas and urban metropolises and between impoverished and war-torn countries and wealthy nations. This migration presents opportunities (e.g. the vitality of new immigrants; the richness when different cultural groups interact) as well as challenges (e.g. disruptions of communities experiencing an influx of migrants). Successful navigation of these challenges will require a new generation of citizens with the abilities and dispositions to listen, take the perspectives of others, and collaborate. It will require people and communities to act with a shared sense of humanity and fairness; to be able to act and solve problems democratically. In this chapter we focus on how children's sense of democratic responsibility can be promoted through storytelling and story acting.

If the democratic nature of a particular early childhood activity could be measured, storytelling and story acting as enacted in Vivian Gussin Paley's classroom would surely score high. Cooper (2009), McNamee (2015) and Nicolopoulou and her colleagues (2015) have all described how Paley's storytelling and story acting promotes skills and dispositions essential to democracy. While not naming democracy explicitly, Nicolopoulou et al. (2015) list the democratic characteristics of storytelling and story acting, including its child-initiated, voluntary, shared, collaborative and public nature. McNamee (2015) explains how storytelling and story acting helps create a democratic atmosphere in Head Start classrooms. Cooper (2009) describes how a 'pedagogy of fairness' is deeply engrained in Paley's teaching, of which storytelling and story acting is an essential part. Paley concurs, commenting that the storytelling and story acting involves 'doing favors for each other and creating community. There is no room in this community for favouritism … [Storytelling and story acting is an] opportunity for supreme intimacy' (Paley,

2010). Elsewhere she writes, 'Even more than play itself [storytelling and story acting] brings us several rungs up the ladder in our classroom democracy' (personal communication, 1/3/14). At a time of increasing direct instruction in early childhood settings (Bassok and Rorem, 2014), and declining opportunities for children to play (Miller and Almon, 2009), it is essential to recognize and support practices that sustain and strengthen democracy.

Storytelling and story acting originated in a specific context – one particular classroom – and until recently efforts to expand it have involved individual or small groups of teachers who embraced the practice voluntarily. With increased interest in storytelling and story acting in the UK (e.g. MakeBelieve Arts), the USA (e.g. the School Literacy and Culture Project and, in particular, the inclusion of storytelling and story acting in mandated curriculum in the Boston Public Schools *Focus on K2* kindergarten curriculum), the issue of maintaining the democratic character of storytelling and story acting takes on particular urgency, and is the impetus for this chapter.

We begin the chapter by examining how storytelling and story acting can foster democracy, including its support for individual voice and agency, as well as promotion of learning communities. Attention is then turned to risks to the democratic character of storytelling and story acting in publicly funded settings. Special attention is given to the scaffolding of storytelling as an opportunity to either support or undermine children's agency and voice. Concerned with the risks and opportunities present in efforts to scale up storytelling and story acting, we conclude by drawing on experiences in the Boston Public Schools, theorizing about professional development practices that support teachers in preserving the democratic character of storytelling and story acting.

Storytelling and story acting as a democratic classroom practice

In discussions of democratic classroom practices, the distinction between democracy on national and local levels is useful (Moss, 2011). On a national level, democracy is operationalized through voting and majority rule, an independent judiciary, adherence to the rule of law, and a free press. On a local level – in clubs, community organizations, and schools – relationships play a prominent role in actualizing democratic values. While adherence to agreed rules and laws remain important, democracy also depends on the members of a group listening to, trusting, and treating each other fairly and with respect. It is on this local level that Eleanor Roosevelt (1958) explained human rights begin 'where every man, woman and child seeks equal justice, equal opportunity'.

Early childhood classrooms operate on the local level and creating democratic communities here involves managing the tension between individual needs and desires, and the requirements of the group. In accord with the United Nations Convention on the Rights of the Child (1989), in a democratic classroom community each child should have an equal opportunity to express his or her opinions and, to the degree appropriate to their development, have input on issues that impact his or her life. At the same time, a democratic early childhood classroom is not a free-for-all, with each individual doing what he or she pleases. Rather, it is a place where individuals act with sensitivity to the needs of other community members; where children learn to develop control over impulses, and make decisions based on reason (Dewey, 2004).

Most importantly, a democratic classroom community is a community where children have the opportunity to collectively create ideas and make meaning together. This involves far more than children voting for what kind of crackers they want for snack. It involves children and teachers creating a culture together by establishing the rules, rituals, stories, artefacts and ideas that define the group. It involves a collective 'who are emotionally, intellectually and aesthetically engaged in solving problems, creating products and making meaning' (Project Zero and Reggio Children, 2001: 285).

With this in mind, it is clear why storytelling and story acting would score highly on a hypothetical democracy meter. The opportunities to tell a story, to choose whether or not to participate in story acting, and to have the license to decide how to portray characters in story acting, allows for individual voice, choice, and agency. In addition, storytelling and story acting allows for children's creative ideas and impulses, while encouraging children to coordinate their ideas and actions with others. Storytellers and actors need to take turns. Children must agree that others can take the coveted roles of princess or superhero. They have to watch and listen carefully in order to synchronize the enactment of stories on the classroom stage.

This tension between individual impulses and the needs of the group have led some to maintain that in order to promote democracy, teachers must, at times, be anti-democratic. Covaleskie (2003) labels this the 'Paley's Paradox', arguing:

> The deepest habits of democratic life are, in a real sense, forced on children. If democratic citizens are to exhibit the sort of self-restraint and self-discipline, even at times self-denial, that are the cornerstones of a substantive democracy, this can happen only if responsible adults require of children that they are inclusive in the public spaces of our schools ... This is just why the classroom that restricts children's freedom in the right ways is the best way to prepare children for the later exercise of responsible freedom in a democratic society.
> *(Covaleskie, 2003: 336–337)*

Covaleskie (2003) is right to point out the importance of self-restraint and self-discipline, but he is underestimating the power of stories and play in the lives of children. While the tensions between individuals and the group can never be fully resolved, the high level of children's investment in storytelling and acting can result in their voluntary self-restraint in order to insure the smooth functioning of the activity.

Paley's concept of 'stage rules' provides a good example. While each classroom establishes its own rules, these stage rules often include: actors stay on the 'stage' while audience members stay off the stage, and when the story says characters are fighting, an actor's punches need to stay one arm's-length away from other actors. True, a rule dictating that even when you are a ninja you cannot slug a classmate is a restriction on individual volition. However, it is a restriction children readily embrace in order to proceed with the activity and avoid hurting friends.

Importantly, storytelling and story acting builds the trusting relationships that are the glue of democratic classroom communities. By listening to the stories of others, children get to know each other. They can examine each other's ideas and co-construct how to enact characters. For example, over time, a group may decide on the best way to enact a house, deciding how to position one's arms to depict the roof. As Cooper (2009) explains, the children's stories are invitations to classmates to play. Finding shared meaning is their point, and dramatizations enable cooperation and allow children to safely practice friendship.

The possibilities afforded by storytelling and story acting lead to a different conception of the relationship between the individual and the group; a conception articulated by Seidel (2001) when describing learning groups:

> It is possible to see the group as holding the individual in its arms with care, respect and love … The group that embraces the contributions of each member, however diverse and contradictory, may well provide exactly the right context for the emergence of strong individual identities. Through the debate, experimentation and negotiation that characterizes the work of these learning groups, each member comes to see, and in time to value, the particular, even idiosyncratic, qualities of the others. The valuing of each member's contribution means that each person not only develops respect for the others, but also has the experience of being valued for what he or she brings to the problem at hand.
>
> *(Seidel, 2001: 313)*

Paley (1997) captures this sense of democratic classroom communities, writing, 'The whole point of school is to find a common core of references without blurring our own special profiles' (Paley, 1997: viii). In sum, storytelling and story acting provides a powerful context for a collection of children to find common references while maintaining their special profiles. It is democracy in action.

Risks to the democratic character of storytelling and story acting in publicly funded settings

Paley created storytelling and story acting in the hospitable and relatively sheltered context of the University of Chicago Lab School, a historically progressive, well-resourced, private PreK through Grade 12 setting (children aged three through eighteen). What might happen to the democratic character of storytelling and story acting when it is brought to scale in publicly funded classrooms? To shed light on this question, in this section we:

- name two competing perspectives on evaluating young children's narratives;
- discuss the question of teachers' scaffolding of children's stories;
- describe the climate of publicly funded early childhood classrooms in the USA and UK;
- present anecdotal evidence on how the democratic character of storytelling and story acting fares in public settings.

Our conclusion is that storytelling and story acting face pressures in publicly funded settings that can erode its democratic character.

Stories in early childhood: One kind or many?

Asked to tell a story, four-year-old Gabriella responds:

> Once upon a time there was girl who didn't find a flower at the backyard cause she was planting a flower that she didn't saw it. Then a fairy come. Then she talked to the girl who didn't have flower in the backyard. The end.

What should we make of Gabriella's story? Is it a lovely fantasy about a girl playing in her garden, or an immature narrative that is lacking a clear conclusion and with grammatical errors, or both? Judgements about Gabriella's story are shaped by one's perspective on evaluating young children's narratives.

One perspective, from the field of narrative studies, defines *story* as a chronological recapitulation of successive events, that is to say as two or more events logically connected over time (McCabe and Peterson, 1991). From this definition emerge several systems to evaluate children's stories. Peterson and McCabe's (1983) High Point Analysis evaluates children's narratives in terms of their structural components (orientation, evaluation, and appendages) and overall structure (e.g. does the story have a high point?). Story grammar analysis (Stein and Glenn, 1975) evaluates stories on whether they have a beginning, middle, and end, with a story climax in the middle. From this perspective, Gabriella's story would be evaluated as typical for her age, and in need of development (in that it lacks a clear conclusion).

An alternative perspective on stories is associated with Moll and colleagues, who refer to 'funds of knowledge' (Moll and Cammarota, 2010), which acknowledges the diversity of families' practices and children's skills. In the early 1990s, research with immigrant families living in the United States started a new branch of literacy studies, which placed a strong emphasis on the cultural-historical context of literacy instruction. Whilst children in the Hispanic homes visited in Moll and colleagues' work were commonly considered 'disadvantaged', as their families were reputed not being able to provide the rich and engaging environments offered by other more 'advantaged' families, Moll's research showed that, in reality, these families and their communities contain extensive 'funds of knowledge'. Funds of knowledge are described by Moll as 'historically accumulated and culturally developed bodies of knowledge and skills essential for household or individual functioning and well-being' (Moll et al., 1992: 133). Moll and colleagues used this term to refer to the skills, strategies, and information utilized by households, which may include information, ways of thinking and learning, approaches to learning, and practical skills. Examples given include knowledge related to farming, construction, and household maintenance, such as shopping, meal preparation, gardening, and socializing with wider family and community members.

We use funds of knowledge as an umbrella term to celebrate the difference and diversity in children's narratives. Although Moll and colleagues did not talk about children's narratives specifically, we borrow their term to embrace children's locally constructed narratives. From this perspective, Gabriella's story is seen as a creative amalgam of story structures gleaned from home and school, reflecting her own personal interests.

How should Gabriella's teacher respond to her story? Should she simply accept Gabriella's utterances as told? Should she try to steer Gabriella towards a more mature, 'correct' form of storytelling? Should she engage Gabriella in a conversation about her story to learn more and potentially elicit more ideas? And how should the knowledge that Gabriella is a dual language learner from a Spanish-speaking home influence the answers to these questions?

In storytelling and story acting, teachers face the classic tension of whether to guide children towards certain outcomes or celebrate their achievements. Complicated by these two contrasting views of narrative, the teacher's scaffolding of children's storytelling is where this tension plays out particularly clearly.

Scaffolding

Scaffolding refers to paired adult–child activities (such as storytelling), where the adult supports the child's learning. The term was first used by Wood et al. (1976), to describe an interaction between an adult and a child constructing a wooden pyramidal puzzle. They referred to this process as 'a "scaffolding" process that enables a child or novice to solve a problem, carry out a task or achieve a goal which would be beyond his unassisted efforts' (Wood et al., 1976: 90). The term has gained a wider usage, including structuring and guiding a child's reasoning in a given task (e.g. Van de Pol et al., 2010).

It should be acknowledged that the idea of scaffolding is based on Vygotskyan ideas, even though he didn't use the term himself. In Vygotsky's theory (1978), the notion of the zone of proximal development (ZPD) relates to the scaffolding idea in that adults (or the 'more knowledgeable others') structure activities so that children are able to engage in more complex behaviours than they could on their own. Through feedback, adults provide support according to a child's current knowledge and gradually increase the task complexity, extending, or 'scaffolding', children's learning (see Wood et al., 1976).

In storytelling and story acting, scaffolding of story dictation can support or undermine children's agency and voice. Agency can be undermined by teachers asking numerous questions and offering many suggestions, ultimately taking control and ownership of the story away from the child. Alternatively, the teacher's questions and suggestions may support the child in sharing the story he or she wants to tell.

Examination of an example of scaffolding clarifies the risks and opportunities inherent in scaffolding children's storytelling. In this episode, the first author supports four-year-old Gabriella in telling her story. A video of our example can be found on the Boston Public School Early Childhood website (http://bpsearlychildhood.weebly.com/dictation.html). As seen in the video, the session begins with the adult asking a question:

Adult: You have a story to tell?

Gabriella: Ah ha.

A: OK. Why don't you tell it to me.

G: Once upon a time there was girl who didn't find flower at the backyard cause she was planting a flower that she didn't sawed it. Then

A: You got to slow down a second. Cause I haven't got in the backyard. So once upon a time there was a girl who didn't find a flower in the backyard. She was planting a flower?

G: Yes.

A: She was planting a flower. OK.

G: Then a fairy come. Then she talked to the girl who didn't have flower in her yard. Then end.

A: The girl who didn't have flowers. Cool. You know what? I want to read you back the story and see if there is anything you might want to add or change.

G: OK.

A: And I have a question for you too. So you said: Once upon a time there was girl who didn't find a flower in the backyard. She was planting a flower. Then a fairy comes. She talked to the girl who didn't have flowers in the backyard. The end. You know what I'm wondering? What the fairy said to the girl?

G: The fairy said to the girl, "I'm going to make magic and put you a lot of flowers for you to pick."

A: And make lots of flowers for you to pick. Did the fairy do that?

G: Yes.

A: Should I put that in the story?

G: Yes.

A: What do you want to say? The fairy made the flowers?

G: Yes.

A: OK. The fairy made the flowers. And what did the girl do?

G: She picked all the flowers for herself and her mommy.

A: She picked all the flowers for herself and her mommy. Can I read it to you again?

G: Yes.

A: OK, and see if you like it. Once upon a time there was girl who didn't find a flower in the backyard. She was planting a flower. Then a fairy comes. She talked to the girl who didn't have flowers in the backyard. The fairy said to the girl, "I'm going to make magic and make a lot of flowers for you to pick." The fairy made the flowers. She picked all the flowers for herself and her mommy. The end.

G: Thank you.

Interpreting the nature of this conversation, there is evidence of little initial scaffolding. Other than the adult's inadvertent correction of grammar (changing 'at the backyard' to 'in the backyard'), the adult simply writes down what the child is saying. This changes in line nine. First, the adult explains he is going to read back the story to see if 'there is anything you might want to add or change', signalling to Gabriella that her story has permanence (is captured in writing and can be recounted verbatim) and can be modified. Then, beginning in line eleven, the adult begins asking a series of questions about the story. The story expands through Gabriella's answers.

Members of the storytelling and story-acting community would evaluate this conversation differently, in part, influenced by their understanding of narrative in early childhood. In the UK, Lee's Helicopter Approach favours the interactions seen in lines 1 through 8, with teachers providing no input into the child's story (Lee, 2015). On one hand, this position is explained by the fact that often children have little agency in school; storytelling and story acting is a chance for them to express themselves. On the other hand, this position guards against the overzealous teacher whose multiple suggestions will rob children of their voice in storytelling. From this perspective, Gabriella's story was no longer hers after all the adult's questions.

In contrast, educators in Boston espouse the idea of 'gentle scaffolding'. In line with Cooper's (2009) notion of a 'participatory scribe', the teacher should, along with writing down and echoing the child's words, ask 'editorial questions'. The goal, for the child, is a story that will be understandable when dramatized. For the teacher, story dictation is understood as an opportunity to support children's narrative development. The questions the adult asks beginning in line 11 are consistent with these goals. Importantly, the questions asked are motivated by a desire to better understand the child's thinking. In the spirit of Duckworth's (2006) clinical interviewing, scaffolding is provided by asking for clarifications and the desire to know more. Gabriella's 'thank you' in line 24 suggests that her voice was supported in this interaction.

Yet both groups would agree that scaffolding is the place where storytelling and story acting risk losing their democratic character. If teacher's questions and comments have an instructional intent, the focus can move from helping children tell their story to getting a story with correct grammar or with a beginning, middle, and end. This is a particular concern in public settings because of the current climate of standards and high-stakes accountability.

The climate of standards and high-stakes accountability

In the 1980s, a consensus emerged among educational policy makers and political leaders in the USA and UK that the way to solve the ills of K–12 education was to create standards for schools and to deploy tests to insure the standards were being met. In recent years, efforts have been made to link these tests with rewards and punishments for teachers and administrators.

In parallel, a growing awareness about the importance of the early years has led to efforts to link early childhood education to K–12 systems (Key stages 0–5 in the UK) and the application of these standards and accountability paradigm to preschool (now often called pre-kindergarten in the USA). While their defenders are clear that standards are not intended to standardize curriculum, this can be an unintended consequence. In the USA, Common Core State Standards (CCSS), voluntary national standards that can be adopted by each state, name 75 standards for kindergarten English Language Arts. These include: participate in collaborative conversations with diverse partners about *kindergarten topics and texts*; continue a conversation through multiple exchanges; with prompting and support, retell familiar stories, including key details; recognize and name all upper- and lower-case letters of the alphabet; and read emergent-reader texts with purpose and understanding.

While some educators worry that these standards themselves will cause teachers to focus on the acquisition of discrete skills, to the detriment of creativity, what is more problematic for democracy is how these standards are evaluated. As even the small sampling of the CCSS illustrates, it is possible to have standards on a wide range of skills and dispositions, but if the accountability system measures only a small number of the most discrete skills, other, unmeasured skills, will be undermined. As Frede et al. (2011) explain:

> Rather than measuring what we value, it may be accurate to say that we all too often value what we measure. Whatever is measured tends to become a focus of concern for preschool providers, policy makers, and the public. Therefore, assessment systems have the potential for driving much of what goes on in early education classes, simply by increasing the saliency of the measured areas of the curriculum relative to the unmeasured (or less well measured) areas.
>
> *(Frede et al., 2011: 157)*

In the USA and the UK, what are measured are generally literacy and numeracy skills, beginning in early childhood and even more so in the later grades. However, children's democratic dispositions and the democratic climate of the classrooms – for example whether children collaborate and have voice – are not assessed. With teachers and administrators facing sanctions in the current accountability system, the result is a climate that can be described as anti-democratic.

A report from the US Alliance for Childhood (Miller and Almon, 2009) finds that in early childhood settings, standards and high-stakes accountability has led to a narrowing of the curriculum, where open-ended play, the arts, and social studies are sidelined; additionally it reports, 'In an increasing number of kindergartens, teachers must follow scripts from which they may not deviate. These practices, which are not well grounded in research, violate long-established principles of child development and good teaching' (Miller and Almon, 2009: 11). Similarly, research by Bassok and Rorem (2014) finds that since the onset of the current school reform movement, kindergartners play less, have less art and music, and more direct literacy and math instruction. In the UK, Cremin (2006) concludes that tests and targets have fostered in teachers 'a mindset characterised more by conformity and compliance than imagination and inventiveness' (Cremin, 2006: 3).

These pressures have particular implications for storytelling and story acting. The view of 'one kind of story' with a beginning, middle, and end creates pressures to scaffold story dictation towards one particular goal. Indeed, the Boston Public School kindergarten report card includes the line 'tells and dictates stories with clear narrative structure (beginning, middle, end)'. There is thus a concern that if teacher's scaffolding becomes overly emphatic, the democratic character of storytelling and story acting could be lost.

Anecdotal data about when storytelling and story acting meet standards and high-stakes accountability

If teachers are being monitored and rewarded for adhering to standards and rubrics, they are likely to interpret and implement storytelling and story acting in this light. In other words, they are not going to look for storytelling and story acting's democratic potential, but rather for links to specific, discrete literacy skills.

While we know of no studies to date on the impact of school climate on the implementation of storytelling and story acting, anecdotal evidence from the field is worrisome. In the UK, Cremin et al. (2013) conducted classroom observations as part of an evaluation study of storytelling and story acting. In one visit to a primary school in rural England, a teacher scribed a boy's story about knights who 'tooked' all the treasures. When transcribing the story, the teacher made her own decision in situ and corrected 'tooked' to 'took'. Similarly, Lee (2015) describes an observation of story dictation where the teacher repeatedly corrected the child's grammar as he tried to tell his story. Ultimately, in frustration, the child got up and left the table.

In the USA, we have seen signs posted in four-year-old classrooms which read, 'Good stories have beginnings, middles and ends'. We have seen graphic organizers such as charts and webs created to illustrate to kindergartners how their stories should proceed in this direction. We have talked to teachers expressing frustration with children not meeting this goal.

Such interpretations of storytelling and story acting are far from universal. However, they inject a note of caution to those aspiring to bring the practice to more classrooms, especially those in public settings. Nevertheless, in our work in Boston over the past three years, we have found some strategies which open up the curriculum and assessment practice for preserving the democratic character of storytelling and story acting and which acknowledge different ways of storytelling and story acting. In the next section we summarize these strategies.

Strategies to preserve the democratic ethos of storytelling and story acting

How a curriculum is operationalized is influenced by the experiences and backgrounds of the children, school leadership and climate, and community values, as well as by the experiences, abilities, and beliefs of a particular teacher. Given that individual teachers have agency, professional development can help preserve the democratic ethos of storytelling and story acting. Others have written with valuable insights on supporting teachers in implementing storytelling and story acting (Cooper, 1993, 2009; McNamee, 2015). Here we draw on experience in the Boston Public Schools (BPS), which are unique in: a) the size of the effort (involving 250 kindergarten teachers, and beginning in 2016, 150 pre-K teachers); and b) the mandatory nature of storytelling and story acting, as part of a prescribed curriculum.

The history of storytelling and story acting in Boston is described in Chapter 2. Regarding professional development, the focus on this section, author Mardell and his BPS colleague Marina Boni led seminars for three years that included over 100 teachers. During each seminar session, the teachers were presented with information about storytelling and story acting, and had time to discuss practices with colleagues. They also completed a reflection exercise that asked: What is something you learned and/or are taking away that you can use in your classroom from today's session?; What is a key question you are leaving with?; What feature(s) of today's session would you keep or change to enhance your learning?

Based on the experience of facilitating the seminar, interviews with participating teachers, and a review of the teacher reflections, we have developed several hypotheses about professional development strategies that can help teachers maintain the democratic character of storytelling and story acting. Specifically, we believe it is important to provide teachers with:

- information about narrative development in early childhood;
- continuous support regarding the logistics of implementing storytelling and story acting;
- a democratic adult learning environment.

We discuss each of these three elements next.

Information about narrative development in early childhood

Bringing storytelling and story acting to scale is not a matter of instillation; simply including it in the weekly curriculum plans and training teachers on the approach would not work. For teachers to embrace storytelling and story acting they need to understand why it is in the best interest of their children. Knowledge of how narrative development unfolds in early childhood is also important in maintaining the democratic nature of the activity.

As mentioned, the pressures to advance children's literacy skills are strong. 'Yes, children love storytelling and story acting, but I need them to meet the benchmarks' is not an uncommon refrain among teachers asked to implement storytelling and story acting. An understanding that storytelling and story acting promotes language and literacy skills allows teachers to embrace the practice, reassuring them that it is *not in addition* to their literacy programme, but a central part of it. The research basis is an important element helping teachers understand the reasons for including storytelling and story acting in their practice. In their reflections, a third of teachers expressed appreciation about hearing the research basis of storytelling and story acting during the initial session of the school year. Interestingly, this appreciation grew over time – 57 per cent wrote positively about a review during a mid-year session, with one teacher explaining, 'Now I get it'.

The pressure to move children's literacy abilities forward often takes the form of expecting young children to tell stories with a beginning, middle, and end (paralleling the writing they will be expected to do on high-stakes tests beginning in third grade). Teachers new to storytelling and story acting often voice impatience with children's stories that do not match this expectation. Knowledge of narrative development in early childhood helps teachers adjust their expectations.

As a body of research by McCabe and colleagues has shown, there are important developmental stages in children's narratives. Three-year-olds' narratives often have an unstructured 'leap-frog' nature. Four-year-olds' stories often consist of the telling of event after event, chronologies, or what some call 'and then and then stories'. It is not until the age of five that children reliably *begin* to tell stories that have a problem that is resolved (McCabe and Peterson, 1991). One needs to bear in mind that this is the developmental trajectory based on data of middle-class children of European ancestry. Given that storytelling is a cultural construct and story structure varies based on children's backgrounds, there are important cultural differences in children's stories. For example, African American, Japanese, and Taiwanese children sometimes produce performative narratives that consist of multiple related events (Champion and McCabe, 2015).

Learning about the development of narrative in early childhood proved liberating for teachers in the BPS seminar. Knowing that four-year-olds typically do not tell stories with beginnings, middles, and ends – and that this absence does not represent a problem – freed teachers to listen to what the children were saying. Teachers could enjoy and celebrate the many ways children tell stories. Consequently, 63 per cent of teachers expressed appreciation for learning about this research.

Continuous support regarding the logistics of implementing storytelling and story acting

On one level, storytelling and story acting is a simple activity; a teacher writes down a child's story and then brings it to a group time to be acted out. On another level, storytelling and story acting is a complex practice, with teachers having to make multiple decisions, including when and how to respond to a child's dictation and how to manage and support a group of young children in dramatizing a narrative.

Teachers beginning to work with storytelling and story acting have numerous questions and worries about specific parts of the practice, often asking whether they and their children are 'doing it right'. These concerns can lead more to a focus on behaviour and management rather than on stories and ideas. We found that an effective way of overcoming this hurdle is to provide teachers with continuous support regarding the logistics of storytelling and story acting.

Naturally in our work, the first seminar of the year focused on logistics – the basics of storytelling and story acting – which teachers found useful. Ninety-five per cent of teachers listed logistical information as something they learned/were taking away from these initial seminar sessions. Appreciation remained high throughout the year, with 79 per cent of teachers naming logistical considerations as helpful. How the information was shared was also commented on, with teachers writing they were, 'Glad it isn't a lecture'.

Indeed, seminar leaders went to great lengths to provide information in an engaging manner. One particularly effective technique, introduced by Trish Lee, had teachers taking part in storytelling and story acting. Seminar leaders marked out a stage with tape, took story dictation from a teacher, and then had the teachers act out the story. The facilitator's strategies and the rationale behind these strategies were then discussed. In subsequent seminars, the seminar leaders asked seminar members to lead the activity and to bring in children's stories in order to foster a deeper and more nuanced practice of supporting story acting.

A democratic adult learning environment

We believe that the learning environment for children often parallels that of the adults, and therefore hypothesize that creating a democratic learning environment for teachers is an important way to maintain the democratic ethos of storytelling and story acting. While not easy or straightforward in the context of a large bureaucracy, in the BPS storytelling and story-acting seminar efforts to create a democratic learning environment included:

- use of protocols for small groups where teachers can learn from and with one another;
- an ethos of flexibility about the details of storytelling and story acting.

After the initial seminars session, all subsequent sessions featured small group conversations about documentation from teachers' practice. Teachers brought documentation from their classrooms – either video of story dictation or acting or transcripts of children's stories. The small group conversations were structured with either See–Think–Wonder or (where participants share 'objective' observations before their evaluations) Ladder of Feedback (clarifying questions, appreciations, concerns, and suggestions) protocols (Visible Thinking Project, 2015). To help teachers gain familiarity with these conversational structures, they were modelled in whole group conversations.

The small groups were very well received. In their end of session surveys, 65 per cent of the teachers listed the small groups as something to keep, or requested even more time to hear from colleagues. One teacher explained that hearing from colleagues is a 'great way to recharge my creative teacher brain'. Another expressed appreciation for 'suggestions and feedback along with knowing others have similar struggles and puzzles'. A third teacher was more effusive, writing, 'Love! Love! Loved! Seeing other classes acting out stories.' Teachers also noted that the protocols were very helpful in supporting productive conversations.

An often-cited critique of small group learning, both with adults and children, is that peers might provide wrong information. In this case the seminar leaders have taken the stance that there is no one right way of doing storytelling and story acting. Instead, an ethos of flexibility about the details of storytelling and story acting was adopted. The stance of flexibility was expressed in an introductory quote from Vivian Paley (2012) on the storytelling and story-acting guide provided to the teachers: '[the teacher's] own observations will inform her best about all these details'.

The question of violence in children's stories captures well this stance of flexibility. When children, boys in particular, are allowed to tell their own stories, fights and battle scenes almost inevitably arise, with the carnage that ensues. Teachers brought this to the seminar. Seminar leaders framed the question as one of 'community standards'; that every community has norms and rules about how stories (books, plays, and movies) can be expressed and how the emotions and the realities of life are expressed. Leaders quoted Paley, who noted that, 'Boys, like Shakespeare, seem to have a need to see moments of violence acted out' (Paley, 2012) and a four-year-old BPS student who explained to his teacher, 'this is the only time we get to pretend to be killing and dying'. And then they returned to the notion of community standards, noting that each teacher is the guardian of her or his classroom community, and along with the children, needs to help negotiate their community standards. In other words, to ban, limit, or accept violence in stories was ultimately up to the individual teacher.

As one BPS teacher explained, when she joined the storytelling and story-acting seminar she worried about 'doing it right'. After a few sessions she realized that she was allowed to create structures that served her children best. The result, as she explained, was that 'I could make it [storytelling and story acting] my own. Now I love it.'

This stance is not always easy. Seminar leaders have strong opinions about storytelling and story-acting practices (e.g. scaffolding) and issues that arise when children tell and act out stories (e.g. violence in stories). When implementing storytelling and story acting in Boston kindergartens, the leaders did not shy away from explaining their positions, but also made clear that teachers' own observations will best inform the practice in their classrooms. Seminar leaders recognized the risks associated with giving teachers this license; that it might be done 'wrong', or at least become something not recognized as storytelling and story acting. To date, this has not been the case.

Lytle (2013) has spoken about the importance of teachers being allowed to make mistakes. While our current educational climate is not hospitable to mistakes (by teachers or children), mistakes are an integral part of the learning process. A school district culture where teachers know they, as professionals, can experiment, learn from colleagues, be supported by experienced coaches and, yes, make mistakes, seems to us the environment best suited to preserve the democratic character of storytelling and story acting.

Conclusion

In *The Boy Who Would be a Helicopter* (1990) Paley tells the story of Jason, whom she describes as 'the quintessential outsider'. With some regularity, Jason fills the classroom with 'wails of fright' and 'earsplitting noises'. Every classroom, indeed every society, must determine how to deal with their Jasons; with those who don't fit in. It is easy to imagine, even in a high-quality classroom, Jason being ostracized or even expelled. The suspension rates in early childhood classrooms in the USA are at a disturbingly high level (Gilliam and Shahar, 2006).

Expulsion is not an option for Paley. As she explains, '[Jason] is the one we must learn to include in our school culture if it is to be an island of safety and sensibility for everyone. What happens to Jason in school is the mirror of its moral landscape' (Paley, 1990: xi). In her efforts to include this child, Paley leverages storytelling and story acting as a way for the children and teachers to learn about Jason and, in turn, for Jason to learn about his classmates. Over the months, the progress is erratic, but in the end, by sharing his own stories and listening to and helping enact the stories of his friends, Jason becomes a valued member of the community. He has, in Steve Seidel's parlance, 'the experience of being valued for what he brings to the problem at hand' (2001: 313), and in Paley's, 'an island of safety and responsibility' (Paley, 1990: xi).

Making storytelling and story acting part of the curriculum of large public school districts opens the possibilities to enhance the democratic character of hundreds and even thousands of classrooms. It also requires facing the tensions named in this chapter:

- the classroom tension between individual children and the group;

- the instructional tension between supporting children's emerging storytelling abilities and taking away children's voice;
- the professional development tension between fidelity of implementation and teachers finding their own way with storytelling and story acting;
- the evaluative tension between measuring success through standardized tests of literacy sub-skills and the creation of a democratic classroom culture.

It is within this final tension, and belief that the creation of democratic classroom cultures receive high priority, where Jason's experience is relevant. How the Jasons of these classrooms are treated will serve as a measure to see if storytelling and story acting's potential is achieved.

References

Bassok, D. and Rorem, A. (2014) Is Kindergarten the new first grade? The changing nature of Kindergarten in the age of accountability. EdPolicyWorks Working Paper Series, No. 20. Retrieved from: http://curry.virginia.edu/uploads/resourceLibrary/20_Bassok_Is_Kindergarten_The_New_First_Grade.pdf

Champion, T. B. and McCabe, A. (2015) Narrative structures of African American children: Commonalities and differences. In S. Lanehart, L. Green and J. Bloomquist (eds.), *Oxford Handbook of African American Language*. New York: Oxford University Press.

Cooper, P. (1993) *When Stories Come to School: Telling, writing and performing stories in the early childhood classroom*. New York: Teachers and Writers Collaborative.

Cooper, P. (2009) *The Classrooms All Young Children Need: Lessons in teaching from Vivian Paley*. Chicago: University of Chicago Press.

Covaleskie, J. (2003) Paley's paradox: Educating for democratic life. *Philosophy of Education Yearbook*, 330–337.

Cremin, T. (2006) Creativity, uncertainty and discomfort: Teachers as writers. *Cambridge Journal of Education, 36*(3): 415–433.

Cremin, T., Swann, J., Flewitt, R. S., Faulkner, D. and Kucirkova, N. (2013) *Evaluation Report of MakeBelieve Arts Helicopter Technique of Storytelling and Story Acting*. Available at: http://www.makebelievearts.co.uk/docs/Helicopter-Technique-Evaluation.pdf

Dewey, J. (2004) *Democracy and Education*. New York: The Free Press (first published 1916).

Duckworth, E. (2006) *'The Having of Wonderful Ideas' and Other Essays on Teaching and Learning*. New York, NY: Teachers College Press.

Frede, E., Gilliam, W. and Schweinhart, L. (2011) Assessing accountability and ensuring continuous program improvement: Why, how and who. In E. Zigler, W. Gilliam and S. Barnett (eds), *The Pre-K Debates: Current controversies and issues* (pp. 152–159). Baltimore, MD: Brookes.

Gilliam, W. and Shahar, G. (2006) Preschool and child care expulsion and suspension rates and predictors in one state. *Infants & Young Children, 19*(3): 228–245.

Lee, T. (2015) *Princesses, Dragons and Helicopter Stories: Storytelling and story acting in the early years*. London: Routledge.

Lytle, S. (2013) *Teacher-Research and the Inquiry Stance*. Washington, DC: National Association for the Education of Young Children Annual Conference.

McCabe, A. and Peterson, C. (1991) *Developing Narrative Structure*. New Jersey: Lawrence Erlbaum.

McNamee, G. (2015) *The High-Performing Preschool: Story acting in Head Start classrooms.* Chicago, IL: University of Chicago Press.

Miller, E. and Almon, J. (2009) *Crisis in the Kindergarten.* Available from: http://www. allianceforchildhood.org/sites/allianceforchildhood.org/files/file/kindergarten_report. pdf

Moll, L. C. and Cammarota, J. (2010) Cultivating new funds of knowledge through research and practice. In K. Dunsmore and D. Fisher (eds.), *Bringing Literacy Home.* Newark, DE: International Reading Association.

Moll, L. C., Amanti, C., Neff, D. and Gonzalez, N. (1992) Funds of knowledge for teaching: Using a qualitative approach to connect homes and classrooms. *Theory into Practice, 31*(2): 132–141.

Moss, P. (2011) Democracy as first practice in early childhood education and care. In R. E. Tremblay, M. Boivin and R. De V. Peters (eds.), *Encyclopedia on Early Childhood Development* [online]. Montreal, Quebec: Centre of Excellence for Early Childhood Development and Strategic Knowledge Cluster on Early Child Development. Available at: http://www.child-encyclopedia.com/documents/MossANGxp1.pdf

Nicolopoulou, A., Cortina, K. S., Ilgaz, H., Cates, C. B. and de Sá, A. B. (2015) Using a narrative- and play-based activity to promote low-income preschoolers' oral language, emergent literacy, and social competence. *Early Childhood Research Quarterly, 31*: 147–162.

Paley, V. (1990) *The Boy Who Would Be a Helicopter: The uses of storytelling in the classroom.* Cambridge, MA: Harvard University Press.

Paley, V. (2010) *Storytelling and Story Acting with Vivian Paley.* Ball State University, IN: Child Care Collection.

Paley, V. (2012) *Storytelling/Story Acting.* Boston Public Schools kindergarten conference, Boston, MA. http://bpsearlychildhood.weebly.com/the-wisdom-of-vivian-paley-and-trish-lee.html

Peterson, C. and McCabe, A. (1983) High Point Analysis. In *Developmental Psycholinguistics* (pp. 29–47). New York: Plenum Press.

Project Zero and Reggio Children (2001) *Making Learning Visible: Children as individual and group learners.* Reggio Emilia, Italy: Reggio Children.

Roosevelt, E. (1958) 'In Our Hands' speech delivered on the tenth anniversary of the Universal Declaration of Human Rights. http://www.un.org/en/globalissues/briefingpapers/humanrights/quotes.shtml

Seidel, S. (2001) To be part of something bigger than oneself in Project Zero and Reggio Children. In *Making Learning Visible: Children as individual and group learners.* Reggio Emilia, Italy: Reggio Children.

Stein, N. L. and Glenn, C. G. (1975) An analysis of story comprehension in elementary school children: A test of a schema. http://files.eric.ed.gov/fulltext/ED121474.pdf

United Nations Convention on the Rights of the Child (1989) http://www.ohchr.org/en/professionalinterest/pages/crc.aspx

Van de Pol, J., Volman, M. and Beishuizen, J. (2010) Scaffolding in teacher–student interaction: A decade of research. *Educational Psychology Review, 22*(3): 271–296.

Visible Thinking Project (2015) http://www.visiblethinkingpz.org/VisibleThinking_html_files/03_ThinkingRoutines/03c_Core_routines/SeeThinkWonder/SeeThinkWonder_Routine.html

Vygotsky, L. S. (1978) *Mind in Society: The development of higher psychological processes.* Cambridge, MA: Harvard University Press.

Wood, D., Bruner, J. and Ross, G. (1976) The role of tutoring in problem solving. *Journal of Child Psychology and Psychiatry, 17*(2): 89–100.

CONCLUSION

Storytelling and story acting: Rays of hope for the early years classroom

Ben Mardell and Joan Swann

Introduction

Forty years ago Vivian Gussin Paley, a kindergarten teacher in Chicago, was faced with an important decision. The administration of her school had decided her class would go from half to whole day. What to do with the additional time? Should children have more time for free play? Should they engage in developmentally appropriate, teacher-led activities? Or should they participate in a practice she was developing at the time, which has come to be known as storytelling and story acting?

The question of how young children should spend their time in the classroom – be that in public schools, nurseries, Head Starts and childcare centres – is one teachers continue to face. The research in this volume confirms that it would be wise to include the choice Paley made all those years ago when she picked the option of storytelling and story acting. The chapters demonstrate, in various ways, the educational value of Paley's approach: a glance at the titles shows that storytelling and story acting are seen to promote oral narrative skills, but also cognitive and social development, print awareness and literacy, agency and creativity, equity and inclusion, and democratic classrooms. The authors consider storytelling and story acting from a range of disciplinary perspectives. Developmental psychology, applied linguistics, literacy studies and early childhood education are among the fields represented. In addition, the research reported here was conducted in a range of locations – urban, suburban and rural settings in the USA and the UK; in different types of educational programmes; and among children of different economic, cultural and linguistic backgrounds. The diverse and complementary perspectives adopted across chapters enable the volume to contribute new, critical and sometimes challenging insights to the body of empirical and theoretical knowledge about the value of storytelling and story acting, discussed earlier in Chapter 2.

Chapters also highlight occasional tensions, unfinished business and continuing questions that future research should address. These questions include debates within the storytelling/story-acting community about details of practice. Indeed, once Paley had made the choice of storytelling and story acting, she continued to reflect on and revise the practice, making changes to best meet the needs of her students. This process continues to this day in classrooms around the world. In this concluding chapter we discuss how the work in this book adds to our knowledge and consideration of implementing storytelling and story acting. We end by speculating about what the future holds for this vibrant and powerful practice.

Storytelling and story acting observed

Through close observation, documentation and analysis, chapters document a range of classroom practices, experiences and achievements in the field of storytelling and story acting. Many also introduce us to individual children and their stories. In Chapter 4, for instance, we meet Fiona, who brilliantly scribes her friend Will's story using the one letter she knows best (F). In Chapter 5, Alan's story of a dragon falling in the bin and being 'splatted' by an orange provides striking imagery that is drawn on by children in his class over the following eight weeks. Chapter 6 introduced George, initially reticent, who blossoms as a confident storyteller with the support of attentive adults. Jessica, in Chapter 7, uses story to navigate an emotionally charged home life. In Chapter 8, Oscar's one-word story helps him explore the developmental issues involved in being three. And for Jaime and Wang Tai, in Chapter 9, the practice of storytelling and story acting supports their participation in a classroom whose language they are just learning. Here children's development as narrators is understood to involve literacy and cognitive abilities *and* social and emotional development. The experiences of these children are viewed holistically. What do we learn from such closely observed children? We consider below some themes that recur across the chapters, and contribute new insights to our understanding of storytelling and story acting. Themes include:

- pathways to literacy;
- agency, creativity and collaboration;
- cognitive, social and emotional development;
- the interdependence of storytelling and story acting;
- story and multimodality;
- equity, inclusion and democracy.

Pathways to literacy

In storytelling and story acting the interplay between spoken and written language is important. Storytelling allows children to express themselves through speech, attended to and supported by an adult; and story acting encourages children's attentive and focused listening. Children also observe the process of writing, and recognize the importance of this in capturing their stories. The potential benefits for children's spoken and written language have been a major focus of earlier research by Nicolopoulou, reviewed in Chapter 2. In Chapter 3, Nicolopoulou discusses a recent study focusing on children from low-income and otherwise disadvantaged backgrounds. The children had exceptionally weak language skills by comparison with others she had studied and were building up many of their narrative skills from scratch. Nicolopoulou comments that 'if storytelling and story acting could work successfully in such difficult circumstances, it should be able to work anywhere'. In fact her quantitative analysis was able to demonstrate the positive impact of storytelling and story acting on these young children's oral narrative development along several measures of complexity and sophistication.

In her discussion Nicolopoulou also points to the established association between the development of young children's narrative skills and literacy development: while they are predominantly oral practices storytelling and story acting may, therefore, also promote children's emergent literacy. There is some evidence for this claim in another study by Nicolopoulou and her colleagues (2015). In this case a hierarchical linear modelling analysis found that engagement in storytelling and story acting was significantly associated with increased print and word awareness. Nicolopoulou's work on narrative development and literacy is complemented by other chapters in this book that focus on children's participation in storytelling and story acting, in this case drawing attention to the keen interest children display in seeing their words take shape in written form. Cremin, in Chapter 4, examines this issue more substantively, documenting the process of print and word awareness as this unfolds through storytelling and story-acting sessions. It is particularly gratifying to read about preschool boys, who are often seen as disengaged from pen and paper tasks, taking on the mantle of writer. In many ways Cremin's contextualized, ethnographic account of emergent writing provides a companion piece to Nicolopoulou's larger-scale quantitative study of children's narrative texts.

Agency, creativity and collaboration

Despite their different analytical approaches, Nicolopoulou and Cremin both draw attention to children's agency in storytelling and story acting. Nicolopoulou notes that while these activities are teacher-initiated they are also voluntary – children make choices and control their own participation. Cremin comments on the agency involved in children's 'self-initiated authoring', in which they take ownership of storytelling and story acting: many children have been observed to extend this by writing and illustrating their own stories, and eliciting and scribing stories from others. While not all contributors to the book use the term 'agency', the idea of children exercising choice and taking ownership is evident in all chapters.

There is also, however, an emphasis across chapters on storytelling and story acting as collaborative processes. While emphasizing children's agency, for instance,

Cremin sees authoring as occurring collectively between children. Collaboration is a major focus of Chapter 5, where Faulkner refers to storytelling as a form of collective meaning-making. Children learn from the 'guided participation' of the adults who support and scribe their stories, and their own stories are also affected by their participation in the storytelling of other children. An analysis of story themes shows the outcomes of these joint participative processes, as children recycle common tropes and narrative structures. Faulkner sees this as a form of sociocultural transmission: she argues that children are learning how to construct stories that will be popular with their immediate peer group, and that this process engenders the development of symbolic 'communities of minds'. In Chapter 6, Swann provides a detailed moment-by-moment analysis of the subtle processes by which stories and their performances are jointly constructed by all participants: the child narrator; the adult scribe (in actively encouraging the child or even remaining silent and motionless); and the adult 'stage manager', along with actors and audience members in performance. Swann goes outside education (to research on conversational narrative, the study of performance and language creativity) to explore this process. Contemporary understandings of creativity in language, for instance, have emphasized collaboration over individual agency. Swann argues that the collaboration evident in storytelling and story acting both values, and adds value, to individual children's narratives.

There are however, potential tensions between the ideas of individual agency and collaboration, or the collective, in storytelling and story acting, and these are explored by Mardell and Kucirkova in Chapter 10 in relation to the development of democratic classrooms (see further below).

Cognitive, social and emotional development

As noted in Chapter 2, the focus on collaboration between participants in storytelling and story acting is consistent with ideas on child development associated with the Russian psychologist Lev Vygotsky (e.g. Vygotsky, 1978). It is perhaps not surprising, therefore, that several chapters in the book take a Vygotskyan sociocultural approach to children's learning, in which cognitive development is rooted in children's relationships with others. The ideas of collective authoring (Cremin) and collective meaning making (Faulkner), for instance, derive in part from Vygotskyan theory. Chapters 7 (McNamee) and 8 (Cooper) explore in greater depth the association between Vygotsky, storytelling and story acting. McNamee engages in an intellectual conversation with Vygotsky to shed light on the learning that takes place in a single classroom. And Cooper's exploration of Paley's 'pedagogy of meaning' relates this to Vygotskyan theories of development. Vygotsky's focus on social interaction as fundamental to cognitive development has clear relevance to the collaborative processes involved in storytelling and story acting, where children's learning is supported in interaction with adults and peers. McNamee, for instance, points out that while teacher-initiated and teacher-guided activities are 'the building blocks' of the school day, children also learn from their peers: 'learning ebbs and flows in relationships among many people'.

McNamee and Cooper also engage with Vygotsky's ideas on imaginary or pretend play as a way of enabling and supporting children's learning. With Vygotsky, Cooper sees play 'as the young child's natural option for the acquisition and practice of symbolic thinking, as well as the best preparation for later acquisition of scientific concepts and abstract reasoning'. And McNamee argues that dramatization in story acting is a step forward from pretend play: 'it uses the power of speech to reorganize our perception of the world, and create new forms of thinking'. For these authors Vygotsky provides a powerful theorization of the learning potential of storytelling and story acting. Cooper in particular is also concerned to mount a defence of play and imagination against contemporary curricula in the USA that discourage fantasy content in young children's oral and written narratives. We return below to some of the tensions between storytelling and story acting and contemporary curricular settings.

As essentially collaborative processes, storytelling and story acting foster cognitive development alongside social and emotional development: seeing learning as socially situated suggests these are closely integrated. This is acknowledged by McNamee and Cooper, and is also addressed by Flewitt in Chapter 9. Flewitt argues that the social nature of learning means that learning processes are not shaped merely by individual competence but also by cultural and social factors: learning takes place in 'a complex web of social, historical and cultural beliefs that the individual encounters through everyday practice' (Nind et al., 2014: 345).

Illustrations of the integration of cognitive, social and emotional development occur throughout the book. Faulkner's analytical framework discussed in Chapter 5, for instance, includes an interpersonal focus, suggesting that relationships between children affect their participation in learning activities. In scribing other children's stories (Cremin, Chapter 4), children are taking on particular identities – as writers and guides. These are validated by other children who dictate stories to them, and by teachers who accept the stories for acting out. Chapters 6 (Swann) and 9 (Flewitt) show children increasing in confidence through their participation in storytelling and story acting. These chapters also document the close interpersonal negotiation that underpins both storytelling and story acting. The stories themselves enable children to explore social relations – for instance, as Faulkner argues, recycling narrative structures and themes helps to build community, and the act of reproducing another child's character or motif is also a positive acknowledgement of the child and his/her choices. The stories often reflect popular culture and their gendering in this case (discussed in Chapter 2 and also by Cooper in Chapter 8) allows children to explore gendered identities. Sometimes stories help children to work through difficult or complex social and emotional issues. McNamee comments on the child who narrated a disturbing family incident, and Cooper argues that the themes frequently recycled in children's narratives allow the 'use of fantasy to integrate and explore fear, friendship, and fairness in the effort to grow up'. In all these examples, children's deep engagement in storytelling and story acting leads to what Seidel

(2001) describes as 'learning in many directions at once', in this case a combination of social, emotional, cognitive and intellectual development.

The interdependence of storytelling and story acting

Storytelling and story acting are sequential but integrated practices, and chapters document the interplay between these. In Chapter 3, for instance, Nicolopoulou refers to the importance of the interrelated roles taken up by children: composing and dictating stories, taking part in group enactment of their own and others' stories, and watching the performance of others' stories. She argues that, while children typically enjoy storytelling for its own sake, looking forward to the acting out of their stories provides an additional motivation; furthermore, stories are produced in the public setting of the classroom peer culture, enabling children to borrow and rework elements from each others' stories, a process that facilitates narrative cross-fertilization. Faulkner (Chapter 5) demonstrates that cross-fertilization occurs as children observe others' storytelling as well as in the public performance of stories. In Chapter 4, Cremin notes that, in a class she observed, children who scribed stories from their peers, or created their own 'Helicopter' stories, often wished to read these during story-acting sessions. Where this occurred it gave 'real purpose to their writing'. For Swann (Chapter 5) and Flewitt (Chapter 9) children's increasing confidence is enabled across both storytelling and story acting, as their stories are demonstrably valued by teachers and other children. And for McNamee (Chapter 7) and Cooper (Chapter 8) the developmental potential of children's story making is evident as they tell and then perform their stories with others. In their consideration of democratic classroom practices, Mardell and Kucirkova (Chapter 10) comment that 'the opportunities to tell a story, to choose whether or not to participate in story acting, and to have the license to decide how to portray characters in story acting' in combination promote individual voice, choice and agency.

All the contributors to this volume would, then, agree that an essential element of Paley's approach is the combination of storytelling and story acting. Storytelling without acting, or acting of narratives not written by the children, are not as powerful as bringing the two together. Indeed, the highly specific marriage of dictation and dramatization – their mutual interdependence – underpins the potency of Paley's approach.

Story and multimodality

Storytelling and story acting, and indeed all the processes outlined above, are better understood if researchers acknowledge the range of ways in which children and adults communicate. This is something that has only recently been acknowledged, and it is explored in Chapter 9 (Flewitt) through the lens of two young boys with an emerging command of English, the classroom language. Flewitt shows that participation in storytelling and story acting enables these and other young children to gain in confidence and engage more fully in classroom life. To understand this process, however – and to see the potential of the children's stories – we need to take account of their use of multiple communicative modes, such as body orientation and posture, body movements, gesture, facial expression, gaze, tone of voice, and verbal language, referred to by Flewitt as a 'multimodal ensemble'.

Flewitt argues that multimodality is compatible with sociocultural Vygotskyan approaches to learning. Mental processes, social in origin, 'are mediated through interaction using diverse symbolic tools, including language and material artefacts'. Thus Jaime's initial one-word story is accompanied by a gesture that contributes to its meaning; the teacher's attention to and respect for a later story is indicated through her body posture, direction and length of gaze, hand position, tilt and proximity of her head.

While Flewitt explicitly takes a multimodal perspective throughout her analysis, other chapters also consider the multimodal nature of storytelling and story acting: in Chapter 4, Cremin sees children's writing as a multimodal activity; Faulkner, in Chapter 5, comments on the role of 'non-verbal' communication in teachers' support for children and children's participation in storytelling; and Swann, in Chapter 6, sees the collaborative creativity inherent in storytelling and story acting as a multimodal achievement.

Equity, inclusion and democracy

Flewitt argues that the adoption of a multimodal perspective, in which children's achievements are recognized and valued, can promote equity and celebrate diversity in the early years classroom: all children are enabled to share ideas, 'building each child's sense of identity and worth in an inclusive community of peers and teachers'.

Such ideas are explored further by Mardell and Kucirkova (Chapter 10) in relation to the political ideal of democracy. Democracy in the classroom is related both to the promotion of individual agency and choice, and to the establishment of a community, with 'children and teachers creating a culture together by establishing the rules, rituals, stories, artefacts and ideas that define the group'. We mentioned above certain tensions between individual agency and the collective, and Mardell and Kucirkova attempt to resolve these. In relation to 'Paley's paradox' – that in order to promote inclusivity and democracy teachers need to restrict children's freedom (Covaleskie, 2003) – they argue that the high level of children's involvement in storytelling and story acting leads to their voluntary self-restraint, embraced to support the smooth running of the activity. Just as in play, children abide by the rules because they understand their necessity. Storytelling and story acting also promote a conception of the collective that values the contributions of individuals, and so allows children to retain their 'special profiles'.

For Mardell and Kucirkova, democracy is not just about practices in the here and now of the classroom, but also about the creation of citizens of the future, equipped to face the challenges of social changes such as migration and increasing diversity. The contributors to the volume share a common answer to the question: What kind of citizens do we want to create? The answer is citizens who are engaged, caring, creative and able to work with others to solve community problems. The descriptions of classrooms provided by Cremin (Chapter 4), Faulkner (Chapter 5), McNamee (Chapter 7) and Flewitt (Chapter 9) provide solid evidence that storytelling and story acting can support the development of such citizens.

The democratic potential of storytelling and story acting is, however, under threat from a contemporary climate of 'standards and high-stakes accountability', a situation explained in Chapter 1. Mardell and Kucirkova argue that this climate may lead teachers to focus on the development of a particular set of discrete, easily measurable skills, to the detriment of creativity and open-ended play. In storytelling and story acting, a restrictive definition of 'story' would threaten children's choices, and democratic principles in the classroom. Earlier chapters express similar concerns. We mentioned above Cooper's (Chapter 8) discussion of contemporary curricula that discourage fantasy in young children's narratives. And in Chapter 4, Cremin points to the 'downward pressure of performative cultures', with their focus on discrete skills and 'the basics'. Cremin sees storytelling and story acting positively, as a complementary way forward in the current, standards-based context. Mardell and Kucirkova proactively identify strategies to support the inclusion of storytelling and story acting within contemporary early years curricula: providing information about narrative development in early childhood (to counter the expectation that young children should adopt fully fledged narrative structures); providing continuing support with the logistics of storytelling and story acting; and instituting a democratic learning environment in seminars for teachers. Given the evidence presented in this volume on the value of storytelling and story acting, it is essential to develop local strategies to secure a place for these initiatives, with their democratic principles, at the heart of early years language and literacy curricula.

New and continuing questions

The chapters in this volume offer a solid, if not complete, insight into the knowledge base regarding storytelling and story acting. Reading across these chapters raises new theoretical, empirical and practical questions that future research should address.

Dual language learners

Given the large-scale migration that is occurring around the globe, it is not surprising that the researchers contributing to this volume encountered children participating in storytelling and story acting in a language that was not the language of their home. The experiences of Fernando and Isabella (Chapter 7), Oscar

(Chapter 8) and Jaime and Wang Tai (Chapter 9) illustrate that the practice has much to offer children learning a new language at school. Supports include the possibilities of recognizing young children's multimodal communicative strategies, and valuing how they skilfully orchestrate gesture, facial expression, gaze, tone of voice, and body movements in addition to verbal language. Paley has described such support as a 'life line of participation' (see http://bpsearlychildhood.weebly.com/the-wisdom-of-vivian-paley-and-trish-lee.html).

At the same time, the growing number of children being supported in learning another language through storytelling and story acting raises questions about if and how the practices should be adapted. Should children be able to share their stories in their home language? Would it be helpful to act out stories in two languages – first in a child's home language and then the main language of the classroom? Are there special techniques that teachers could or should use to introduce storytelling and story acting to children not fluent in the main language of the classroom?

In addition, it would be valuable to extend the methodological look at the issues of dual language learners to include quantitative methods. Impact studies such as Nicolopoulou's in Chapter 3 would provide important additional evidence to the qualitative and theoretical information currently available.

Children with special educational needs

While not addressed in this collection of chapters, similar questions could be asked about children with special educational needs. Children with specific language impairment would benefit from the non-verbal support that story acting provides. Children with pragmatic social difficulties might benefit from the scaffolding story acting provides. While practitioners have, by necessity, confronted these issues[1] it would be useful for researchers to explore these questions as well.

'Dosage'

How much storytelling and story acting is needed for it to have an impact? Are there diminishing returns, or is more storytelling better? In Paley's classroom children told and acted out stories every day, which is the recommendation in Boston Public Schools. Nicolopoulou and her colleagues' (2015) research found that the benefits of a programme were related to the number of stories a child had told. It seems likely that some 'density' to the experience is necessary.

Yet teachers often note that they do not have the time for daily storytelling and story acting. Indeed, in Nicolopoulou's research in this volume (Chapter 3), stories were told and enacted in approximately 50 per cent of their school days, which may not be possible to replicate in other classrooms. While the intuition of many proponents of storytelling and story acting is that more is better, the question of dosage remains important for those deciding large-scale educational policy.

To scaffold or not to scaffold

Scaffolding is a point of disagreement among proponents of storytelling and story acting. Trisha Lee (2015), the founder of the UK's Helicopter Stories approach, argues that children's stories should be taken down verbatim without any guiding questions from teachers. The Boston Public Schools advocate 'gentle scaffolding', where teachers can ask the child storyteller a small number of clarifying questions. In addition, in Boston a teacher may support a child in starting their story, and, especially with children who have difficulties telling stories in English, co-construct a story using photographs and other supports.

The work in this volume does not provide unambiguous guidance here. Nicolopoulou (Chapter 3) concludes that the development of narrative abilities found in her research is due to peer culture, not adult support. Yet Swann's idea of co-construction (Chapter 6) between teacher and child suggests that scaffolding can be part of the scribing process. Where it involves best practice, it is also fascinating to note that Fiona's interaction with her friend Will as she takes down his story (discussed by Cremin, Chapter 4) can be described as scaffolding.

Ultimately, as noted by Mardell and Kucirkova in Chapter 10, we see the question of scaffolding as part of a healthy dialogue about storytelling and story acting, a dialogue we hope this volume supports.

Story content – restrictions and repetitions

As Cooper points out in Chapter 8, teachers new to storytelling and story acting often ask questions about story content. Is it all right for children to tell stories based on popular culture? Are stories with violence permissible? What does it mean that all the boys are telling superhero stories, or all the girls are telling stories about princesses? It is not uncommon for teachers, as Cooper admits she did when she was a classroom teacher, to restrict or censor children's story content.

To the question of popular culture, Cooper provides a compelling argument for allowing such stories and also for allowing children to tell similar stories again and again. While many educators may be comfortable with this answer for princess and superhero stories, stories with violence and sometimes killing provoke stronger opposition. In arguing for a higher level of tolerance towards stories with violence, Paley likens boys' fascination for violence with Shakespeare's and suggests that allowing such themes in stories provides a forum where the community can establish its own standards (see her answer to the question from a Boston Public School teacher at http://bpsearlychildhood.weebly.com/the-wisdom-of-vivian-paley-and-trish-lee.html).

Of course, there are limits. McNamee's description (Chapter 7) of how a teacher guides a child away from telling a story of domestic violence is a good case in point. Such examples, as well as the dialogue we hope that they promote, are a part of a healthy storytelling and story-acting community.

For those teachers at their wits' end on hearing what seems to be the same story week after week, the good news from this volume is that stories mature. As Nicolopoulou (Chapter 3) found in tracking Deena's stories over the course of the year, narrative development occurs within the repetition of themes. And there are the moments of extraordinary stories: for example George, who Swann introduces us to in Chapter 6, whose initial story captures something essential about the world.

The future of storytelling and story acting

What does the future hold for Paley's approach to storytelling and story acting? Forty years from now, will it be thriving, surviving or a distant memory of the educational past? Our crystal ball reading has us to believe that three interrelated factors will be instrumental in determining the future of storytelling and story acting:

- how play is viewed;
- conceptions of early childhood educators;
- the rights of children.

How play is viewed

Virtually every contribution to this volume mentions play. For example, Cremin (Chapter 4) talks about creating textual playgrounds for children while Faulkner (Chapter 5) mentions children playing with language. As explained in Chapter 2, there is a close relationship between story and play, and how story acting draws upon elements of children's dramatic play. Cooper (Chapter 8) also notes that Paley sees storytelling and story acting as a natural extension of children's dramatic play. Play and storytelling and story acting conjure up the same words: agency, choice, collaboration, joy and delight.

Cooper discusses how play has long been a central pillar of early childhood education and why this should remain so. Yet the future is far from guaranteed. As discussed in Chapter 1, an educational landscape dominated by standards and high-stakes accountability measures has led to the movement towards more direct instruction, and less play, in early years classrooms. These and other global trends in early years curricula spell an uncertain future for play, both within and outside formal educational settings (LEGO Learning Institute, 2013).

At the same time, it is important to recognize that play has always had an uncomfortable relationship with school (Kuschner, 2015). In play the players lose their sense of time, and schools are governed by schedules. Play can be messy and loud while schools aspire to be places of order. In play the child is in charge, whereas at school it is the adults who set the agenda. Talented early years teachers have long been able to manage these tensions and successfully advocate for children to play in educational contexts. Storytelling and story acting's future depends, in part, on the continuing recognition of the value of play.

Conceptions of early childhood educators

As described in Chapter 1, the educational landscape in the USA and the UK has shifted the conception of the teacher from educator towards technocrat; the implementer of a scripted curriculum. This shift can be seen as part of a long-standing struggle between those who see teachers as transmitters of skills and culture and those who see teachers as guides to children's inquiry, and as co-creators of culture with their students.

While these struggles are occurring throughout schooling, there are issues that are particular to early childhood education. As a field, early childhood teachers are less well paid and so generally less credentialled. In the USA, despite growing recognition of the early years, and greater demands on early childhood educators, compensation remains substandard. The perception of an unqualified workforce provides justification for some to advocate 'teacher-proof' curricula.

Storytelling and story acting represent anything but a teacher-proof curriculum. The stories children tell are unpredictable. Supporting twenty four-year-olds in acting out stories can be loud, and occasionally chaotic. It is the opposite of scripted. It is an activity that requires a professional to manage it. Whether early childhood educators are seen as professionals, and supported through educational opportunities, professional development and compensation, will have a significant impact on the future of storytelling and story acting.

The rights of children

In classrooms where children are seen as citizens – with the right to express their opinions and the right to be children – they are given the opportunity to explore creative ideas for discovery and play, generate theories of how the world works, and develop insights into the feelings of others. They are allowed to play. They are allowed to tell stories. They are, in Cooper's words in Chapter 8, actualizing their 'natural and immediate need for imagination-based learning'.

In the future will children be seen as contemporary citizens, with rights and responsibilities? Or will they merely be seen as future citizens who need to be prepared to be contributors to the national economy?

Storytelling and story acting depend on children being seen as contemporary citizens. In these activities children have the right to tell a story or not, and act in a story or not. They are allowed to tell the kinds of stories they want. The adults are not the only teachers in the room and children learn from and with one another about story themes and ways of acting. In storytelling and story acting children are seen as capable of directing their own learning. They are doing what they want to do. In enlightened classrooms, this is exactly what the adults want children to be doing.

The idea that young children have rights, have opinions, can learn from each other and should be able to direct their own learning may seem like radical notions in an era that favours bureaucratic control, fidelity of implementation and centralized authority (and we thought the Soviet model had collapsed!). Yet there are many who continue to advocate children's rights as enshrined in the United Nations Convention on the Rights of the Child, whose Article 12 recognizes the child's right to express opinions and Article 31 recognizes the right to play (see http://www.ohchr.org/en/professionalinterest/pages/crc.aspx).

Kindergarten teacher Vivian Paley's 40-year-old experiment with storytelling and story acting offers rays of hope to those seeking to build and nurture early years classrooms where creativity, agency and democracy thrive. Our hope is that this volume, drawing on new research, serves to support those who seek to understand and promote such practices.

Note

1   See the video interviews with preschool inclusion teacher Megan Nason and multiple disability teacher Erica Lilley on the Boston Public Schools' Early Childhood Department website: http://bpsearlychildhood.weebly.com/boston-listens-seminar.html; in Cremin et al., 2013 see the examples of stories told by a boy with limited verbal language, using a sign-supported communication system.

References

Covaleskie, J. (2003) Paley's paradox: Educating for a democratic life. In K. Alston (ed.), *Philosophy of Education Yearbook* (pp. 330–337). Urbana, IL: Philosophy of Education Society.

Cremin, T., Swann, J., Flewitt, R., Faulkner, D. and Kucirkova, N. (2013) *Evaluation Report of MakeBelieve Arts Helicopter Technique of Storytelling and Story Acting*. MakeBelieve Arts and The Open University. http://www.makebelievearts.co.uk/docs/Helicopter-Technique-Evaluation.pdf

Kuschner, D. (2015) Play and early childhood education. In J. Johnson, S. Eberle, T. Henricks and D. Kuschner (eds), *The Handbook of the Study of Play*. Lanham, MD: Rowman & Littlefield.

Lee, T. (2015) *Princesses, Dragons and Helicopter Stories: Storytelling and story acting in the early years*. London: Routledge.

LEGO Learning Institute (2013) *The Future Play: Defining the role and value of play in the 21st century*. Billund, Denmark: LEGO Foundation.

Nicolopoulou, A., Cortina, K. S., Ilgaz, H., Cates, C. B. and de Sá, A. (2015) Using a narrative- and play-based activity to promote low-income preschoolers' oral language, emergent literacy, and social competence. *Early Childhood Research Quarterly, 31*: 147–162.

Nind, M., Flewitt, R. S. and Theodorou, F. (2014) Play and inclusion. In K. Cologon (ed.), *Inclusive Education in the Early Years: Right from the start* (pp. 341–357). Australia and New Zealand: Oxford University Press.

Seidel, S. (2001) To be part of something bigger than oneself. In Project Zero and Reggio Children (eds), *Making Learning Visible: Children as individual and group learners*. Reggio Emilia, Italy: Reggio Children.

Vygotsky, L. (1978) *Mind in Society: The development of higher psychological processes*. Cambridge, MA: Harvard University Press.

INDEX